1 CORINTHIANS

ABINGDON NEW TESTAMENT COMMENTARIES

1 CORINTHIANS

RICHARD A. HORSLEY

Abingdon Press
Nashville

ABINGDON NEW TESTAMENT COMMENTARIES:
1 CORINTHIANS

Library of Congress Cataloging-in-Publication Data

Horsley, Richard A.
    1 Corinthians / Richard A. Horsley.
      p. cm — (Abingdon New Testament commentaries)
    Includes bibliographical references and index.
    ISBN 0-687-05838-4 (alk. paper)
    1. Bible. N.T. Corinthians, 1st—Commentaries. I. Title.
  II. Series.
  BS2675.3.H67   1998
  227'.207—dc21
                                              98-12727
                                                  CIP

98 99 00 01 02 03 04 05 06 07—10 9 8 7 6 5 4 3 2 1

MANUFACTURED IN THE UNITED STATES OF AMERICA

*To the many many women
and slaves who suffered
because of what "Paul" wrote
and how that was used.*

CONTENTS

FOREWORD

The *Abingdon New Testament Commentaries* series provides compact, critical commentaries on the writings of the New Testament. These commentaries are written with special attention to the needs and interests of theological students, but they will also be useful for students in upper-level college or university settings, as well as for pastors and other church leaders. In addition to providing basic information about the New Testament texts and insights into their meanings, these commentaries are intended to exemplify the tasks and procedures of careful, critical biblical exegesis.

The authors who have contributed to this series come from a wide range of ecclesiastical affiliations and confessional stances. All are seasoned, respected scholars and experienced classroom teachers. They take full account of the most important current scholarship and secondary literature, but do not attempt to summarize that literature or to engage in technical academic debate. Their fundamental concern is to analyze the literary, socio-historical, theological, and ethical dimensions of the biblical texts themselves. Although all of the commentaries in this series have been written on the basis of the Greek texts, the authors do not presuppose any knowledge of the biblical languages on the part of the reader. When some awareness of a grammatical, syntactical, or philological issue is necessary for an adequate understanding of a particular text, they explain the matter clearly and concisely.

The introduction of each volume ordinarily includes subdivisions dealing with the *key issues* addressed and/or raised by the New Testament writing under consideration; its *literary genre, structure, and character;* its *occasion and situational context,* including its wider social, historical, and religious contexts; and its *theological and ethical significance* within these several contexts.

In each volume, the *commentary* is organized according to literary units rather than verse by verse. Generally, each of these units is the subject of three types of analysis. First, the *literary analysis* attends to the unit's genre, most important stylistic features, and overall structure. Second, the *exegetical analysis* considers the aim and leading ideas of the unit, deals with any especially important textual variants, and discusses the meanings of important words, phrases, and images. It also takes note of the particular historical and social situations of the writer and original readers, and of the wider cultural and religious contexts of the book as a whole. Finally, the *theological and ethical analysis* discusses the theological and ethical matters with which the unit deals or to which it points, focusing on the theological and ethical significance of the text within its original setting.

Each volume also includes a *select bibliography,* thereby providing guidance to other major commentaries and important scholarly works, and a brief *subject index.* The New Revised Standard Version of the Bible is the principal translation of reference for the series, but the authors draw on all the major modern English versions, and when necessary provide their own original translations of difficult terms or phrases.

The fundamental aim of this series will have been attained if readers are assisted, not only to understand more about the origins, character, and meaning of the New Testament writings, but also to enter into their own informed and critical engagement with the texts themselves.

Victor Paul Furnish
General Editor

PREFACE

How can we understand a letter by a third-world missionary to a new community of marginalized people in a cosmopolitan city of the Roman Empire? To highlight even more the difficulties, it is well to remember that other missionaries had come to visit during that missionary's absence, and many in the community had come to embrace views very different from the ones he had taught. Christians look back at 1 Corinthians as one of the founding scriptures of their faith. But at the time Paul wrote the letter, the term *Christian* had not yet been coined, and it was not yet certain that the communities Paul "founded" would survive. The people whom Paul addressed in 1 Corinthians and other letters were just beginning to work out the community relations, celebrations, beliefs, and attitudes toward the larger imperial society that would provide some basis for the expansion of the social movement that later became Christianity. First Corinthians gives us a window onto the beginning struggles in one unusually contentious community of that movement in one of the most wide-open cosmopolitan centers of the Roman order. Reading the arguments comprised in the letter makes our heads spin. From the numerous innuendoes, plays on words, and even flashes of sarcasm, we sense that Paul and at least some of the Corinthians did not understand each other. In fact, they seem at times to be "talking past" each other. So how can we even begin to read, let alone understand, this letter?

It will not be easy. Nor will it be satisfying to simplify, to pretend that the disagreements and conflicts are not there in section after section of the letter. On the contrary, in reading what has been researched as the most informative of Paul's letters for a variety of issues in "early Christianity," we have an opportunity precisely to discern the different viewpoints and conflicting concerns that struggled for prominence in the nascent movement. To do so, we must take into consideration where rival missionaries and Corinthians' viewpoints that differ from Paul's may have been coming from. We also need to recognize that the movement Paul was attempting to organize was not a religion. There was no such concept yet. The religious dimension of life among ancient peoples and in ancient Roman cities was inseparable from other aspects of life, such as economics and politics and kinship and household. A "religion" may have been something that emerged as the movement Paul started adjusted to continuing coexistence with the Roman Empire. From Paul's letters, however, it is clear that the movement thought of itself in political terms as an *ekklesia,* which was not a "church" but an "assembly" alternative to the established city-assembly that represented the citizens and, indirectly perhaps, the mass of resident aliens. Most important, perhaps, we need to keep in mind that Paul was spreading from house to house a "gospel" of an ignominiously executed third-world prophet whom he claimed had been exalted as the Lord of the world, the diametrical opposite of the imperial "gospel" of Caesar as the savior who had brought peace and security to the world. The trouble was that many people in Corinth had been looking rather for a more personal spiritual transcendence of their miserable lot in life.

Two apologies to the readers may be in order. Since Paul's language reflects the patriarchal and "andromorphic" assumptions of his culture, it seemed inappropriate to gloss his formulations with "inclusive language," even though he surely included women in terms such as "brothers." Also, since Paul's arguments are often long, it would be misleading to break them up into shorter units that might fragment the longer trains of thought. But the long sections of commentary covering his long arguments may try the readers' patience.

I would like to express gratitude to several persons who helped me directly or indirectly in the preparation of this commentary. I owe a special debt to those colleagues whose analyses and interpretations of Paul's letters have informed and stimulated my own analysis, in particular Elisabeth Schüssler Fiorenza, Antionette

Wire, Neil Elliott, Stanley Stowers, Gordon Fee, and Jerome Murphy-O'Connor. With generous and, surely, often painstaking effort and remarkable patience, Vernon Robbins and Victor Paul Furnish kept the commentary in bounds and on track. Macus Aurin, Heather Kapplow, and Jane MacIntosh provided research assistance. Laura Whitney and the circulation staff at Andover Harvard Library and the circulation staff at the EDS-Weston Libraries were consistently helpful, as well as patient. Ann DiSessa helped immeasurably with the repeated processing of the manuscript. Neil Elliott and Cynthia Kittredge read over a draft of the commentary and offered many helpful suggestions. Finally, the many University of Massachusetts Boston students in a seminar on 1 Corinthians, particularly Tom Gilmore, Jane Paquet, and Jane Souza, and those in a seminar on religion and imperialism in antiquity, particularly Jane MacIntosh, Jack Reynolds, and Chris Tuttle, should know how stimulating their reflections and reactions to Paul's arguments have been for my own struggles to understand this strange and powerful figure.

Richard A. Horsley

LIST OF ABBREVIATIONS

1 Enoch	Ethiopic *Book of Enoch*
1QH	*Thanksgiving Hymns* (Qumran Cave 1)
1 QpHab	*Pesher on Habakkuk* (Qumran Cave 1)
1QS	*Rule of the Community* (Qumran Cave 1)
2 Apoc. Bar.	*Syriac Apocalypse of Baruch*
AB	Anchor Bible
Alex.	Plutarch, *Alexander*
Anim.	Philo, *On Husbandry*
ANRW	*Aufstieg und Niedergang der römischen Welt*
Apol.	Apuleius, *Apology*
Apology	Plato, *Apology*
AT	Author's translation
BA	*Biblical Archaeologist*
Ben.	Seneca, *On Benefits*
Bib. Ant.	Pseudo-Philo, *Biblical Antiquities*
BTB	*Biblical Theology Bulletin*
CBQ	*Catholic Biblical Quarterly*
CD	Cairo text of the *Damascus Document*
Cher.	Philo, *On the Cherubium*
Congr.	Philo, *On Mating with the Preliminary Studies*
Det.	Philo, *The Worse Attacks the Better*
Did.	*Didache*
Diss.	Epictetus, *Discourses*
Ebr.	Philo, *On Drunkenness*
EKKNT	Evangelisch-katholischer Kommentar zurn Neuen Testament
Ep.	Seneca, *Epistles*
Epis.	Horace, *Epistles*
Fuga	Philo, *On Flight and Finding*
Geogr.	Strabo, *Geography*
Gig.	Philo, *The Giants*

GNS	Good News Studies
Gorg.	Plato, *Gorgias*
Heres	Philo, *Who Is the Heir of Divine Things?*
Hist.	Livy, *History*
HNTC	Harper's NT Commentaries
HTR	*Harvard Theological Review*
Ign. *Eph.*	Ignatius, *Letter to the Ephesians*
Is. et Os.	Plutarch, *On Isis and Osiris*
JAAR	*Journal of the American Academy of Religion*
J.W.	Josephus, *The Jewish War*
JBL	*Journal of Biblical Literature*
JRH	*Journal of Religious History*
JSNT	*Journal for the Study of the New Testament*
Leg. All.	Philo, *Allegorical Interpretation of the Laws*
LWC	Living Word Commentary
LXX	*Septuagint*
m. Abot	Mishna, tractxate *Abot*
Med.	Marcus Aurelius, *Meditations*
Met.	Apuleius, *Metaphorphoses*
MeyerK	H. A. W. Meyer, Kritisch-exegetischer Kommentar über das Neue Testament
Migr. Abr.	Philo, *On the Migration of Abraham*
Mut.	Philo, *On the Change of Nature*
NICNT	New International Commentary on the New Testament
NJB	*The New Jerusalem Bible*
Nom.	Philo, *On the Change of Names*
NovT	*Novum Testamentum*
NRSV	New Revised Standard Version
NTS	*New Testament Studies*
Op. Mundi.	Philo, *On the Creation of the World*
Or.	Dio Chrysostom, *Orations*
Phaed.	Plato, *Phaedus*
Pol.	Aristotle, *Politics*
Post. Cain	Philo, *On the Posterity and Exile of Cain*
Praem.	Philo, *On Rewards and Punishments*
Quaes. Gen.	Philo, *Questions and Solutions on Genesis*
RB	*Revue biblique*
Sacr.	Philo, *On the Sacrifice of Abel and Cain*
SBLDS	SBL Dissertation Series
Sobr.	Philo, *On Sobriety*

Somn.	Philo, *On Dreams*
Spec. Leg.	Philo, *On the Special Laws*
Symp.	Plato, *Symposium*
T. Naph.	*Testament of Naphtali*
Tim.	Plato, *Timaeus*
VC	*Vigiliae christianae*
Virt.	Philo, *On Virtue*
Vit. Phil.	*Diogenes Laërtius, The Lives of Eminent Philosophers*
Vita Cont.	Philo, *The Contemplative Life*
Vita Mos.	Philo, *On the Life of Moses*

INTRODUCTION

THE CHARACTER OF THE LETTER

First Corinthians, like Paul's other letters, was meant to be read aloud to the assembly addressed—the next best thing to his appearing before it in person. Although here, as elsewhere, Paul has followed a standard epistolary form, the body of the letter is unusually long and highly structured. This structure and the issues Paul addresses are clearly discernible:

1:1-9	address, greeting, and opening thanksgiving
1:10–4:21	divisiveness in the community
5	how to deal with a man living with his stepmother
6	on not taking disputes to official courts
7	marriage and separation for community members
8:1–11:1	eating food sacrificed to idols
11:2-16	hair arrangement when prophesying
11:17-34	procedure at celebration of Lord's Supper
12–14	use of spiritual gifts, particularly "tongues"
15	resurrection of the dead
16:1-4, 5-12	collection for Jerusalem, travel plans, Apollos
16:13-24	closing exhortation, greetings, and grace

As a personal communication addressed to a particular community, this letter contains arguments intended to persuade the hearers, not doctrinal treatises formulated to define Christian belief. In order to accomplish his objective Paul uses forms of argumentation or rhetoric common in the dominant hellenistic culture of the day. Deliberative rhetoric (which argues for or against some future course of action) predominates, but at particular points he employs forensic or judicial rhetoric (which was used in law courts to defend or condemn past actions) or epideictic rhetoric (which was designed for public speeches or funeral orations to praise or blame persons, cities, or ideas).

The highly distinctive language of 1 Corinthians reflects its ad hoc character. Because it is focused on issues that arose in the life of a particular community at a certain point toward the beginning of its development, the "typically Pauline" language of law, sin, righteousness, and faith hardly appears. Instead, oppositions such as wisdom versus foolishness, mature versus infant, rich versus poor, strong versus weak, and pneumatic versus psychic, dominate whole sections. In 1 Corinthians, moreover, Paul discusses issues that he either does not mention or issues that he treats in very different ways in other letters. Perhaps because it relies heavily on distinctive and non-Pauline language, this letter has been less susceptible than the Letters to the Romans and the Galatians of interpretation according to the Lutheran Protestant theology that has tended to dominate scholarly readings of Paul.

Paul wrote this letter to address the problem of divisions that had arisen within the recently founded Corinthian assembly. However, we know from his subsequent correspondence with the Corinthians, in the collection of letters now combined into 2 Corinthians, that the conflicts became worse and came to involve his own conflict with some in the community. Therefore, if we are to focus on 1 Corinthians at the time in which it was written, we must read its arguments as windows onto the situations and conflicts of a divided community.

THE CONTEXT OF PAUL'S CORINTHIAN MISSION

The patricians of Rome built up their empire over a period of several centuries of violent conquests and intimidation of subject peoples by slaughter, terrorism, and enslavement. Their empire building also entailed displacement of millions of people. They brought massive numbers of slaves into Italy from conquered lands to work the grand estates they built up by forcing off their ancestral lands the very peasants who had fallen heavily into debt while serving in the Roman legions. The displaced Roman peasants then swelled the ranks of the urban poor. The Roman state therefore founded colonies in conquered lands, providing land for veterans and exporting the urban poor and freed slaves—potential sources of discontent in Rome itself. Roman imperial practices of violence and displacement thus provided the conditions for both Jesus' ministry in Galilee and Paul's mission in Corinth.

The vicious Roman treatment of ancient Corinth served notice to the rest of the Greek cities that Rome would brook no opposition to its interests in and control of Greece and the eastern Mediterranean. Rome maneuvered Corinth and the Achaean league into war and, in 146 BCE, ruthlessly sacked and torched the city, slaughtered its men, and sold its women and children into slavery. In one massive stroke of violence the Romans terminated the life of one of the most illustrious classical Greek cities, carrying off many of its cherished cultural treasures to Rome.

The Roman establishment of a colony at Corinth in 44 BCE, named *Colonia Laus Julia Corinthiensis* in honor of its founder Julius Caesar, was a decisive step toward the Romanization of Greece. By founding Corinth and other colonies in the area, Caesar and Augustus simultaneously secured the area militarily, promoted more efficient administration and economic exploitation of the area through its "urbanization," and facilitated trade and communications with the eastern empire. While they never carried an overtly Romanizing mission, Roman colonies such as Corinth, which remained steadfastly faithful to Rome, provided the structure for the perpetuation of imperial rule in Greece.

Whereas most Roman colonies were settled almost entirely by army veterans, many of those sent to Corinth were recruited from the urban poor in Rome and fully half of them were freed slaves (Strabo *Geogr.* 8.6.23). However, the Roman destruction of classical Corinth had not left the site utterly desolate. Recent archaeological explorations and critical reassessment of literary sources indicate that descendants of the traditional Greek population and its culture remained on the site (Wiseman 1979, 493-94). After a visit to the site in 79–77 BCE, the Roman lawyer Cicero commented on the productive farms in the area. There was also continuing activity, for example, in the temple of Aphrodite, the sanctuary of Demeter and Kore, and the sacred precincts of Asclepius, the god of healing. The majority of the colonists sent to Corinth in 44 BCE, moreover, were only superficially "Roman." Many of those taken from the urban poor in Rome had likely been displaced from their farms in the Italian countryside. The freed slaves, moreover, would probably have been originally (or descended) from peoples conquered by the Romans when they took control in the eastern Mediterranean—perhaps from Syria, Judea, Asia Minor, and Greece itself. Reflecting aristocratic Greek attitudes, the poet Crinagoras lamented that Corinth had been "wholly abandoned to such a crowd of scoundrelly slaves" (Crinagoras, *Greek Anthology* 9.284). By the second century CE Corinth had grown to a city of about eighty thousand in an area of 725 hectares, with roughly twenty thousand more villagers living in the surrounding area.

Its strategic location at the principal juncture in the best sea route between Rome and Italy in the west and Greece and other areas to the east meant that Corinth became a center of trade and political communications between Italy and the eastern empire, as well as the capital of the Roman province of Achaia. Like its "classical" predecessor, the new city of Corinth became envied as " 'wealthy' because of its commerce" (Pindar, *Eulogies* 122; Strabo, *Geogr.* 8.6.20). Lechaeum, the western port on the Gulf of Corinth, lay about two miles directly north of the city. Cenchreae, the eastern port, was situated on the Saronic Gulf about six miles to the east. Goods in the transit trade were either unloaded from one port and reloaded in the other port, or the ships were dragged along a track across the narrowest part of the isthmus (about four miles). Corinth itself was known for its bronze works and for manufacture of small utilitarian and decorative items.

Politically and, to a degree, culturally the new Corinth would have been patterned after Rome. Municipal government consisted of a council *(boulē)* on which freedmen could serve, with two annually elected chief magistrates *(duoviri)* presiding. The official language was Latin, which predominated in inscriptions well into the second century CE. Since Corinth soon became the capital of the Roman province of Achaia, it was also the administrative base for the governor of the whole province. Accordingly, while the old civic center became the center of commercial activity, the forum of the reconstructed city served more as an administrative center. In religious practice as well as layout and organization, Corinth was initially Roman, not a restoration of a Greek city. Extant records of priesthoods and the majority of dedicatory inscriptions concern Roman gods or the imperial cult. One of the most elaborate temples (Temple F, to Venus), apparently the first erected in the new forum at the very center of the city, represented not nostalgia for the Aphrodite of old, who had protected the city from atop Acrocorinth, but Venus the Mother of the Roman Nation, who was also understood as the Mother of the Roman colony. Control of the Isthmian Games, with their contests honoring the emperor, returned to Corinth near the beginning of the first century CE, and provided a major means through which the city became the center of Roman imperial culture in Greece.

By the second century, however, it was said that Corinth, though Roman, had become thoroughly hellenized. Under Hadrian, in the early second century, the official language was finally changed from Latin to Greek. Despite the predominance of Latin inscriptions in the middle of the first century—the time during which Paul founded the Corinthian assembly—hellenistic culture must have already been dominant among those of indigenous Corinthian stock, those from elsewhere in Greece itself, and those from the rest of the eastern Mediterranean. Although Corinth remained a center of Romanitas in Greece, because of its central location, administrative role, and commercial importance, it also became the principal "Mother-city" among Greeks.

The Romans maintained minimal administrative staff and no standing army in Greece, by contrast with its extensive standing army along its eastern and northern frontiers. In Greece the empire seems to have been held together through a combination of patronage relations and the emperor cult that took hold quickly under Augustus and his successors. That imperial power was structured by patronal relations and ceremonies honoring the emperor may illuminate what Paul was up against in his mission and why he came into such conflict in Corinth.

The key role in the patron-client system was played by the local and provincial elite. A distinguished family pedigree and wealth were ordinarily the prerequisites of local and regional power and honor. In Corinth wealth counted for more, since even rich freedmen could hold public offices, and they competed with more established and pedigreed aristocrats for multiple honors from the city. Perhaps the most prominent freedman whose wealth won him honor and power in first-century Corinth was Babbius Philinus, who donated several buildings around the city, was elected to two public offices, *aedilis* and *duovir,* and held the important priestly offices of *pontifex* and priest of Neptune.

In Corinth and other provincial cities vertical networks of power and influence were headed by elite families. The aristocratic patron provided protection, resources, influence, and other benefactions. In return, the clients provided loyal popular support for the patron, bolstering his social status by appearing at his door for the morning "salutation" and forming a crowd around him as he went about his rounds of public business during the day. As Seneca noted, this hierarchical exchange of favors and services bound society together, effectively mitigating the conflicts created by steadily increasing political-economic divisions and inequalities (*Ben.* 1.4.2). More "horizontally" based groups or associations (Lat. *collegia*), in which ordinary people such as artisans provided mutual support for one another, were gradually pulled into the patronage system. Even freedmen, having escaped the utterly despised status of dishonor associated with the condition of slavery, remained at the bottom of the patron-client hierarchy, since they still had the duty of serving their former master in certain capacities and could do nothing to in any way diminish the former master's prestige. The powerful and wealthy, finally, often served as the patrons of philosophers and (other) religious teachers, who might even become "resident" in the household of their patron.

Only recently have we begun to realize how important the emperor cult was in cities such as Corinth. Representations of the emperor and imperial family, honors for the emperor, and worship of the emperor pervaded the whole context of public life. Not only was the emperor cult the most widespread and ubiquitous religious practice—embodied in temples, shrines, statues, images, coins, inscriptions, sacrifices, citywide and provincial celebrations, and even the calendar that regulated the rhythm of social-political life—but the imperial presence even came to dominate public space at the very center of urban life, the arena for political and commercial activity. The transformation of the city center of Corinth during the early empire was typical. Major building and rebuilding were undertaken under Augustus and continued well into the first century.

The new shape of Corinth was set by the time Paul arrived in the city. Archaeologists find striking the amount of construction that was related to the imperial presence and the degree to which previously open public space was now ordered with very particular orientation. While the old civic center may have served still as a commercial area, a newly constructed area became the new center for political activity as well as public and commercial life generally. The new Roman-style Temple E at the west end of the *agora* (forum or plaza) was erected specifically in honor of the emperor as a commanding presence in and extension of the city center. Shrines and images of Augustus and his successors were placed at significant places around the forum in front of and in between buildings, in front of temples to other gods, and at points in the surrounding porticoes. Public inscriptions dedicated to the emperors graced the facades of public buildings. Whether or not residents of Corinth participated in an active way in the emperor cult, the imperial presence surrounded them, particularly at the sites of public life. At public festival times such as the Imperial Games, of course, it was virtually impossible not to participate.

Traditional Greek religion was relativized but not displaced by the empire. As with the emperor cult, it is impossible to separate the indigenous religious life and institutions of an ancient city from its political-economic institutions and practices. Private and public life, household and city alike, depended upon the favor of the gods. Among the archaeological finds of traditional Greek religion continuing at new Corinth are a bronze statue of Athena, a temple of Apollos, and evidence of the cult of fertility forces represented by Demeter and Kore. Besides the famous temple on Acrocorinth—the mountain that rises fifteen hundred feet above the forum toward the south—another temple of Aphrodite, goddess of love and fertility, was found in the forum. Also prominent, among traditional cults, were the temples of Asclepius, the god of emotional as well as physical healing, and the sea god Poseidon, whose sanctuary was located on the isthmus, to the east of the city.

Joining the emperor cult and the traditional Greek cults in the rich and eclectic cultural life of Corinth were also Egyptian and other foreign deities, whose transformation and diffusion were facilitated by the empire. Already worshiped during the hellenistic period in Greece, the Egyptian goddess Isis had a temple in the port of Cenchreae, east of Corinth, in the first century CE. The second-century writer Pausanius claims to have seen two more temples dedicated to Isis and two dedicated to Serapis on his ascent of Acrocorinth (2.4.6).

PAUL AND THE CORINTHIANS

Only when Paul went to Corinth did he encounter a hellenistic urban ethos that was both the product of and fully assimilated into the Roman imperial order. This is the context we must keep in mind if we are to appreciate Paul's Corinthian mission, subsequent developments in the assembly he founded in Corinth, and 1 Corinthians. The only way to proceed, admittedly somewhat circularly, is to reconstruct the historical (and "rhetorical") situation of and in the Corinthian assembly through a critical reading of Paul's arguments in 1 Corinthians. Many aspects of the historical reconstruction that follows will be justified and clarified in the commentary below.

In 44 CE the emperor Claudius had restored Achaia as a senatorial province with its capital at Corinth. Thereafter the Senate was represented by an annually appointed proconsul (governor). An inscription mentioning Gallio as proconsul from July 51 to June 52 is virtually the only ascertainable basis for a chronology of Paul's mission in general (see Acts 18:12-16). Reckoning with this date, most scholars have concluded that the eighteen months Paul spent in Corinth ran from the beginning of 50 to the early summer of 51.

Paul's Mission in Corinth

As in Galatia and Thessalonica (see Gal 3:5; 1 Thess 1:5), Paul's preaching in Corinth was accompanied by a "demonstration of the Spirit and of power" (2:4). The Corinthians took a particular fancy to manifestations of the Spirit, especially ecstatic prophecy and "speaking in tongues," perhaps already during Paul's work there, but certainly within a short time after he left (see 12; 14). Paul remembers having himself administered the baptismal ritual of entry into the new society of God in Christ to only a few of the Corinthians (1:14-16; 16:15). He did, however, instruct the Corinthians in the basic practices and convictions of the movement, such as the Lord's Supper and the crucifixion-resurrection creed (11:2, 23; 15:3-5). We must assume also that Paul instructed the Corinthian assembly, as he had the Galatian and Macedonian assemblies, in the history and traditions of Israel, for the very content of the gospel was that the promises to Israel were in the process of being fulfilled in the events of Christ's crucifixion, resurrection, and *parousia*.

Paul was teamed in the mission with a number of coworkers. Timothy and Silvanus, who had worked with him earlier, joined him in Corinth (1 Thess 1:1; 2 Cor 1:19). In the expansion and organization of the movement in Corinth a fuller cadre of workers emerged, including women as well as men. One of the most prominent among them, apparently, was Phoebe, minister *(diakonos)* of the assembly in Cenchreae (seaport town to the east of Corinth) and benefactor of many, including Paul himself (Rom 16:1-2). Moreover, Paul formed a special collaborative bond with Prisca and her husband Aquila, perhaps because they plied the same "trade" of tent making (Acts 18:2-3). This couple provided Paul with a residential base in Corinth and continued in collaboration

with him when he moved on to Ephesus. Contrary to the historically unwarranted popular and scholarly image of Paul preaching
the gospel in public places, he almost certainly would have avoided
the marketplace of religious competition for the more intense
personal interaction of small groups in people's houses. Indeed he
was adamant that he was "not [a peddler] of God's word like so
many" (2 Cor 2:17).

From Paul's passing comments about "Prisca and Aquila" and
the "assembly in their house" (Rom 16:3-5; the NRSV translates
"assembly" as "church," see 16:19; cf. Phlm 2) we may surmise
that the movement in Corinth and again in Ephesus took the form
of several small "assemblies" based in particular households. Paul's
further passing comment about "the whole assembly" coming
together (14:23; cf. 10:20; Rom 16:23) suggests that at other times
only a subset, a portion of the whole community, functioned
separately in some way. That appears to be the basis for the
supposition that the households of Stephanas, Gaius, and perhaps
Crispus hosted such house-based assemblies. Understandably, the
heads of these households—who were sufficiently well-off to have
a larger house than most but hardly need have been wealthy—became leaders and, in effect, additional coworkers in the movement
on whom Paul could rely for communication, coordination, and
group discipline (see especially Paul's reliance on Stephanas in
16:16-17). The movement as a whole then may have taken the form
of a network of such house-based assemblies, which met periodically for special occasions such as the Lord's Supper and discussions (11:18; 14:23; Rom 16:23). Presumably the assembly at
Cenchreae, of which Phoebe was the principal leader, provides an
illustration of how the network expanded into the wider area,
becoming the assembly (or the saints) in "Achaia," while still
centered in Corinth itself.

In contrast with Paul's previous mission fields in Galatia and
Macedonia, the social-cultural ethos of Corinth involved an atom-
ized individualism, an obsession with status, and a competitive
spirit. Here, as in ancient hellenistic and Roman society overall, a
huge gulf separated the tiny wealthy and powerful elite from the
great mass of the very poor, whether slave or free. Despite this, or

perhaps partly because of this, Greek society—and even more so Roman society—was obsessed with rank and status. Within the same ranks at all levels, even among slaves, significant status variations marked some people off from others (Garnsey and Saller 1987, 199). At all levels, moreover, women were subordinated to and under the power of their husbands and masters. In Corinth the lower strata must have been every bit as concerned with their status as the elite scrambling for provincial honors and imperial favor. As the descendants of former slaves they would have been made to feel acutely the despised and dishonored position of their origins.

By the end of the first century CE Corinth had a reputation as the most competitive of all cities, even in economic matters, a city of unprincipled profit takers who would stop at nothing to outdo their rivals (Apuleius, *Met.* 10.19, 25). In Roman times the famous proverb, "not for everyone is the voyage to Corinth," referred to losing one's shirt in the intense commercial competition of this urban emporium, not losing one's virginity in the temples to Aphrodite, which was by then merely a legend from classical times (Horace, *Epis.* 1.17.36). Thus, amidst all the luxuries of Corinth, the people seemed uncultured and lacking in social graces, partly because the wealthy so grossly exploited the poor of the city (according to Alciphron, *Letters* 15, 24 [3.51, 60]). The recently founded city full of uprooted people yet striving for the appearance of culture had an atmosphere of spiritual emptiness, of a hunger for status and security.

The distinctive language Paul uses in 1 Corinthians and the issues he discusses appear to belong in precisely such a situation. A key text to consider is 1 Cor 1:26, especially the comment that "by human standards, not many [of you] were powerful, not many were of noble birth." The terms "powerful" *(dynatoi)* and "nobly born" *(eugeneis)* originally referred to the traditional Greek aristocracy in their political-economic and social dimensions, the "magnates and nobles." By Paul's time these terms had long since come to be used in a spiritualized sense in reference to an intellectual or spiritual aristocracy: the *truly* "powerful" and "nobly born" and "wealthy" were "the wise"—the other term Paul uses in 1 Cor 1:26! The original sense of the terms does not fit the situation in Roman

Corinth, where the old Corinthian nobles had given way to new magnates, who were hardly "nobly born," in some cases even being sons of freedmen. Taken in connection with the rest of the rhetoric in chapters 1–4, Paul's reference in 1:26 is most likely to some in the Corinthian assembly who claimed to have attained a certain aristocratic *spiritual* status. Indeed, as we shall see in the commentary below, Paul is dealing with issues of spiritual status in several sections of the letter. Behind or underneath the issues of spiritual status, of course, were issues of concrete social status. The latter, however, were rooted in particular patterns of social power relations. It is thus highly unlikely that conflicts over eating "food offered to idols" and conduct of "the Lord's supper" discussed in 1 Cor 8–11 can be reduced to a simple economic conflict between rich (the "strong") and poor (the "weak"). Since particular Corinthians, whatever their "status inconsistency," were embedded in patterns of social power relations, we cannot understand the composition of the Pauline assemblies (and behavior within those assemblies) simply in terms of choices by individuals to "join" a "voluntary association."

Paul's passing references to households, and the possibility that the movement in Corinth took the form of several house-assemblies as well as "the whole assembly," suggest we should not look simply for the social status of individuals in order to determine the composition and spread of the movement. Most probably the movement spread through already existing networks, whether households, neighborhoods, contacts among people in the same trade, or friendships. It seems highly unlikely that the movement comprised a cross section of the society as a whole, and it is particularly unlikely that any truly highborn or wealthy people joined. People did not have to be rich to travel, as the movement of the apostles themselves illustrates. Heads of households who joined the Corinthian assembly may have been people of moderate means, but need not have been wealthy. Most were probably from the mix of urban poor and involved in one or another form of dependency. A large percentage of the Corinthian community appear to have been women. In addition to those known to have played highly visible leadership roles, such as Phoebe in Cenchreae, a number of the women in the Corinthian community appear to have broken with the traditional subordination and disabilities imposed on women in the dominant social patterns.

The Writing of 1 Corinthians

After apparently being thrown out of Achaia by Gallio, Paul moved on to Ephesus, where he established another base from which to spread the movement in the province of Asia (western Asia Minor). During the more than three years of his mission in Ephesus, Paul continued his close relationship with the Corinthian assembly through periodic correspondence and visits by delegations. First Corinthians, which is the second of his letters to the community, was probably written at least two years after he left Corinth for Ephesus.

Paul had learned what was happening in the Corinthian community from two or three sources of information. After he had written to the Corinthians (5:9), they had written him a letter inquiring about several issues (see 7:1). He had also received reports from "Chloe's people" about "quarrels" among the Corinthians (1:11; see 1:13). He may also have heard reports from Stephanas, Fortunatas, and Achaicus, apparently a delegation of Corinthians who were visiting Paul when he wrote 1 Corinthians, and who may have been the bearers of the letter from the Corinthians, or may have delivered Paul's letter back to the Corinthians, or both (16:17).

A great deal of information related to these matters emerges from a close reading of Paul's arguments in response, in which he often cites Corinthian slogans, or counters or strongly qualifies their language, or both. The divisions among the Corinthians were closely connected with attachment to particular apostles (1:12) and claims to exalted spiritual status (as "wise, powerful, of noble birth," "mature, spiritual," and "filled, rich, kings" [1:26; 2:6-16; 4:8-10]), and "wisdom" (1:17-31). Those separating from their spouses argued "it is well for a man not to touch a woman" (7:1). The eating of food sacrificed to idols was rooted in the "knowledge" that "no idol in the world really exists," that "there is no God but one" (8:1, 4), and that "all things are lawful" (10:23; cf.

6:12). Clearly there had been major developments in the Corinthian assembly since Paul departed the city over two years earlier.

Various explanations have been offered for the emergence of the beliefs and behavior Paul is addressing in 1 Corinthians. According to an older view, Jewish Christian missionaries were responsible. Another suggestion is that the Corinthians had somehow become Gnostics. More recently, the problems have been attributed to the Corinthians' "overrealized" eschatology or hellenistic "enthusiasm" that caused them, for example, to spiritualize the idea of the resurrection of the dead (cf. 2 Tim 2:18). However, all of these explanations were developed well before the recognition that historical reconstruction must take into account Paul's rhetorical formulations. A very recent and socially more concrete approach working from Paul's rhetoric—although not in its ancient Greek forms—argues that Corinthian women in particular, caught up in the free flow of the Spirit, had experienced liberation from their confinement to subordinate and demeaning roles in the traditional patriarchal Greco-Roman households. While clearly discerning that the effect of Paul's arguments is to reinforce certain traditional patriarchal patterns, this suggestive recent approach cannot account for all of the distinctive language in 1 Corinthians and important issues in the "rhetorical situation" that Paul's arguments address.

The approach followed here will attempt to take the Corinthian beliefs and behavior addressed in all sections of 1 Corinthians into account and to understand them in the particular context of the social-cultural ethos of first-century Corinth. Attention will be given both to the rhetoric of Paul's arguments in the letter and to the larger social context of the assembly to which it was addressed. In particular, we will see that Paul's argument against divisiveness not only devotes considerable attention to Apollos (1:12; 2:4, 5-9; 4:6), but includes a sharp warning about how Apollos had "built" upon the foundation Paul had laid (3:10-15). The inclusion of Peter and Christ among the gurus with whom the Corinthians were supposedly identifying (1:12) is almost certainly for rhetorical effect, and Paul's generous but noncommittal response in 16:12 to the Corinthians' desire for his return can hardly be taken at face value. The division that required such extensive discussion and evoked both sarcasm (3:1-4) and threats (3:10-15; 4:18-21) was apparently largely between the partisans of Apollos and those of Paul.

We will also note the importance of Paul's insistence, while he was in Corinth, that he supported himself by working with his own hands. This was looked upon as demeaning in the dominant Greco-Roman culture (see below on 9:3-14; cf. 2 Cor 11:8-9; 12:13). Whatever his reasons, he was clearly deviating from the standard in the movement, that of the communities supporting the apostles who worked among them. Was the emergence of this as an issue with the Corinthians related to the entrance into the community of another "minister" whose practice was more in accord with the patronage pattern so important in Roman imperial society generally and in Corinth particularly?

Reconstruction of such relationships and developments enables us to understand the beliefs of the Corinthians as more may be inferred from Paul's arguments and from what can be known about their concrete social circumstances. As will be noted regularly in the commentary, the distinctive language and apparent religious devotion of the Gentile Corinthians is paralleled in hellenistic-Jewish devotion to heavenly Wisdom (Gk. *Sophia*), as attested in the Wisdom of Solomon and the treatises of Philo of Alexandria. Particularly striking are the parallels between the Corinthians Paul addresses and the contemporary Therapeutics described by Philo *(Vita Cont.),* Jewish ascetic mystics living near Alexandria in Egypt, who had left their spouses behind for an intimate, transcendent relationship with heavenly *Sophia.* Apollos, who worked for some time in the Corinthian community after Paul had departed, provides a direct link with this hellenistic-Jewish devotion to *Sophia* in and around Alexandria (see Acts 18:24). It would appear that he had encouraged a devotion to heavenly *Sophia* that brought exalted spiritual status as "wise, powerful, of noble birth, rich, and so forth" along with "knowledge" of the one true God, freedom in earthly behavior, and ecstatic spiritual experiences. From what we know of the cultural background of the Corinthians, the *Sophia*-devotion, spiritual status, and personal transcendence taught by

Apollos would have been far more readily assimilated than the gospel of the crucifixion and resurrection presented by Paul, embedded as it was in a historical-eschatological orientation toward reality.

THEOLOGY AND ETHICS

In the broadest terms, Paul worked from the conviction—derived from the sacred traditions of Israel—that God willed justice for humankind, which would be realized in a new social order. Indeed he was driven by the conviction that God had finally fulfilled the promises to Abraham in the crucifixion and resurrection of Christ, which meant that all peoples could now inherit God's righteousness in a new social order imminently to be established at Christ's "coming" *(parousia)*. Apollos and some of the Corinthians, on the other hand, more in tune with the general hellenistic culture, believed that the divine was concerned primarily with the inner, spiritual essence of the individual, with any ethical or social implications following from that spiritual essence. Paul, convinced that God had now begun implementing his plan to terminate the imperial order, was energetically establishing communities among the various peoples of the world in anticipation of an imminent new age of righteousness. In 1 Corinthians Paul's main concern, thus, is the solidarity and mutual edification of the community. Some of the Corinthians, on the other hand, had experienced a personal transcendence of the troublesome social order. They had attained spiritually the aristocratic status denied them by the dominant social order, an individual experience of transcendence that included knowledge of the nature of the divine and personally fulfilling spiritual gifts such as ecstatic prophecy or speaking in tongues.

The means by which God had finally begun the termination of the imperial order, Paul insisted, was in the martyrdom of Christ by death on a cross, the mode of execution used by the Romans for slaves and those who rebelled against the pax Romana. But God's vindication of Christ as the "first fruits" of the resurrection of the dead was the guarantee of the imminent completion of the resurrection as the eschatological event by which the dead would be raised to join in the new society, the kingdom of God. The Corinthians primarily addressed in 1 Corinthians, on the other hand, focused on their personal relationship with heavenly *Sophia* (Wisdom), the personified and reified essence of the divine known through the Jewish Scriptures spiritually understood. As revealed apparently by the wisdom teacher Jesus and his disciple Apollos, *Sophia* provided her devotees with true spiritual knowledge of the divine and immortality of the soul once they attained the highest spiritual advancement as truly wise, mature, and "spiritual."

The Corinthians' exalted spiritual status and immortality gained from their intimate relationship with *Sophia* had significant implications for mundane social relations. On the one hand, for some Corinthians the all-important cultivation of their relationship with heavenly *Sophia* required devoting their energies to the spiritual life. Thus, intimacy with *Sophia* meant avoidance of marital/sexual relations, and perhaps, by implication, liberation from confining subordination in a traditional patriarchal marriage for women. On the other hand, for some Corinthians the security in their possession of immortality and knowledge in the divine world provided them the enlightenment that anything was possible/permissible in the mundane social world. Their strong enlightened consciousness freed them from the parochial prejudices of conventional moral codes. Spiritual experiences in particular were given for the satisfaction, illumination, and personal fulfillment of the individual. Paul, however, urged that primacy be given to relations among community members, partly in order to reinforce the solidarity of the community as an alternative to social relations in the established order. Spiritual gifts were to be used for the edification of the community. Individual behavior should take into account its effect on others. And while remaining open to outsiders—indeed, even attempting to bring them into the community—the community must maintain its solidarity in avoiding the values (idolatry/the "gods and lords") and dehumanizing interpersonal relations (sexual immorality) of the dominant society.

Finally, we may note the ways in which both Paul and the Corinthians are still products of the society and values they are attempting to transform or transcend. The Corinthians, in their attempt to escape or find a personal alternative to the aristocratic values of the imperial order that held them in subjection, appear to have replicated aristocratic values on the spiritual level, with the corresponding implications for social relations within the community. Some of them also were still participating in the larger society, ironically out of the conviction that their true self was secure in its transcendence. Paul, in his attempts to persuade the Corinthians, is largely careful and even sensitive at points, although he also resorts to sarcasm, threats, and assertions of his own apostolic authority. Moreover, at some key points the net effect of his arguments for consideration of others in personal behavior is to reinforce the very patriarchal and authoritarian social relationships that the alternative society he was building was ostensibly attempting to transform.

COMMENTARY

SALUTATION AND THANKSGIVING (1:1-9)

Like most Greco-Roman letters, Paul's letters usually begin with a threefold salutation followed by an opening thanksgiving. In the salutation the writers identify themselves, then name the addressees and offer greetings. The thanksgiving often is a prayer to god(s) for the well-being of the addressee(s). Also it often praises the addressees and attempts to elicit their goodwill. In prolonged rhetorical arguments such as Paul's letters, the thanksgiving can function as the introduction to the argument in the body of the letter, establishing major themes that the subsequent discussion amplifies. The expanded salutation and thanksgiving here suggest that Paul is anticipating the issues at stake in the Corinthian community.

Salutation (1:1-3)

In identifying himself more elaborately as "an apostle of Christ Jesus by the will of God" (v. 1), and not simply listing his own name along with those of cowriters, as in 1 Thess 1:1, Paul is already responding to the challenge to his authority among the Corinthians (cf. 3:1-4, 5-15; 4:1-20; 9; 15:8-10). Not yet limited to the twelve disciples, "apostle" was the title given to leaders of the expanding movement(s) who preached the gospel and founded communities. In connection with his own authority as an apostle, Paul is emphasizing a point with each of three terms, over against some Corinthians whose focus he finds problematic: he was "called" to his historic role, "by the will of God" who is accomplishing purposes through him, and his apostleship is "of Christ Jesus," whose lordship over the movement and its assemblies he is eager to assert repeatedly in the letter. Sosthenes is not necessarily the same as the officer of the Jewish synagogue in Corinth in Acts 18:17. Acts is not a trustworthy source for the existence of a Jewish "assembly" in Corinth because the author repeatedly stereotypes "the Jews" as attacking Paul and other apostles. If he had been a Jew in Corinth, Sosthenes must have joined the movement Paul started there and become a coworker in his subseqent ministry.

First Corinthians 1:2 is the most elaborate address of the genuine letters. Here Paul is already framing his argument to the Corinthians. The Greek term *ekklēsia,* usually translated "church," has a basically political meaning. It was the standard term for the assembly of the citizens of the Greek city-state *(polis)*. As a virtual synonym for "synagogue" *(synagōgē)*, *ekklēsia* also had connotations of the assembly of Israel as a whole or that of its local village communities in the biblical tradition or both. Given its basically political meaning, the "assembly" that Paul had founded in Corinth constituted an alternative to the established assembly of the city of Corinth. Paul's Corinthian assembly, moreover, was part of an international network of assemblies, an expanding movement that Paul also called "the assembly." (The term *assembly* will thus be used instead of the NRSV's *church* in this commentary.) In a phrase peculiar to the Corinthian correspondence and aimed surely at the divisiveness he is about to discuss (cf. 1:10-13; 3:9, 21-23), Paul characterizes the Corinthian assembly as "of God" (contrast Gal 1:2; 1 Thess 1:1). By adding "together with all those who in every place" he attempts to expand the perspective of the Corinthians— who were focused on their own divisions—to the broader movement of all the assemblies.

"Called to be saints" (v. 2) introduces the hope of imminent fulfillment of a world of justice ruled by God. This hope, prominent in Jewish revelatory (apocalyptic) literature such as the book of Daniel (on "saints" see esp. Dan 7:18-27) and the Dead Sea Scrolls, is inherent in the ethical definition of the Corinthian assembly as "those who are sanctified" (cf. 1 Thess 4:3). In addition to the references in the formal phrases "an apostle of Christ Jesus" (v. 1) and "grace . . . from . . . the Lord Jesus" (v. 3), Paul adds references to an instrumental role of Christ Jesus as the agent of their sanctification and to Christ's political role as the exalted universal Lord (v. 2). This anticipates later assertions of the centrality of Christ as the focus of faith and the basis for unity (1:23-25; 3:22-23; 6:15; 8:6; 10:4, 16; 12:27; 15:20-28, 45-49; 16:22-24). In verse 3 Paul changes the traditional hellenistic greeting "rejoice" to "grace" and combines it with the traditional Jewish greeting "peace."

Thanksgiving (1:4-9)

The thanksgiving is even more pointedly oriented toward the Corinthian situation and the arguments Paul is about to make. In contrast with the faith, hope, love, and partnership in the gospel for which Paul offers thanks in 1 Thess 1:3 and Phil 1:5, 9, Paul focuses here on "speech" *(logos)*, "knowledge" *(gnōsis)*, and "spiritual gifts" *(charismata;* vv. 5, 7), anticipating his critique of them later in the letter (1:18–2:4; 8; 12–14). Paul evaluates the Corinthians' spiritual gifts of speech and knowledge in this highly positive evaluation at the outset of the letter in order to elicit their positive disposition to the arguments that follow. Here, as throughout the letter, Paul addresses the assembly as a whole, even though it is divided. He never dignifies or blames any particular faction by naming specific people. The opening thanksgiving sets a tone for the whole letter by focusing on Christ, and especially on the full "revealing" of Christ as the world ruler on the day of his return.

"As you wait for the revealing of our Lord Jesus Christ" (v. 7*b*) and the parallel relative clause (v. 8, a new sentence in NRSV) place the Corinthians' spiritual gifts in the context of the "day of [the] Lord." This is the typically Pauline orientation toward the imminent completion of the final events of history now underway (cf. 1 Thess 1:10; 2:12, 19; 3:13; 4:14-17; 5:23). Although Paul ordinarily speaks of the "return" or "coming" *(parousia)* of Christ, he may have used "revelation" *(apokalypsis)* in verse 7*b* to emphasize that the final or full revelation involved still-awaited future events, in contrast with the partial revelations of prophecy and knowledge already experienced by himself and the Corinthians. Paul is not addressing people who believed that expectations about the future had already come about, but people for whom the notion of world-transforming historical events would have been relatively new, strange, and difficult to understand. The relative clause in 1:8 (cf. 1 Thess 3:13) elaborates the anticipation of Christ's return, repeating a legal metaphor from verse 6: he will "confirm" ("guarantee"; NRSV: "strengthen") you (in whom the testimony of Christ has been confirmed) until the end, so that you will be "blameless" at the judgment that "the day of our Lord" will bring. In a play on the Greek term "blameless" (*anegklētous,* v. 9), Paul refers to the ultimate agent, God, by whom "you were called" *(eklethētē)* and focuses not only on Christ again, but also on "the fellowship" (*koinōnia,* "community") of Christ (v. 9), in transition to the main theme of the first major section of the letter: divisiveness.

◊ ◊ ◊ ◊

Paul places the distinctive gifts of the Corinthians firmly in the context of his own focus on Christ and Christ's imminent return. He saturates the salutation and thanksgiving with repetitive references to Jesus Christ as the instrument of salvation and the exalted and returning political Lord. Christ is also now the content of the "testimony" that is "confirmed" (or "guaranteed"—a legal metaphor) among them (v. 6). Paul is suggesting here that the eloquence and knowledge with which the Corinthians are enriched is the evidence that confirms the testimony of the gospel of Christ presented to them.

DIVISIVENESS AND UNITY (1:10–4:21)

Three or four closely interrelated oppositions stand out in this section: the divisions Paul sees among the Corinthians *versus* the unity he would like to see established (1:10-11; 3:1-3); their boasting in their favorite "guru" *versus* his concern for the cohesion of the community under its common Lord (1:12, 31; 3:4, 5-17, 21-23; 4:1-7); their attachment to wisdom *(sophia) versus* his gospel of the crucified Christ (1:17, 18-25; 2:1-5, 6-9; 3:18-20); and their excitement over the exalted spiritual status that seems closely related to their possession of wisdom *(sophia) versus* the low social status of the members and leaders of the movement (1:26-29; 2:3, 6, 14-16;

4:8-13). Underlying the argument is Paul's concern with his own authority, which has been threatened by a rival servant of the movement who has been building on the foundation Paul laid (3:5-10) and by Corinthian criticism (4:3-5).

Paul's rhetorical strategy unfolds in five major steps. (1) After issuing a formal appeal in 1:10-17 to overcome their divisiveness, he moves (2) in 1:18–2:5 to counter the wisdom *(sophia)* that he sees lying behind the divisiveness with the foolishness of the gospel that features the crucified Christ. (3) In 2:6–3:4 he resorts to the standard rhetorical device of sarcasm to attack the exalted spiritual status in which he believes the divisive attachment to particular apostles is rooted. (4) In 3:5-17 Paul presents his view of the relationship between his ministry and the ministry of Apollos in Corinth. (5) In the final step of his argument for unity, 4:1-21, he defends himself against Corinthian criticism and asserts his fatherly role in the foundation of the community. Each of these five steps is an integral component of the overall argument in 1:10–4:21.

In the course of this argument Paul employs some of the standard forms of ancient hellenistic-Roman oratory: persuasian (deliberative rhetoric), praise and blame (epideictic rhetoric), and sarcasm (a subcategory of irony). In particular, his use of censure and sarcasm serves his overall deliberative rhetorical strategy of calling the assembly to think and act in concord. As he indicates explicitly at the end (4:14, 16), he is admonishing them to change and calling them to imitate him in the appropriate humility that will foster concord (4:16). In the latter appeal he is again following a standard deliberative procedure in which the speaker calls for imitation of himself as a model of appropriate moral character *(ēthos)*. Yet he displays a decisive substantive difference as well. Paul's presentation of his own character, as being in utter "disrepute" and "the rubbish of the world" (4:8-13) is diametrically opposite to the standard aristocratic paradigms of the imperial hellenistic-Roman culture.

First Step in Paul's Argument for Unity (1:10-17)

In this introduction to his argument Paul states that divisions in the assembly are obvious from their slogans about attachment to favorite "gurus" (vv. 11-13), perhaps having something to do with their baptism by particular apostles (vv. 13-16). Finally (v. 17), he indicates that these divisions and slogans are related to a polarity between wisdom *(sophia)* and the cross of Christ.

◊ ◊ ◊ ◊

Paul's formal appeal to the Corinthians for unity in 1:10 articulates his dominant concern in the whole letter as well as in the first major argument. "I appeal" is common in calls to political concord. Like later leaders and members of popular protest or revolutionary movements, Paul frequently addresses his fellow believers as "brothers" using the masculine plural in an inclusive sense (NRSV: "brothers and sisters"). The formal phrase "by the name of our Lord Jesus Christ" constitutes Paul's appeal to the source of his own apostolic authority, which he considers to have been called into question by the divisions in the community. Contrary to his practice on other matters in the letter (5:1; 11:18; 15:12), Paul mentions his source for the information about quarreling among the Corinthians (v. 11). We have virtually no information about "those of Chloe" (NRSV: "Chloe's people"), although this phrase suggests members of Chloe's household, perhaps slaves or freedpersons (but "Chloe" was itself a name often given to female slaves). That Paul does not mention them along with the representatives from the Corinthian community named later (16:15-18) suggests that they were probably not from Corinth. They probably lived in Ephesus, from where Paul was writing, and likely belonged to the movement.

The phrases "I belong to Paul . . . Apollos, and so forth" (v. 12) have been the principal bases for reconstructions of the situation in Corinth and interpretations of Paul's response, but nothing requires us to posit the existence of identifiable "factions" or "parties." Nothing similar in form has been identified in ancient literature that could qualify as a political party slogan. Although Paul introduces the statements with "each of you says," his introductory phrase "what I mean is" may indicate that he is telling the Corinthians how their quarrelling sounds to him. That Paul is setting the stage, rhetorically, for the rest of the letter is evident when he cites two of these same statements again in 3:4 and mentions all four names in his recapitulation of the argument in 3:21-23. Subsequent steps in the argument (especially 3:4 and 3:5-15) show that Paul believes the quarrel is between his followers and the followers of Apollos. So far as we know, Cephas (Peter) had not visited Corinth; hypotheses about his role in the Corinthian community are based on either chapters 10–13 or the now discredited theory of "Judaizers" as the opponents of Paul wherever he went or both. Paul himself may be responsible for the inclusion of Cephas in the list of names in verse 12.

How shall we explain the slogan, "I belong to Christ"? That Paul later makes a point of subordinating the whole community to Christ (3:21-23) and that he reasserts in no uncertain terms his own fundamental gospel of Christ's crucifixion and resurrection (1:18–2:5; 15:1-28) suggests that at least some Corinthians did not understand Christ in the way Paul would have liked. Again, most likely Paul himself is responsible for this slogan, used as a rhetorical device to set up the rhetorical questions in verse 13. With the implied negative answers, he in effect reasserts the unity of the assembly in (under) Christ. From what follows, it appears that the Corinthians may have understood Christ as a wisdom teacher somewhat like Apollos or Paul, and not as the crucified, resurrected Lord.

In an aside (vv. 14-16) Paul rejects partisanship by discounting his own role in baptism. He is not devaluing baptism in general (cf. Rom 6:3-7). He has in mind the importance of baptism for some in the Corinthian assembly who practiced a "baptism on behalf of the dead" (see on 15:29 below). That Paul baptized these particular people or their household(s), however, may have some significance for understanding the situation in Corinth and later sections of the letter.

Precisely with reference to Crispus, Gaius, and Stephanas (vv. 14-16) it has been argued that early Christianity was a religious movement sponsored by wealthy patrons for their social dependents—wives, children, clients, slaves or freedpersons—and not a movement of the disinherited poor, as previously thought. Luke's later portrayal of Crispus as an "official" (not "ruler") of the Jewish synagogue and head of a household (Acts 18:7-8) is part of a historically unreliable theme in the book of Acts. We have no information about him beyond Paul's passing mention. That Gaius is later the "host" of Paul and "the whole assembly" (Rom 16:23) suggests that he has a house large enough to accommodate at least a small group of people. The "household" of Stephanas (v. 16) could have included some slaves or freedpeople along with his wife and children, perhaps including Fortunatas and Achaicus, the two men with slavelike names mentioned along with Stephanas in 16:17-18. As heads of households that joined the assembly or owners of houses large enough to host "the whole assembly" or both, Stephanas and Gaius were relatively well-off in comparison with ordinary artisans and freedpersons. Yet men who had a modest-sized house and owned a few slaves would hardly have been considered wealthy in a city such as Corinth. However modest their economic circumstances, they may nevertheless have been playing the role of patrons in the fledgling assembly. As head of the household that became the "first converts of Achaia" (the area of Greece around Corinth) and the apparent bearer of the Corinthians' letter to Paul (16:15-16), Stephanas was clearly a leader in the Corinthian assembly.

In verse 17 Paul moves into what he sees as the root of the divisiveness in Corinth. The combination of the Greek words *sophia logou* (wisdom of word/speech) as a mode of proclamation evidently refers to "eloquence" or, more precisely, "eloquent wisdom." The last phrase identifies this "wisdom of word" as a threat to the "cross of Christ" and sets up the dominant antithesis that Paul explores in the next step of his argument. In opposing "wisdom of word" to the cross of Christ or power and Spirit in (see also 2:1, 4, 13; 4:20), Paul is not simply subordinating the means of communication to the efficacy of the gospel. Nor is he merely using the typical rhetorical device of an orator deprecating his own ability in eloquence. Rejection of "persuasive wisdom" is integral to the rejection (or transformation) of *sophia* itself, particularly in 1:17–3:4 and 3:18-20. In Paul's day, eloquent speech was of special importance in public discourse and entertainment and was also associated with other marks of high social standing (such as those Paul mentions in 1:26-28).

The close association of eloquent "speech" with wisdom *(sophia)* is most strikingly paralleled in the hellenistic-Jewish wisdom-devotion represented by Wisdom of Solomon and Philo of Alexandria. Hellenistic Jews readily fused the importance of eloquence in hellenistic public discourse and philosophy with the high evaluation of speech in the Jewish wisdom tradition (e.g., Prov 1:2-7; Sir 6:5; 18:28-29; 38:33; 39:1-6). Most striking in connection with chapters 1–2 is Wis 8:8, 12, 18, where turns of speech and skill in public discourse are important benefits of a personal relationship with *sophia.* Philo elaborates the connection between eloquence and a close relationship with *sophia* in a number of images paralleled later in 1 Corinthians. Spiritual "maturity" or "perfection" depends on having "speech" along with reason. Eloquence is God's gift to the soul who has transcended mortal things for the contemplation of the immortal (*Migr. Abr.* 70-85; cf. 1 Cor 2:6–3:4). Those who desire "knowledge" and put their faith in "wisdom" display "bold speech" (*Heres* 14-21; cf. 1 Cor 8:1).

Second Step in Paul's Argument for Unity (1:18–2:5)

Here a quotation from Isaiah followed by numerous plays on the word "wisdom," which include its demotion to mere "wisdom of the world," establishes a sharp opposition between wisdom *(sophia)* and God's power manifested in the crucified Christ (1:18-20). With multiple plays on the principal terms he is using, Paul illustrates how God's "foolishness," which is "wiser than human wisdom," and God's "weakness," which is "stronger than human strength" worked through the low status Corinthians to shame the pretentious wise and powerful aristocracy who dominate the world (1:25-31). To conclude this step in his argument for unity Paul emphasizes the contrast between wisdom and the gospel of the crucified Christ by referring to the manner of his own preaching (2:1-5).

◊ ◊ ◊ ◊

Throughout much of 1:18-25 Paul plays on the word *sophia* and its opposite, *folly,* with different twists and turns. But while the meaning of *sophia* keeps shifting, that of the cross/Christ crucified

47

remains stable, from the thesis statement in 1:18 to the climactic statement of the paragraph in 1:23-24: it is the power of God for those who are being saved/the called. By contrast, Paul moves the term *sophia* from opposition to the cross and opposition by God in 1:18-20 into apposition with the crucified Christ (and the power of God) and into identification as the wisdom *of God* in 1:23-24. The final statement in 1:25 reasserts the point with which he started, encompassing the paradox that God's saving action in the crucifixion is foolishness to human wisdom in the larger paradox that God's folly/weakness is wiser/more powerful than humans. In between, in 1:21, where *sophia* appears twice in opposed senses, Paul makes the transition from wisdom *opposed to and by God* to wisdom *of God*.

The Greek participle in 1:18*a* translated "those who are perishing" in the NRSV has the more permanent sense of "those who are being destroyed," as in the next verse: "I will destroy" (cf. 8:11; 10:9-10; 15:18). "Saving/being saved" in 1:18*b* is Paul's comprehensive general term (with roots in scriptural accounts of historical events of deliverance) for the work of God in the Christ events and gospel; it has a broad historical sense, not a separable "religious" sense. Of Paul's fifteen references to the cross or Christ crucified, six come in this passage, with another six grouped in Galatians. It would appear that Paul mentions the cross or Christ crucified when he feels some threat to the implications of his gospel for the current life of the communities he has founded: these are found only in Galatians (3:1; 5:11, 24; 6:12, 14) against the threat he feels from "Judaizers"; briefly in Phil 3:18; and here in 1 Corinthians (1:13, 17, 18, 23; 2:2, 8; with 2 Cor 13:4 probably derivative). Paul focuses on the cross in this context because he finds the *sophia* of some of the Corinthians to be a serious threat to the community. In 1:19-20 he sharply rejects the Corinthians' *sophia* first by adapting Isa 29:14: God "will destroy the wisdom of the wise"!

The rhetorical questions in 1:20 continue the point of verse 19: Now that God has fulfilled his intention to destroy the wisdom of the wise, what is left of the wise, the scribes, and the debaters of this age? "The wise" are probably not Greek philosophers, and "the scribes," are not Jewish teachers of Torah (no connection with

1:23). Along with "the debaters" they stand for the wise "of this age" in general. "Of this age" (language of Jewish revelatory literature) and "of the world" are synonyms for the historical era that God has brought to an end through the crucifixion (cf. "the present form of this world is passing away," 7:31). In this context of oppositional rhetoric, Paul's insinuation that the Corinthians' wisdom was "worldly" suggests that they claimed it was "heavenly"! That Paul's concern was not about some "secular philosophy" is confirmed by 2:6-16 (see below).

In 1:21, the crucial statement of the paragraph, the two opposed uses of *sophia* must be clarified from rhetorical context. With regard to the second *sophia* (used only here without a qualifier "of word," "of the world," and so forth), the sense is that "the world did *not* know God *through sophia* contrary to the assumption of the Corinthians (and others). Insofar as "in the *sophia* of God" occurs in the explanatory phrase beginning "for since," it must be related to the preceding quotation and rhetorical questions stating God's destruction of wisdom and the wise of this age (1:19-20). In 1:24 Paul virtually identifies "the *sophia* of God" with the crucified Christ, and in 2:7-8 he speaks of Christ's crucifixion as the key event in God's plan for the fulfillment of history. Thus "the *sophia* of God" in 1:21*a* must allude to God's plan for fulfillment through Christ. Events of world-historical significance are happening: Some people are being destroyed, others are being saved. In the more distant past, God announced his intention through an oracle of the prophet Isaiah that he would destroy the wisdom of the wise (1:19). In the more recent past, God has carried out that intention (1:20). The explanation comes in 1:21: Since, in the *sophia* of God, the world did not know God through *sophia,* God decided to work through the foolishness of Paul's proclamation of Christ crucified.

Two further explanatory statements complete the argument. In 1:24-25 Paul restates the thesis of 1:18 with full ecumenical scope and implications: Although scandal to Jews and folly to Gentiles, to the called—both Jews and Greeks—the proclamation of Christ crucified is the power of God *and* (finally commandeering the term *sophia* for God) the *wisdom* of God. "Jews . . . and Greeks" (vv. 22, 24) represents the human world in its basic division culturally, from the (Palestinian) Jewish point of view—"Jews . . . and Gentiles" (v. 23) being somewhat more ecumenical. "Jews demand signs" is probably a reference to scriptural tradition in which God was portrayed delivering the people with signs and wonders. "Wisdom" *(sophia)* or philosophy was characteristically a personal quest of well-off people of the Greek cultural heritage in cities of the eastern Roman Empire.

Christ's crucifixion and its proclamation would indeed have been foolishness to the dominant culture in its understanding of wisdom and power. Crucifixion was a Roman form of torture, an execution by slow, excruciatingly painful death. As the most extreme form of capital punishment, it was reserved for the lower class, usually inflicted upon slaves and rebellious peasants in subject provinces such as Judea. Like modern acts of terrorism, crucifixion was done primarily for its demonstration effect on those who witnessed the torturous death. As state-sponsored terrorism it was intended as a means of social control, such as breaking the will of conquered people who, after any disruption of the pax Romana ("peace" imposed by Rome), would witness hundreds, even thousands of so-called bandits or rebels prominently displayed in public execution. As Paul writes in Gal 3:1: "it was *before your eyes* that Jesus Christ was *publicly exhibited* as crucified!" (emphasis added). Far from being sympathetic with those subjected to such terror and execution, the dominant hellenistic culture was concerned for law and order and considered those crucified as despicable. In a cultural climate dominated by traditional aristocratic Greek values, it would indeed have been "folly" (1:23) to proclaim and organize around a crucified political criminal as a central symbol.

That Christ crucified would also be "a stumbling block" (a cause of falling) to Jews may be a more ambivalent matter. Hellenistic Jews who had assimilated into the dominant hellenistic culture would have shared most of its assumptions. Although there is little evidence of expectations of an "anointed *(messiah)* king" in Palestinian Jewish texts of the time, some Palestinian Jews may have looked for a messiah as a political leader against Roman domination. That such a *messiah* (Gk. *christos*) had been crucified would have been a *skandalon,* and this may be the background of Paul's rhetorical counterpart here to the Greeks and wisdom/folly, his main interest. The concluding play on both wisdom/folly and power/weakness in 1:25, reasserts the paradox that God's work in the cross appears as utter foolishness and weakness to humans.

In 1:26-31 Paul explains this paradox by characterizing the Corinthians' own call into the salvation now underway by God's action in the crucified Christ. (The NRSV partly obscures this connection by leaving the opening "for" untranslated.) Discussion of the social status of the Corinthians and other early Christians generally has focused on the statement in 1:26 that "not many" in the Corinthian assembly were "wise, powerful, of noble birth," assuming these terms to be indicators of concrete social standing and that *some* of them did enjoy higher status. Even though Paul's statement may be an indication of the concrete social status of most members of the Corinthian assembly (inauspicious), to focus only on social status misses the point of his rhetoric, obscuring both the implied contrast of "then" and "now" and the multiple levels of meaning in the terms "wise, powerful, of noble birth." We must recognize that Paul's rhetoric in 1:26-31 works at two levels.

At one level the terms in 1:26, 27-28, along with the closely related terms in 4:8, refer to the principal attributes of the wealthy and powerful aristocracy of a given city or state in antiquity, basking in honor at the apex of the imperial order. It was precisely those whom God had "shamed" and "destroyed." The terminology of "things that (do not) exist" (v. 28 AT) even lends an ontological dimension to the historical political-economic transformation God has effected in wiping out the ruling aristocracy in the call of the lowly members of the Corinthian assembly. This idea of God's overturning the established order is deeply rooted in Jewish biblical traditions, such as the great songs of God's victory over the powerful and wealthy rulers on behalf of lowly Israel (e.g., Exodus 15; Judges 5; 1 Sam 2:1-10; cf. Luke 1:46-55).

Rhetorically, however, in the framing of the argument in 1:26-31, the aristocratic terms cited in 1:26 must be related to the reference to boasting in 1:29. This suggests that there may be some connection between the aristocratic terms and the "boasting" about which Paul warns the Corinthians. It is noteworthy that boasting was a standard feature of eloquence in public oratory and closely associated with eloquent speech. Hellenistic and Roman philosophers had long since relativized and spiritualized aristocratic attributes and values. Best known for this were the Stoics, who taught that only the wise man was truly "wealthy" and a "king." Hellenistic Jews then assimilated this philosophical spiritualization of the old aristocratic ideals into their own devotion to God or God's *Sophia*. Thus, in the Wisdom of Solomon it is said that heavenly *Sophia* confers on pious souls a kingdom (6:20, 21; 7:7; 10:14), riches (7:8, 11, 13-14; 8:5, 18; 10:11), noble birth (8:3), and, of course, being "wise" (cf. the opposites also, e.g., a "nothing," 9:6). The Jewish philosopher Philo also employs such terminology, often in characterizing the exalted spiritual status that *Sophia* or the *Logos* provides to devoted souls.

That the aristocratic qualities "wise, powerful, of noble birth, rich, and so forth" were commonly used in this spiritualized sense, particularly in close connection with *sophia,* is highly suggestive for Paul's argument in 1:26-31, which is addressed to his assembly in what was perhaps the most status conscious city in the Roman Empire. He has just completed an argument displacing *sophia* as the means of knowing God (see especially 1:21). Believing that the divisions in the assembly were also rooted in (some of) the Corinthians' excitement over the high spiritual status they attained through their attachment to *sophia,* Paul pointedly inverts and transvalues the symbols of their spiritual status in 1:26: *At the time of their call,* few of the Corinthians were "wise, powerful, and of noble birth." With rhetoric that works on two levels Paul is making two points simultaneously in 1:26-29. In addition to illustrating the effectiveness of the salvation working through the crucified Christ (and not through *sophia*) in the call of the lowly Corinthians that shamed the ruling aristocracy, he is rejecting the high spiritual status that some Corinthians have attained through *sophia.*

Paul completes this step of the argument by again replacing *sophia* as the means of salvation with "Christ Jesus" as the real "*sophia* from God" (1:30-31). He now relativizes *sophia* by placing it in a series along with three other benefits provided by God in the crucified Christ. "Righteousness" could have either the sense of

God's final act of bringing justice in the crucifixion of Christ (Rom 3:21-22) or the forensic sense that believers are now able to stand before God's judgment. The sacral but also ethical term "sanctification," as in the letter's opening (1:2), indicates being set apart by and to God, with certain expectations of subsequent behavior (cf. 1 Thess 4:3; 5:23). To anyone familiar with basic biblical stories such as the Exodus, "redemption," as in giving freedom from slavery or debt slavery, would connote God's liberation of the Israelites from Egypt. In 1:31, Paul adapts a quotation from Jer 9:23-24, in order to turn the focus to God, the agent of the saving action (both negative, 1:19, 27-28, and positive, 1:21-24, 30) in the crucified Christ, as the object of trust/boast. Having called them to be united "in the same mind and the same purpose [gnōmē]" (1:10), he is now also presenting a "gnomic" maxim (in ancient Greek rhetorical terms) on which they are to focus that mind and purpose.

In 2:1-5 Paul provides a second illustration of his argument, returning to his own manner of preaching without persuasive wisdom, with which he began the whole discussion in 1:17. Here he contrasts persuasive wisdom not only with the message of the cross of Christ (2:1-2) but with "Spirit and . . . power" as its effective mode (2:1, 4-5). The alternative readings listed in the NRSV footnotes are to be preferred in 2:1, 4. The occurrence of "mystery" (mystērion; NRSV: "secret and hidden") in 2:7 could easily have influenced its substitution for "testimony" (martyrion) in 2:1; and using "mystery" in 2:1 would have spoiled its effect in 2:6-7, where Paul suddenly claims to be speaking wisdom after all (but of a certain kind: "in a mystery"). The reading "persuasiveness of wisdom" in 2:4 is the obvious basis from which all other variants could have arisen, many of which have a form of the adjective "persuasive" otherwise unattested in Greek literature (Conzelmann 1975, 55; Fee 1987, 88).

In sharply disclaiming the use of eloquence in 2:1, 4, Paul is again implying (see 1:17) that some Corinthians highly value it. A strikingly similar statement from the near-contemporary orator, Dio Chrysostom, shows Paul's familiarity with current rhetorical practice: "For they are clever persons, mighty sophists, wonder-workers; but I am quite ordinary and prosaic in my utterance, though not ordinary in my theme" (*Or.* 32.39). However, Paul's self-deprecation is specific to the Corinthian situation and his own preaching and movement rooted in the traditions of Israel. The disclaimer of eloquence may be similar, but in contrast with Dio his preaching features "demonstration of the Spirit and of power" (2:4).

In 2:1 the term translated "lofty" modifies both "speech" and "wisdom" and may have more the sense of "excellence of," the combination again suggesting "eloquence" or "eloquent wisdom" as in 1:17. Paul clearly formulates 2:2 for rhetorical effect, again in opposition to *sophia,* doubling both the verb ("I decided to know") and the object ("Jesus Christ, and him crucified") and focusing the statement on the Corinthians themselves ("among you"). Paul emphasizes his "weakness" for the first time in 2:3, and he will elaborate on it later (4:9-13; see also 2 Cor 6:4-10; 12:7-10). Not merely a rhetorical device, his "weakness" and "suffering" were rooted in his identification with the Christ and with the disreputable popular movement in which he became a leading apostle. What it meant concretely that he "came to [them] in weakness and in fear and in much trembling" is unclear.

Also unclear is the concrete reference to "demonstration of the Spirit and of power" that he opposes to "persuasiveness of wisdom" (2:4). This may be an allusion to the "signs and wonders" that accompanied God's great historical acts of redemption, according to biblical narratives. But Paul may also be referring to dramatic manifestations of the Spirit (with which "power" is virtually interchangeable in his writings) that accompanied the initial changes in the Corinthians' lives as they responded to his mission among them. As indicated also in his comment about manifestations of "the Spirit and . . . miracles among you" in Gal 3:5, the beginning of Paul's mission in a new place was accompanied by "pentecostal" phenomena including ecstatic prophecy.

In 2:5, with another brief swipe at *sophia* as merely "human," Paul recapitulates the main point of the argument so far: The message of the cross (which is foolishness to "the wise") stands over against *sophia* (through which the world did not know God) as the power of God overturning the established order while saving those who respond in faith.

◊ ◊ ◊ ◊

The problems evident in and behind chapters 1–4 include the extreme difficulty that people who are socialized into very different orientations toward reality had in coming to common commitments and agenda. A number of believers in Corinth—probably relatively isolated in a city populated by people who had been displaced from their original social roots by enslavement, emancipation, commerce, or the indirect result of imperial social engineering—had come together into a newly formed community centered in a few houses. Paul's mission, including his preaching with "demonstrations of the Spirit," was probably the original catalyst. These household communities provided support and a sense of belonging, while the gifts of the Spirit provided a sense of excitement and empowerment. There was nothing in the cultural environment of Corinth, however, to indicate that the Corinthians would have understood, let alone have easily come to adopt, Paul's historical view of reality, which framed his basic gospel of Christ's crucifixion-exaltation-return as God's fulfillment of the promises to Israel through Abraham.

The alternative gospel introduced into the Corinthian assembly, apparently by Apollos, was based on the same or a highly similar orientation to reality as that dominant in Corinth and hellenistic culture generally. This can be seen in a number of the Corinthian views that Paul responds to (or attacks) in chapters 1–4. That Christ had been a wisdom teacher was an idea immediately comprehensible against the background of famous philosophers and "eastern" religious teachers such as Moses, who had long since been cast in the role of a revealer of wisdom in hellenistic-Jewish communities. A (semi-)divine heavenly figure of *Sophia,* who dispensed special grace on individuals questing for enlightenment and transcendence was familiar from both the well-known mysteries of Isis, the Egyptian goddess and "queen of heaven," and from hellenistic-Jewish communities in various cities of the empire. Such personal transcendence was found in an exalted spiritual status of the truly powerful, wealthy, nobly born, mature, and wise of the sort that can be discerned in those same hellenistic-Jewish circles. The presentation of Christ as a wisdom teacher offering personal transcendence achieved through intimate relationship with *Sophia* would have had immediate and extensive affinity with the worldview into which the Corinthians would have been socialized, and would have offered spiritual gifts that rivaled the "demonstrations of the Spirit" that Paul had introduced into Corinth.

Another issue is evident in chapters 1–4. When a movement is new, growing, and bursting with energy ("lacking no spiritual gift"), it tends to generate multiple leaders and considerable diversity. People of varied social and cultural backgrounds join the communities. New charismatic leaders emerge from the creative combination of circumstances, catalysts, and spiritual impulses. One innovation opens the way to another. In the case of the Corinthian community, the few years between Paul's initial mission and the writing of 1 Corinthians had been insufficient time for authority structures to be consolidated and for ideas and procedures to become standardized. Although Paul's correspondence with his assemblies served the function of consolidating and standardizing, 1 Corinthians apparently did not achieve this immediately, as we know from the continuing conflict between Paul and the Corinthian community that is evident in the various sections of 2 Corinthians.

Third Step in Paul's Argument for Unity (2:6–3:4)

In 2:6-16 Paul appears to change course. After sharply criticizing *sophia* as a false means of salvation and insisting that he had not indulged in eloquent wisdom, he suddenly announces that, after all, he does speak *sophia*—among the elite. As a result, this paragraph has been the source of serious misunderstandings of Paul: He was suddenly playing the Corinthians' game; he in effect sold out to the Corinthians in his attempt to communicate in their terms; he had an esoteric wisdom teaching entirely separate from his kerygma; he distinguished between ordinary Christians and a spiritually superior class. However, once we consider Paul's whole argument from 1:10 through 4:21, it is evident that the thought begun in 2:6-16 is completed in 3:1-4, that this third step in the argument presupposes what has been said in 1:10-17 and 1:18–2:5, and that it leads to what he is about to say in 3:5-23 and 4:1-21.

Paul's apparent change of course involves his use of the rhetorical device of sarcasm *(sarkasmos)*, which speakers employed when they meant virtually the opposite of what they appeared to say. Here Paul sets up the Corinthians by speaking their language in 2:6-16, only to turn it against them in 3:1-4. Pretending that he too teaches *sophia* to those who have advanced to "mature" spiritual status, he then puts them down as "infants" incapable of such wisdom because of their quarreling and boasting in favorite leaders. This step in Paul's argument is not pure sarcasm, however, because Paul is still advancing his own distinctive gospel (especially 2:6-8).

◊ ◊ ◊ ◊

The language upon which the sarcastic turn of Paul's argument depends is the complex metaphor constrasting the "mature/perfect" *(teleioi,* 2:6) and "infants" *(nēpioi,* 3:1) along with their respective forms of nourishment, "solid food" versus "milk" *(brōma-gala,* 3:2). When he comes to the sarcastic turn in the argument at 3:1, Paul uses the term "spiritual people" *(pneumatikoi)* as an apparent synonym for "mature." This indicates that the contrast in 2:14-15 between "those who are spiritual" and "those who are unspiritual" *(psychikoi)* is parallel and synonymous to the distinction between "mature" (2:6) and "infants" (3:1).

Since these terms occur only or distinctively in 1 Corinthians, they must have been language with which some of the Corinthians expressed their self-understanding. They seem to have thought of themselves as "spiritual" people endowed with "spiritual gifts" and "spiritual" understanding of "spiritual things" (2:14-16; 10:3-4; 12:1; 14:1, 37; 15:44-46). The many parallels to this distinctive Corinthian language in hellenistic-Jewish literature (e.g., Wis 6:15; 9:6; Philo, *Anim.* 8-9; *Somn.* 2.10-11) show that it formed a whole pattern of religious devotion focused on *Sophia.* Although the spiritual-psychic distinction does not appear there, the synonymous term "mature/perfect" in contrast with a mere "infant" refers to the exalted spiritual status achieved by one who receives or is devoted to *Sophia.* "Mature" regularly appears parallel to the "aristocratic" qualities "rich," "powerful," "of noble birth" (see 1:26) as indicators of the "immortality" or understanding of divine things obtained from a close relationship with *Sophia,* often characterized as a heavenly figure (Horsley 1977; 1978b).

In 2:6-13 Paul himself suddenly appears to speak such wisdom (2:6*a,* 13*b*). Only by attending closely to his more precise statement of the content of the wisdom he speaks, in the qualification in 2:6*b* and the assertion in 2:7-9, can we discern just how different his position is from the Corinthians'. Paul purposely places *sophia* first in his opening statement (literally "Yet *sophia* we do speak among the mature"), and by using *sophia* without a qualifying phrase he clearly distinguishes this as the content or means of salvation, as in 1:21*a,* not the "eloquent wisdom" of the previous paragraph and 1:17. In 2:6*b,* he makes more explicit than earlier the historical-eschatological perspective that has structured his thinking since 1:10. By distinguishing "this age" (2:6*b*) from the coming age, he attempts to render historically relative and temporary the Corinthians' *sophia* and spiritual perfection. "The rulers of this age" (2:6, 8) are not primarily demonic forces (*pace* Barrett 1968, 70; Conzelmann 1975, 61; *et al.*), but human political rulers (like the rulers in Rom 13:3 and other NT literature; Carr 1981; Fee 1987). Paul may be referring here to rulers of the Roman Empire generally, whereas in 2:8 he focuses on those responsible for the crucifixion of Jesus. But also, Paul stands in the tradition of Jewish apocalyptic literature in which human rulers act under the influence of superhuman demonic forces.

When Paul describes his *sophia* in 2:7 as "God's wisdom in a mystery, which God decreed before the ages" (obscured in the NRSV paraphrase "wisdom, secret and hidden"), he writes in almost technical Jewish apocalyptic terms (*not* the language of mystery religions). As can be seen in the book of Daniel (especially 2:18-19, 27-28) and the Dead Sea Scrolls (e.g., 1QS 3:13–4:25; 1QpHab 7:1-5), "mystery" (Heb. *raz*; Gk. *mystērion*) referred to God's plan for the deliverance of the people/Israel from imperial domination, which often was expressed in more grandiose terms as the eschatological fulfillment of history. God's mystery, the eschatological plan of fulfillment now revealed to Paul and others, was an integral if not formative concept in Paul's basic orientation to reality (see also 1 Cor 15:51; Rom 11:25-26). In Jewish apocalyptic literature (e.g., 1QS 3:13–4:25), "wisdom" (Heb. *hokhmah*) was frequently used as a synonym for the "mystery(ies)" of God's plan of fulfillment (now revealed). Against this background Paul's playing with the term *sophia* in 1:21 becomes clear in 2:6-8: "In the *sophia* (i.e., according to the apocalyptic mystery or plan) of God, the world did not know God through *sophia*." Not only is Paul being consistent, but he is gradually unfolding his meaning as he moves from one step of his argument to another. The renewal of the people and the vindication of those martyred for the faith, which were separate aspects of God's agenda of deliverance in earlier Jewish apocalyptic literature (e.g., Dan 7; 10–12) have been collapsed in Paul's formulation, "for our glory."

A further explanation of "God's wisdom in a mystery," found in 2:8, indicates Paul's political as well as eschatological orientation. The thought of rulers acting in ignorance when they executed Jesus is also found in the statements of Peter in Acts 3:17 and of Paul in Acts 13:27, as is the motif of fulfillment of a preordained plan of God. That "the rulers of this age" are "doomed to perish" is part and parcel of Paul's political-apocalyptic view (see 1 Cor 15:20-28; especially v. 24). As part of God's plan of deliverance, unknown to the imperial rulers but now revealed to the elect, the Christ they crucified has been exalted as "the Lord of glory," installed by God as the eschatological ruler (further elaborated in 15:20-28). The imperial rulers have been undone precisely by their own repressive terrorizing of subject peoples.

Paul articulates the positive aspect of God's overthrow of the old order in the quotation in 2:9, completing the thought in verse 10a. This preordained "wisdom in a mystery," so wonderful that it transcends human fantasy as well as experience, is not only prepared for those who love God but now revealed to them through the Spirit. Although the tone of the quotation is apocalyptic, its source is unknown. It probably comes from some unknown Jewish apocalyptic writing that had drawn heavily on prophetic motifs, particularly Isa 64:4 [64:3 LXX], but so significant to Paul that he cites it as scripture. The similarity of the last phrase to Paul's expression "those who love God" in a similarly dramatic crescendo in Rom 8:28 suggests that such language was standard in Jewish apocalyptic circles (for the biblical sources of the phrase, cf. Exod 20:6; Deut 5:10; 7:9).

In 2:10-13 Paul moves closer to the language of the Corinthians, perhaps because just at this point it is so similar to his own understanding of the function of the Spirit in revealing the apocalyptic plan of God. In some hellenistic-Jewish circles the divine Spirit was virtually synonymous with divine *Sophia* in teaching or revealing wisdom and understanding. The statement about knowledge of divine things (2:11) may be virtually a citation from the Corinthian "spiritual" people; the principle in verse 11*b* as well as the analogy by which it is formulated appear nowhere else in Paul's letters. The idea that only the inner spirit can truly know inner/higher truths and, by implication, that the inner spirit must be illuminated by the divine Spirit (virtually identified with *Sophia*) to receive true knowledge developed among the same hellenistic-Jewish circles that focused on the achievement of heightened spiritual status through intimate association with *Sophia* (see especially Wis 7:7, 22; 9:17; Philo, *Leg. All.* 1.38; *Gig.* 27, 47). Thus the idea of the Spirit searching "the depths of God" (2:10*b*) may also stem from the Corinthians.

While Paul formulates these general principles in the present tense, he uses the past tense ("God has revealed to us," 2:10*a*) to place them in the context of the revelation of God's plan in the event of Christ's crucifixion. However, Paul's own apocalyptic point of view recedes as he continues his discourse on revelation by the Spirit in 2:12-13, using still more language that the Corinthians would have appreciated. They too would have distinguished the divine Spirit (probably synonymous with *Sophia*) that had bestowed gifts of wisdom and understanding upon them from "the spirit of the world." Still, the restatement of Paul's earlier contrast between "human wisdom" and manifestations of the Spirit (2:13; cf. 2:4-5) indicates that he continues to differentiate the *sophia* he is presenting from the *sophia* claimed by the Corinthians.

In 2:14-15 Paul uses the Corinthians' own principles to set them up for the sarcastic turn of his argument, but he is not just playing with their language. The statement in 2:14, replete with terms distinctive to 1 Corinthians ("unspiritual" [*psychikos*, literally "soul-like"], "foolishness," "spiritually" [*pneumatikōs]*, and "discerned"), appears to express the Corinthians' explanation of spiritual understanding in terms of two levels of people. The spiritual person has achieved a level of spiritual maturity, but the merely psychic person is still in an infantile phase of development, unable to know the gifts (things) of God's spirit because such ethereal matters can be discerned only spiritually. The highly formulaic statement in 2:15 about "the spiritual (person)" (obscured somewhat by the plural in the NRSV) must be a principle of the Corinthian "spirituals" that Paul is quoting, just as he quotes other principles of theirs later on (6:12*a* = 10:23*a*; 7:1*b*; 8:1*b*, 4*b*).

Paul's motives in citing the principles of the Corinthian spirituals about discernment extend beyond this step in his argument. "Discernment/examination/judgment" *(anakrinein)*, a spiritualized judicial term distinctive to 1 Corinthians among Pauline letters, was a multifaceted matter of contention between Paul and some of the Corinthians. It is evident from Paul's defensive statements in both 4:3-4 and 9:3 that some people in Corinth have been examining and judging Paul's apostleship.

Anticipating the explicit reversal of his argument in 3:1, there is a subtle change in tone in 2:16. After seeming to share the Corinthians' excitement about receiving enlightenment by means of the Spirit, Paul suddenly calls such a spiritual quest into question by posing a rhetorical question drawn from Isa 40:13. He then immediately focuses attention back on Christ, that one who was crucified by the rulers (2:2, 8), whose gospel is "foolishness" (1:18, 23).

If Paul's sarcasm was not evident before, it surely becomes so in 3:1-4. The put-down is blunt and sharp. Not only could he not treat them as "spiritual" and "mature," capable of handling the "solid food" of divine things revealed by the Spirit, but they are mere "infants," even fleshly people (stuck in crass materiality). The effect is to reverse his seeming approval of their principles of spiritual knowledge (cited in 2:10-15). Because there is still "jealousy and quarreling" among them, they are behaving all too humanly and are "not ready" for spiritual matters (3:2-3; cf. 1:10-12).

◊ ◊ ◊ ◊

Paul's historical-eschatological orientation and political agenda come increasingly to the fore as his argument proceeds. His emphasis in 1:18–2:5 and 2:6–3:4 on the crucifixion of Christ is meant to counter the heavenly *Sophia* that he sees as a threat both to his gospel and to the unity of his community. In 2:6-8 he also draws out the political basis and implication of the crucifixion, which would have been utterly shameful and despicable to those of any social standing or social pretension in the hellenistic-Roman world. Ironically, by crucifying Christ, the imperial rulers themselves implemented God's plan for their own termination and destruction. The first of God's eschatological actions in Christ, the crucifixion, was a political action by God that defeated the imperial "rulers of this age." Those interpreters, ancient and modern, who have understood these rulers to be demonic powers have missed seeing the political basis and thrust of Paul's own gospel.

Insofar as chapters 1–2 have contributed to Christian theology, it is the result of the interaction of Paul with the Corinthians and the subsequent reading of the letter by the church, not something intended by Paul. Although chapters 1–2 are often read by modern theological interpreters to indicate that Paul himself emphasized the sovereign wisdom of God, *sophia* was the focus of some of the Corinthians' religiosity that he was arguing against. And although 1 Cor 2:6-16, in particular, is sometimes taken as Paul's own cultivation of a higher spiritual teaching for a Christian elite, this is actually what he is castigating in the sarcasm of the paragraph, as is evident finally in 3:1-4.

What is important theologically is Paul's focused attention on the crucified Christ, which is often identified as a key Pauline teaching. At the same time, however, the identification of Christ and Wisdom (along with the statements in 8:6 and 10:4, discussed below) became the basis of the later (Deutero-Pauline) identification of Christ with the preexistent heavenly *Sophia* (e.g., Col 1:15-20). Ironically, although Paul dissociated himself from *sophia* in chapters 1–4, it was so strong and compelling in the culture that his formulations designed to *replace Sophia* by the *crucified* Christ led to a new identification of Christ as Wisdom.

Fourth Step in Paul's Argument for Unity (3:5-23)

Here Paul addresses the Corinthians' understanding of himself and Apollos, their relationship as a community to the apostles, and their relationship to Christ and God. An extended image from agriculture (3:5-9), is followed by an even more extended image of a building (3:10-15). In the latter, Paul identifies himself as the skilled master builder who laid the foundation of Jesus Christ, and warns that other workers must be careful how they build on this foundation, under threat of the fiery test that the day of judgment will bring for the builders and their work. A further metaphor of the community as God's temple reinforces the threat of God's judgment (3:16-17), and then Paul recapitulates the argument he began in 1:10 (3:18-23), again rejecting wisdom, excitement over being wise, and boasting in favorite apostles, thus subordinating the community as a whole to Christ.

◊ ◊ ◊ ◊

"Servants" (*diakonoi*, 3:5) was already a standard term for those charged with preaching the gospel and supervising the assemblies of the movement. Women as well as men shared in this leadership (thus Phoebe was the "servant" of the assembly in nearby Cenchreae, Rom 16:1). *Diakonos* carries none of the implications of a secondary officer of the community subordinate to the higher authority of a bishop (*episkopos* = overseer) that developed later in ecclesiastical order. In Greek society, servants waited table, which was beneath the dignity of citizens with appropriate means, but the word *diakonoi* was also used for courtiers of an eastern king, and even with the meaning "statesman" (Plato, *Gorg.* 518b; cf. the imperial governing "authority" in Rom 13:4). "Apostle" is the more honorable and authoritative title or role in Paul's letters and elsewhere in the movement. While Paul insists that he is an apostle, he never refers to Apollos as an apostle.

The agricultural metaphor of 3:5-9 represents Paul and Apollos engaged as coworkers (cf. Phil 2:25; 4:3; 1 Thess 3:2; Phlm 24) in a common enterprise with a common purpose, producing fruit from God's field, the Corinthian community (3:9). Credit for the growth is given to God, not the servants, clearly over against the "boasting" in favorite apostles. The emphasis here is on the last clause in verse 5, which distinguishes the respective roles of the servants, "as the Lord assigned to each," and on the last clause of verse 8, which distinguishes the respective labor and wages. Paul's role is clearly the primary and more important one: he *planted*, whereas Apollos came along later and only watered. Paul himself was the *founder*, a point repeated in the next paragraph, as well as in 4:14-15.

The metaphor of the Corinthian community as God's building or edifice is abruptly introduced at the end of 3:9, whereupon the edification of the assembly as God's edifice becomes one of the dominant themes of this letter (1:10; 8:1; 10:23; 14:3-5, 12, 17, 26). The metaphor of building was a common one for personal growth and spiritual enlightenment, both in hellenistic philosophy (e.g., Epictetus, *Diss.* 2.15.8) and in the mystical theology of Philo (*Somn.* 2.8; cf. *Gig.* 30; *Nom.* 211). It is at least conceivable that the Corinthians were using this metaphor for their personal spiritual enlightenment and empowerment; but over against that standard cultural sense of the metaphor Paul focuses on the assembly as a social-political community.

Paul himself claims the role of "a skilled (Gk. "wise") master builder" who laid the foundation, and his tone quickly becomes more ominous in the chiasmus of 3:10-11, with unbalanced lines that elaborate on the authority, skill, and importance of his own role, while initiating a terse warning about "someone else" who is building on the foundation he has laid:

A   According to the grace of God given to me,
     like a skilled master builder I laid a foundation,
  B   and someone else is building on it.
  B'   Each builder must choose with care how to build on it.
A' For no one can lay any foundation other than the one
     that has been laid; that foundation is Jesus Christ.

In 3:12-15 Paul makes explicit the warning against an anonymous "anyone" who presumes to build upon the foundation he has laid. The particular building materials with which "anyone" builds will determine whether the builder will receive a reward. Of course, the builder himself will "be saved," but only "as through fire." "The Day" is "the day of the Lord," a phrase taken over by Paul from the Israelite prophets and Jewish apocalypticism. For him, it refers to the judgment at the coming *(parousia)* of Christ (cf. 1:8; 1 Thess 2:19, and so forth). Some interpreters suggest that Paul has shifted the focus from the roles of himself and Apollos in 3:5-9 to the leaders of the Corinthian community who were also supposedly "building on" Paul's foundation. More likely, however, he is using the rhetorical tactic of temporary covert allusion. The goal is to be less offensive as the note of warning becomes explicit, but the shift to "someone else" and "anyone" has the effect of making the warning all the more ominous. After the opening complaint about partisan boasting (1:11-12), the narrowing of the problem to the competition between himself and Apollos (3:1-4), and the explicit references to their respective roles (3:5-9), there can be little question that "anyone" points to Apollos (although in 3:12-15 the warning would apply to the Corinthians as well).

As a result of his revelatory experience of the enthroned Jesus Christ (Gal 1:15-16), Paul understood himself as commissioned to preach the gospel and found communities among the Gentiles. At least in his own view, each apostle had a particular commission for a particular mission area. Paul's going to the Gentiles may have had something to do with his clear feeling that he was a latecomer (see, e.g., 1 Cor 15:8-10). Whether as a result of the conflicts in Corinth or as a general principle, Paul states in Rom 15:20 that he would "not build on someone else's foundation." Besides being driven to work harder than the rest, he was clearly jealous of his own apostolic turf. Apollos, among other things, had invaded his territory in Corinth, just as the "superapostles" were to do somewhat later (2 Cor 10–13). His concern for the cohesion of the Corinthian assembly, based on the foundation he had laid in the crucified Christ, was partly determined by his sense of his own world-historical role as commissioned by his Lord.

At 3:16-17 Paul shifts to yet a third and now explicitly religious metaphor as a further appeal to God's authority for his apostolic mission in Corinth. Besides being God's edifice, the Corinthians are collectively God's temple, in whom God's Spirit dwells (cf. 2 Cor 6:16). The term *naos* refers to the actual sanctuary where God dwells, not the larger temple compound *(hieron)*. Paul may have had the Jerusalem temple in mind, but the Corinthians' understanding of temple would surely have been shaped by the many prominent temples in their own city. A warning about the anonymous "anyone" is again prominent. Note the terse chiasmus of the *lex talionis* (e.g., "an eye for an eye") in what has been called a "sentence of holy law" (3:17*a*), and also that the potential judgment is now more severe than in the preceding paragraph: the offender will be destroyed, not saved. The opening phrase "Do you not know that . . . ," used repeatedly in this letter, indicates that this is a most serious issue for Paul.

In 3:18-23 Paul recapitulates his whole argument thus far. He is explicit and blunt, again playing on the words "wisdom" and "wise" (cf. 1:18–2:5), again citing Scripture (Ps 94:11; Job 5:13; cf. 1 Cor 1:19; 2:9, 16), and again insisting on his own historical-eschatological understanding of reality (cf. 2:6-8). He wraps up the warning about boasting in apostles (1:29-31) by recasting, in 3:21-23, the Corinthians' own slogans (1:12; 3:4). He reverses the relationship expressed in the possessive genitives and shifts the focus from the individual to the communal and universal: from "I belong to Paul" and "I belong to Apollos," to "all things are yours [plural], whether Paul or Apollos . . . all belong to you [plural]."

Except, of course, that "you," the Corinthian community, belong to Christ. Here Christ is no longer the Crucified One, but Lord of the assembly and mediator under God. Paul's careful formulation of this recapitulation, which repeats the same sharp rejection of *sophia* as in 1:18-25, indicates again that he believes the divisiveness was rooted in a devotion to *Sophia* and, surely integrally related, in Apollos' ministry in Corinth. In this step of his argument Paul asserts the priority of his own ministry and Christ as the "foundation" of the community, warns the Corinthians about the validity of Apollos' ministry, and shifts the focus from Christ the Crucified One to Christ the Exalted Lord.

Fifth Step in Paul's Argument for Unity (4:1-21)

Responding to criticisms by at least some of the Corinthians, Paul now explicitly defends himself and reasserts his apostolic authority. His defensive strategy is to go on the offensive, moving from an ominous tone to biting sarcasm to stern paternal admonition. While defending his ministry against the Corinthians' criticism, he applies the warning about the final judgment of his own work and Apollos' work (3:13-15) to the Corinthians themselves (4:1-5) and drives home the implications of his whole discussion for the Corinthians (4:6-7). He then mocks their claims to exalted spiritual attainment (4:8-10; cf. 1:26), contrasting his own experiences as an apostle (4:9-13; cf. 1:27-28). Finally, he presents himself to them as their father in the gospel, and admonishes his children to return to his "ways in Christ Jesus" (vv. 14-21).

◊ ◊ ◊ ◊

In 4:1-5 Paul picks up the discussion of himself and Apollos as servants (3:5-9) and of the judgment of their servants' work (3:13-15). Here the unspoken, overarching metaphor is of God's or Christ's household or society, with allusions to God's building or edifice (3:9, 10-15). The "us" (v. 1) refers to Paul and Apollos (3:5-9, 10-11, 21-22). The terms "servants" *(hypēretai)* and "stewards" *(oikonomoi)* refer either to the steward or slave-manager of an estate or to the administrative officer of a town or a political district. In any case, they indicate someone charged with important administrative responsibility by a higher authority. Thus those who belong to Christ and ultimately to God (3:23) are charged with responsibility for "God's mysteries," by which Paul probably means the overall message of God's fulfillment of history (cf. the singular in 2:7). By implication, such "servants" and "stewards" also held authority over others within the household or jurisdiction. Paul's message to the Corinthians in the rest of the paragraph flows from the extended network of relationships in the household or estate implied by these terms. Thus 4:2 states, almost as a maxim of economics, that the basic requirement of managers or administrators is that they be found trustworthy of the charge entrusted to them by the master (*kyrios,* "lord").

Allusions to Corinthian criticism of Paul's message, or his lack of eloquence, or his adequacy as a leader have been evident before, partly in his own defensiveness (2:1-5, 15-16; 3:13-15). Now, as if in a judicial proceeding, Paul uses the same verb (*anakrinein,* v. 3) as in the principle cited in 2:15 (literally: "the spiritual [person] examines [or: judges] everything [or: everyone], but is himself examined [or: judged] by no one"), thus suggesting that the Corinthian spirituals had been criticizing him. The defensive tone is continued in verse 4, where the assertions "I am not thereby acquitted" and "It is the Lord who judges me" function both as a further defense against the Corinthians' examination (only the steward's master or political authority would judge his performance) and as a transition to his invoking the *parousia* and judgment of Christ (v. 5; cf. 3:13-15). Paul has been given his commission by Christ himself in a revelatory vision *(apokalypsis)* and must face his commissioner at the *parousia.* Employing the biblical theme that God searches even the innermost purposes of the human heart, he implies to his critics that their inner motives will be publicly exposed at the *parousia.*

In verse 6, by placing "all this" in the emphatic opening position, Paul indicates that he is now applying everything since 1:10 to the Corinthians. The rest of this verse, however, is not at all clear. If verse 6*b* (literally "so that you may learn through us the 'not beyond what is written' ") is explained as a gloss resulting from a series of copyists' attempts to correct an obscure text, then the point would be simply (if in English somewhat awkwardly), "so that you learn so that none of you will be puffed up." If, with the NRSV, we retain "nothing beyond what is written" as originally in Paul's text, then it could refer either to all that Paul has written in the letter to this point or to a perhaps familiar proverb, "live according to the Scripture" (elsewhere in Paul's letters "what is written" is used in connection with citation of Scripture). However, assuming that Paul is addressing the same Corinthians throughout most of the letter, there is a more likely possibility. The Corinthian spirituals appear to have cultivated an allegorical or spiritual understanding of the scriptural Exodus-wilderness stories and symbols, to which Paul is reacting (see further on 10:1-4 below). Thus it is possible that, if "not beyond what is written" belongs in the text, Paul is pushing the Corinthians away from the spiritual reading of Scripture, which he sees as integral to their wisdom and spiritual status.

In any case, in a series of rhetorical questions, Paul castigates, in a biting tone, what he sees as the Corinthians' inflation over their spiritual attainment (v. 7). The verb in the first question *(diakrinein)* must be a play on and reference to what Paul sees as the Corinthians' own pride in their "judgment" *(anakrinein)* as spiritual people (2:15; 4:3): "For who differentiates (distinguishes) you (who claim such absolute discernment)?"—as if supposedly saying that God does, but implying the answer "no one." The implied answer to the second question is, similarly, "nothing," leading finally to the third question rejecting their "boasting" (as in 1:31; 3:21).

In 4:8-13 Paul mocks the Corinthians' spiritual attainment with biting sarcasm, an ironic contrast to the sufferings he has undergone as an apostle. Again in verses 8, 10 (cf. 1:26-28; 2:6, 14-15) he uses what are apparently their own characterizations of the exalted spiritual status they have achieved through *sophia*. The terms contrasted in verse 10 repeat those in 1:26-28, with "of noble birth" varied by "in honor" versus "in disrepute." "Rich" and "kings/reigning" in 4:8 are two of the most frequently used terms in the whole vocabulary of spiritual status, derived ultimately from classical Greek aristocratic values, transformed into intellectual-spiritual qualities by hellenistic philosophy, and cultivated in hellenistic-Jewish wisdom-mysticism.

The word "already," which stands in the emphatic position in the first two exclamations in verse 8, is not to be interpreted as reflecting the Corinthians' enthusiasm or (over-)realized eschatology. Rather, it is *Paul's* own formulation, rooted in *his* historical-eschatological worldview. This is perhaps most clearly seen in his continuing play with the third exclamation, in which he alludes to hopes for the realization of the kingdom of God (see 4:20!) when the faithful will finally share in the divine sovereignty (but not themselves as "kings"; see Dan 7:27)—hopes rooted firmly in

Palestinian Jewish apocalyptic expectations. By recasting the Corinthians' language of residual transcendent status (immortal spiritual existence) into his own worldview, according to which a transformed existence would not be attained until the *parousia,* Paul hopes to demonstrate how inappropriate and inflated are their self-images.

The sarcastic mocking of the Corinthians' spiritual status is carried further in verse 9, where he compares his own status as an apostle (despite the plural "apostles," Paul is now thinking primarily of himself, and not including Apollos). In complete contrast with the exalted position of the Corinthians, God has displayed Paul as "last." "As though sentenced to death" refers to one or another of two similar scenarios. In the final events of Roman spectacles, participants condemned to die fought as gladiators or were thrown to the beasts for the entertainment of crowds with insatiable thirst for blood (Seneca, *Ep.* 7.2-5; for gladiatorial contests in Corinth, Dio Chrysostom, *Or.* 31.121). Perhaps a more likely scenario, partly because Paul uses it in connection with his apostleship in 2 Cor 2:14, is the triumphal procession staged by a victorious Roman general, in which the captives of war were publicly executed (as in the triumphal procession of Vespasian and Titus celebrating their glorious victory over the Judean rebels in 70 CE; Josephus, *J.W.* 7.132-57). Particularly the latter would have been a grand "spectacle" for the whole "world" to behold (the image seems to draw directly on Jewish martyrology, 4 Macc 17:14). Why Paul specifies the superhuman dimension to the spectacle, to "angels" as well as "mortals," is not clear. It is tempting to think that this is a reference to the Corinthians' sense of their own spiritual status as associated with the angels (see especially the "tongues of . . . angels" in 13:1). In any case, those beholding the spectacle are understood as hostile (like the "angels" in Rom 8:38). It seems unlikely, as some believe, that Paul is taking over the Stoic metaphor of the philosopher's struggle against adversity as a "spectacle" of courage in which he proves himself before the gods. His point is virtually the opposite of an individual struggle to prove one's strength.

In verse 10 Paul uses the Corinthians' own favorite self-characterizations mentioned earlier (1:26) to portray himself as the opposite. The term behind "wise" *(phronimoi)* is a synonym for *sophos*, but with connotations of "sensible." Paul uses the term elsewhere in a cautionary, even pejorative sense (Rom 11:25; 12:16; 2 Cor 11:19). He may have added "in Christ" merely to balance "for the sake of Christ" in the first half of the comparison. Paul reverses the third contrast, probably in transition to his list of the apostles' (his own) hardships. The contrast between those "held in honor" (often used together with "kings" and "wealthy" for the "wise") and those in "disrepute" may allude to the preceding spectacle scenario, with the honored Corinthians beholding the dishonored apostles among those condemned to death. Certainly it sets up the following characterizations.

Continuing the contrast, Paul introduces a list of tribulations (vv. 11-13). Such lists were common rhetorical and parenetic devices, from Greek historical writings to Jewish apocalyptic literature (e.g. *2 Enoch* 66:6). Most prominently, hellenistic philosophers, particularly Stoics and Cynics, used portrayals of the suffering sage as a pedagogical paradigm for the philosophical life, presenting the sage's struggle with hardships as a manifestation of his transcendence of the dominant cultural values. The ideal Cynic could suffer poverty and dishonor precisely because (and as proof that) he had attained true wealth and kingship, and even shared in the reign of Zeus as his servant (Epictetus, *Diss.* 3.22.59, 95). Paul is almost certainly drawing on or alluding to such catalogues of hardships; he does so again repeatedly in his later Corinthian correspondence (especially 2 Cor 4:8-9; 6:4-10; 11:23-33). However, he tailors the list of hardships to his particular concerns here in 1 Corinthians. Most strikingly, in contrast to the Corinthians he imagines as "puffed up" in their transcendent status, the suffering apostles are imitating a model very different from the ideal Cynic who, despite his hardships, shares in the reign of Zeus as a truly wise and wealthy king.

The list of sufferings is carefully arranged: a list of five commonplace deprivations plus a sixth specific to the Corinthians' criticism of Paul; a set of three antitheses depicting the apostles' response to abuse; and a concluding characterization of how despicable they appear. The whole is framed by similar temporal phrases ("to the present hour"/"to this very day"), which pointedly set the apostles' situation over against the high status already attained by the Corinthians. Most of the deprivations are also pointed contrasts with the Corinthians' exaltation, such as "hungry and thirsty" versus "filled" and "poorly clothed and . . . homeless" versus "rich" and "reigning." "Grow weary from the work of our own hands" is clearly a reference to a bone of contention between Paul and (some of) the Corinthians (see 9:1-18). The antitheses in verse 12b, particularly "when reviled, we bless" (cf. Luke/Q 6:28; Rom 12:14), might allude to or echo the teachings (or example; cf. Luke 23:34) of Jesus. The concluding characterizations, "rubbish of the world" and "dregs of all things" both refer to what was removed in the process of cleansing and are therefore metaphors for what is contemptible. Put simply, the apostles (Paul) are "the scum of the earth."

In 4:14-21, perhaps realizing how sharp his tone has been in the previous paragraph, Paul softens his rhetoric a bit before resuming a threatening tone in the last sentence of this section. Having, in effect, just shamed the Corinthians, he now insists that his aim is not to shame but to admonish them as his beloved children. His concern here is to reestablish his own authority among the Corinthians. If Paul's tone seems authoritarian and paternalistic, that is in accord with the common rhetoric as well as social relations in hellenistic-Roman antiquity. In 4:15, probably still thinking of Apollos' rivalry or challenge to his authority, he now presents himself as the *one* who "in Christ Jesus" had become their "father through the gospel," as opposed to myriads of "guardians" or baby-sitters (another put-down of Apollos!). In Greek and Roman society, the father held the authority, in no uncertain terms, whereas slaves were usually charged with the tasks of disciplining and cleaning up after the children, with the "guardian" *(paidogōgos)* picking up where the wet nurse and nanny left off. In Paul's case, the "father" is also assuming the role of teacher and paradigm, admonishing the children to learn how to change their ways by imitating his example (v. 16; cf. 1 Cor 9; 10:33–11:1; Phil 3:17; 1 Thess 1:6). Presumably he has in mind the pattern of patient suffering just laid out (vv. 8-13) in contrast to their own excitement over newly won spiritual status.

As steps toward more forcefully reestablishing his paternal apostolic authority, Paul announces in 4:17-19 that he is both sending his envoy Timothy and planning to return to Corinth himself. Timothy would have been known to the Corinthians as Paul's coworker and representative, having been with Paul during part of his mission in Corinth, and having been delegated to visit the Thessalonian assembly during that time (1 Thess 1:1; 3:1-6; Acts 18:5). By the end of the letter Paul seems a little more tentative about Timothy's visit and reception (16:10-11). This suggests that the announcement that he has been sent "to remind you of my ways in Christ Jesus" functions here primarily to sanction Paul's admonition. Paul's "ways," include both his teachings and his behavior—the way he "walks" (cf. 3:3; 7:17; 12:31; Gal 5:16). His reference to "some . . . [who] have become arrogant" (v. 18) suggests either that only a few among them were particularly critical of him (cf. 4:3-5) or that only a portion of the whole assembly was caught up in the excitement over wisdom and spiritual status. The concluding sentences (4:19-21) reinforce the latter suspicion, since Paul refers back to the issues with which the whole section began—a falsely placed trust in eloquent wisdom (1:17-20; 2:1-5).

Although Paul seldom refers to "the kingdom of God," his almost offhand use of the phrase (cf. 6:9-10; 15:50; Rom 14:17; Gal 5:21) suggests that it was well established in his evangelical vocabulary. Assuming, therefore, that he had made it a familiar term among the Corinthians, Paul's formulation of the maxim in verse 20 serves as a summary recapitulation of his whole argument since 1:17-18: "The kingdom of God depends not on talk *(logos)* but on power!" The stern, paternal, threatening plea to change their ways (v. 21) both concludes his long opening argument and sets up the rest of the body of the letter, which addresses problematic views and behaviors among the Corinthians.

◊ ◊ ◊ ◊

Throughout Paul's argument for unity we can discern a conflict between personal liberation and self-fulfillment in individual transcendence of the dominant social order, on the one hand, and a disciplined building of a social movement as an alternative to the dominant social order, on the other. As indicated in his comment that "not many were powerful, not many were of noble birth" in 1:26, most of the Corinthians were of inauspicious social origins. The life of urban artisans was one of constant economic struggle and low social standing in adverse circumstances. The life of most women and slaves was simply degrading, sexually as well as socially and economically; they were without personal freedom and dignity, living in downright oppressive circumstances.

The "gospel" of a gracious and loving heavenly *Sophia* who could be known through the Jewish Scriptures, newly revealed by wisdom teachers such as Jesus and his interpreter Apollos, offered transcendence of those adverse and oppressive circumstances. Those who possessed *Sophia,* moreover, gained an exalted spiritual status as "powerful, wealthy, wise, and of noble birth" that elevated them above the actual Achaean elite who dominated Corinth and whom they very likely served, directly or indirectly. Salvation by and devotion to *Sophia,* moreover, meant the discovery and cultivation of their own higher faculties of intellect, enlightenment, and insight, previously denied them because of their social situation. Whereas Paul, in rejecting the oppressive aspects of "the world" seems to demean human culture in general, the Corinthians, in their excitement over the gifts of *Sophia,* affirmed human action, attainment, and aristocratic values, while still affirming their source in God. Their response and devotion to *Sophia* made possible their personal development and self-realization as wise, mature, spiritual beings. They were full of wisdom, rich in spiritual gifts, able even to search the depths of the divine.

Paul, on the other hand, insistently focuses on the unity of the community and on the delay of gratification and enjoyment while building the movement of the new age (until the *parousia* of Christ which, he believed, was imminent [1 Cor 15:20-28]). Paul and "the saints" in Corinth are "called" to be members of "the assembly of God," which has a world-historical role to play. Paul is apparently expecting that, like himself, the Corinthians should find personal fulfillment in commitment to and building up of the assembly. His focus falls not on individual transcendence, but on God's purpose in the fulfillment of history, which is the constitution of the new people (or "temple") of God.

The respective positions of Paul and the Corinthian spirituals thus have different, even conflicting, social implications. Judging from ancient literary sources, hellenistic-Jewish devotion to heavenly *Sophia*, including a spiritualizing or allegorical reading of the Jewish Scriptures, was cultivated among a social-cultural elite. Part of the evidence for this is the very language used to express the personal transcendence and immortality of the soul, attained through intimacy with *Sophia*. As evident in the Wisdom of Solomon and Philo's treatises, hellenistic-Jewish devotees of *Sophia* simply adapted the language of aristocratic values—"wise, powerful/reigning, wealthy, of noble birth," and so forth—which had already been spiritualized by hellenistic philosophy. The Therapeutics who left their families to cultivate *Sophia* (by meditating on Scripture) near Alexandria were clearly people of economic means and some education. Nevertheless, the elite origins of such devotion to *Sophia* and the symbolization of the corresponding spiritual status attained do not mean that the Corinthians Paul addresses were a social or cultural elite. Cultural expressions often move down the social scale to become more popularly operative. Apollos' gospel of *Sophia* and exalted spiritual status could easily have become a catalyst of personal transcendence among poor artisans, freedpeople, and oppressed women and slaves.

Nevertheless, the distinction made between two classes of people, along with the focus on the individual's relationship with *Sophia* and personal transcendence, would probably not have reinforced community solidarity. Having only Paul's construction of the Corinthian viewpoint, we cannot make any directly informed judgment about this. We can only notice the lack of positive expressions of community in the similar religiosity of the Wisdom of Solomon and Philo. Also, in these same sources, emphasis on individual transcendence of ordinary life in intimate relationship with *Sophia* and the spiritualized reading of Scripture indicates an orientation toward a divine world separated from social-political affairs.

Paul may thus have had some grounds for linking divisiveness with devotion to *Sophia* and "boasting" of high spiritual status. His concern about the Corinthians' distraction is probably what led him to emphasize the crucified Christ, which was his way of refocusing on the historical world of rulers and peoples. A number of features of chapters 1–4 indicate the political dimension of both this letter and Paul's mission and movement in general. As noted in the discussion of 2:6–3:4, Paul's gospel was significantly political in content and implication. In their crucifixion of Jesus as a political rebel, "the rulers of this age" had inadvertently brought about the turn of the ages that spelled their own doom. Moreover, the whole argument in 1:10–4:21, is political. Paul was intensely concerned that the "assembly" in Corinth stand in solidarity so that it would more effectively comprise, in effect, an alternative society that was still in but not of "this age," the world that "was passing away."

The rhetoric of chapters 1–4 is also political. Despite Paul's lack of respectability, as well as eloquence, both his terminology and his main themes are strikingly parallel to those of the deliberative political rhetoric of the broader culture (M. Mitchell 1992). All of the principal terms in 1:10—"be in agreement," "divisions," to be united "in the same mind," and to share "the same purpose"—are common in political discussions of the unity and stability of peoples and states. Similarly, the Greek word behind the NRSV "quarrels" in 1:11 and quarreling in 3:3 is the standard term for political discord or conflict, the opposite of political "concord." Moreover, "zeal" (NRSV: "jealousy") also in 3:3, is commonly identified as a cause of civil strife, and the term *(meris)* behind the question, "Has Christ been divided?" (1:13) is frequently used in political discourse with reference to factions. Finally, Paul's image of the assembly as a building (3:10) derives from political discourse, which commonly portrayed the state as a macrocosmic household that needed to maintain its unity. Paul was addressing the assembly of saints in Corinth not only as a religious but also as a political community that stood over against the dominant imperial society in Corinth.

Finally, this section of 1 Corinthians (particularly 3:5–4:21) shows how the leader of a movement or institution, anxious about his own authority, can become authoritarian. Paul portrays himself as a fool preaching foolishness, as weak, and even as "the rubbish of the world, the dregs of all things" (4:9-13; see also 1:21-23; 2:3). His tone, at least in 4:8-13, is mocking, even sarcastic. Nietzsche was surely not the first to hear a certain resentment in Paul's self-descriptions. In Paul's rhetoric one hears a somewhat arrogant tone that matches his high exalted estimate of his importance in God's grand scheme of things, as having a role second in importance to that of Jesus Christ himself. *He* is the one, "called to be an apostle," who is responsible for laying the foundation of Jesus Christ on which others must build accordingly, at the risk of fiery judgment (3:10-13).

Such a tone grates on modern democratic sensibilities. Perhaps it was less so in the highly authoritarian atmosphere of Roman imperial culture. Yet even though we are listening to only one side of the argument between Paul and the Corinthian spirituals, we can discern how heavily his rhetoric must have hit them. Although clothed in a velvety glove of mere admonition, Paul's assertion of his role as father (4:14-15) may have been an affront to the newfound independence of people now viewing themselves as mature spirituals of transcendent achievement. To describe them as his children (4:14) was belittling, as was the insinuation that their favored Apollos was nothing but their slave guardian ("baby-sitter"). Finally, at the very end of this opening section of the letter, apparently insecure that his arguments so far had not been completely persuasive, he asserted his stern paternal role: Shape up or else I will come to you with a stick!

Exhortation About Relations with the Larger Society and Argument Against Immorality (5:1–6:20)

In chapters 5–6 Paul begins his responses to particular Corinthian principles and actions that he views as causes of the crisis of community and authority he had been addressing only in a general, preliminary way in 1:10–4:21. He is still dealing with matters reported to him (5:1; cf. 1:11), not issues raised in the Corinthians' letter to him (7:1). The connection between the three subjects on which he focuses—community discipline in 5:1-13, taking disputes among brothers to court in 6:1-8, and immorality in 6:12-20—is not immediately obvious. Yet Paul makes many particular connections both between the three principal paragraphs in chapters 5–6 and between these paragraphs and other arguments in the letter.

The instructions in 5:1-13 about expelling one of their own number leads directly to the exhortation to handle disputes between community members within the community in 6:1-11. The declaration that wrongdoers will not inherit the kingdom of God in 6:9-11 links both of the preceding paragraphs with the discussion of immorality in 6:12-20, thus also returning to the topic with which 5:1-13 began. By quoting the same slogan of the Corinthians ("all things are possible for me") in his concluding step in chapters 5–6 and 8–10 (6:12; 10:23), Paul suggests that their empowering enlightenment is intimately related to the immorality discussed in 6:12-20 as well as to the "eating of food offered to idols" discussed in chapters 8–10. His concluding exhortation to flee immorality in 6:18 parallels that to flee idolatry in 10:14. And he seems to set up the discussion of food offered to idols in chapters 8–10 by mentioning both idolatry and food prominently in 5:11; 6:9-10; and 6:13. Moreover, Paul seems to discuss the cases of men's immorality to set up his appeal to the Corinthian women to guard against men's immorality by maintaining conjugal rights in their marriages in chapter 7.

Immorality and Community Discipline (5:1-13)

The issue here is what to do about a man living with his (presumably deceased) father's wife. What Paul makes as a suggestion in 5:2 he repeats as a command in 5:13: Expel the man from the assembly. Paul first expresses shock over a man's incest and the community's arrogance and inaction about it (5:1-2). Then he gives explicit instructions about the disciplinary action to be taken (5:3-5), expresses concern for the sanctity of the community

(5:6-8), and explains the difference between internal community discipline and relations with outsiders (5:9-13).

◊ ◊ ◊ ◊

In shocked disbelief Paul reacts to the man's alliance and the community's lack of action despite his previous letter. Their behavior threatens his understanding of his assemblies as a newly sanctified people of God and of his own authority as Christ's apostle and the community's founder.

The "immorality" consists of a man "having" (NRSV: "living with") "his father's wife," that is, his stepmother (not his mother, as in Lev 18:8). Such a relationship between stepmother and stepson was forbidden in both Jewish and Roman law. In hellenistic society, men generally married younger women, and their second wives often were much younger. Thus the son and stepmother may have been virtually the same age. Evidently the woman was not a member of the community, since Paul formulates the verdict of expulsion in the masculine singular. What Paul characterizes as being "arrogant" and "boasting" in 5:2, 6 implies that the alliance was not a secret or discrete affair, but an open relationship carried on with the approval of at least some in the community.

Precisely in that connection we should prefer the more difficult reading of the text in 5:3-4 that the NRSV offers in a footnote, that is, "the man who has done such a thing in the name of the Lord Jesus" rather than the reading that states that Paul has "pronounced judgment in the name of the Lord." Just as Paul called the Corinthians' *sophia* "wisdom of the world" (1:20), so here he suggests rhetorically that the man was living with his stepmother "in the name of the Lord Jesus" (cf. 12:3). Perhaps in the new spiritual status gained through *Sophia,* which made "all things lawful [possible/permissible]" (6:12; 10:23), the enlightened fellow had achieved a freedom from restrictive traditional patriarchal norms such that an alliance of love was now possible.

Shocked as he is about the incest, Paul is far more upset about the attitude and inaction of the Corinthian assembly, the main focus of the rest of this argument in 5:2-13. His driving concern is for the purity and discipline of the community as "those . . . called to be saints" (1:2). Closely related is the threat the Corinthians are posing to his own authority. Impatient at their inaction, he asserts his own authority: "As for me (emphatic), I have *already* judged . . ." (5:3b AT). Yet he is at pains to proceed *with* the Corinthian assembly. He attempts to formulate this in the confusing phrases that explain his presence in the proceeding he expects them to set up: "absent in body . . . [but] present in spirit." It is as present among them that he has already judged (5:3), just as he will be present with them in their proceeding (5:4b). The mode of spiritual presence is like that expressed in the community disciplinary proceedings mentioned in Matt 18:15-20, where Jesus is "among them." The ultimately empowering authority of the formal juridical proceeding of expulsion, of course, is "our Lord Jesus." "Flesh versus spirit" in Paul does not refer to an anthropological dualism of external/body versus internal/soul but to opposing attitudes or orientations in behavior of the whole person (body and soul; as in Rom 8:3-17; Gal 5:16-26). The express purpose of the action to be taken by the assembly is "*so that* his spirit may be saved in the day of the Lord" (emphasis added), whereas "the destruction of the flesh" is only the anticipated eschatological result of his expulsion from the protective sphere of the Spirit in the community (cf. 1 Thess 5:3). A parallel disciplinary admonition from the eschatologically oriented community at Qumran (CD 7:21–8:3) calls for the destruction by Satan of those "traitors" who failed to maintain the communal purity. Paul, on the other hand, anticipates the ultimate salvation of the offender, and conceives of Satan's role not as the destroyer of evildoers, but as the instrument (of God, in effect) of destruction only of the offender's inclination to evil.

In 5:6-8 the reason for this procedure by the Corinthian assembly becomes clear. As (part of) the eschatological people of God it must maintain rigorous communal discipline. They are to expel the offender for their own sake. "A little yeast leavens the whole batch of dough" must have been a popular Jewish proverb (cf. Mark 8:15). In Gal 5:9 Paul uses it in a similar sense of warning about corrupting influence in the community. The warning proverb gives way to the positive image of the central Jewish festival of the unleavened bread (= Passover), celebrating the original historical formation of Israel as the people of God in the Exodus events (a festival with which he must assume they are familiar; see 10:1-13). For the Christocentric consciousness of Paul, this leads immediately to an integrally related image, the other focal image of the Passover, the paschal lamb (the only occurrence of this image in Paul's letters, dependent on this context). To avoid being a lump of dough corrupted by one bit of leaven, they should clean out that yeast to become what they really are, unleavened bread, since "Our paschal lamb, Christ, has been sacrificed." First Corinthians 5:8 shifts the metaphor from the community as the unleavened bread to the community now celebrating the whole festival of redemption by maintaining purity even of motivation (purity and truth) to avoid any behavior of malice and evil that would corrupt its holiness as a redeemed and sanctified people.

As indicated in 5:9, Paul had previously written the Corinthians a "letter." Since we do not have even a fragment of that letter, we do not know what else it contained other than his exhortation "not to associate with sexually immoral persons." It is possible that Paul is here shifting (narrowing?) his application of that exhortation. More likely is that Paul has the sense that they had disregarded or even misinterpreted his previous instructions to avoid immoral persons. That would help explain his strong assertion of his apostolic authority in 4:14-21 and 5:3-5, as well as his clarification in 5:10-12. In his recitation of several types of evildoers in 5:10-11 Paul is not simply reproducing standard lists ("catalogues of vices"). The overlap between one of his lists and another is minimal. While Paul uses conventional forms of public rhetoric, he almost always tailors those forms to the particular situations he is addressing. Notable in this case ("the greedy and robbers, or idolaters" in 5:10 to which he appends "reviler" and "drunkard" in 5:11, with yet others added in 6:9-10) are (1) the close association of immorality with idolatry, conventional in the Jewish biblical tradition in which Paul was rooted, and (2) the move away from sexual concerns to economic matters of theft and coveting ("usurers" and "swindlers" in the NJB give a better sense of the economic dimension), suggesting that the basic social-economic principles of the Mosaic Covenant are not far under the surface. That the

Corinthians continued to accept (proudly even! [5:2]) a sexually immoral person in their midst despite Paul's instruction in the previous letter (5:1-2, 9) suggests that he was someone of importance for the group. Assuming that Paul intended the innuendos of "usurers" and "swindlers" in his list of vices in 5:11, the person would appear to be economically significant. Perhaps, in the imperial society in which most poor people were economically dependent in some way on patrons, some in the assembly were economically dependent on this fellow. The point of Paul's reminder in 5:9-11 is the fundamental distinction between maintaining the ethical discipline of the eschatological community, on the one hand, and keeping open contacts with people in "the world" on the other. As God's newly constituted alternative to the dominant society, they must not even eat with one of their supposed "brothers" who violates the expected ethical discipline. To be an alternative for people of the world, however, they must remain open to contact with them (*in* but not *of* the world).

First Corinthians 5:12-13 pulls this argument together in two parallel sets of paired short sentences centered on "judging" in the same sense that Paul was judging in 5:3. In 5:12, using himself as an example, Paul recapitulates the exhortation of 5:9 about not judging outsiders; he then insists that it is their responsibility to maintain community discipline by judging those within the assembly (which he addresses next, in 6:1-8). In 5:13 he repeats the same contrasting points, referring to God as the (eschatological) judge of the outsiders, then calling upon the Corinthians to "drive out the wicked person from among" them. With this Deuteronomic refrain attached to the sentences for idolatry and other extreme offenses (Deut 13:5; 17:7; 19:9; 22:21-24), Paul again repeats the basic instruction throughout this argument (5:2, 5, 7a).

◊ ◊ ◊ ◊

First Corinthians 5 might be thought of as the beginning of community discipline, except that both the community and the discipline may have existed mainly in the mind of Paul. The situation in Corinth was apparently not a simple matter of an ethical aberration of one member of a community that otherwise had a clear sense of its own identity as a movement and certain norms that could be upheld. Nor was it a matter of a few Corinthians who had gotten carried away in their enthusiasm about the apocalyptic transcendence of the old age that Paul had proclaimed, and who now required guidelines for acceptable new age behavior. The situation in Corinth was thus more complicated than the unilinear sequence detected by anthropologists in certain modern millenarian movements from an original situation of "old rules" through a phase of "no rules" and finally settling down into "new rules." Paul founded the Corinthian assembly only a few years previously. Partly because of subsequent developments in Corinth, such as the work of Apollos, a variety of viewpoints had emerged—which is precisely what Paul was addressing in this letter. Moreover, as will be evident in chapters 8–10 below, at least some of the Corinthians were caught up in a kind of enlightenment that they believed liberated them from observance of traditional religious-ethical norms and taboos. This enlightenment spirituality may be the best explanation for both the alliance of the man with his (former) stepmother and its apparent acceptance by some Corinthians. The "no rules" of the Corinthians may thus have been rooted in an orientation and gospel very different from those on the basis of which Paul was dictating as "new" a continuation of the "old rules." If the Corinthians concerned in this case were primarily Gentiles, furthermore, both the "no rules" rooted in enlightenment spirituality and the traditional Mosaic covenantal principles pressed upon them by Paul were new to them. One came from Palestinian Jewish tradition by way of Paul, the other from Alexandrian Jewish tradition by way of Apollos.

Yet another factor was probably at play. Although the enlightened Corinthians did not share Paul's understanding of their salvation as belonging to an eschatological community of the new age, Paul's message of eschatological fulfillment would likely have contributed to their belief that traditional norms and social relations had been transcended. Elsewhere in 1 Corinthians Paul himself expresses a distinctive personal freedom over against the conventional norms in his own social relations ("unmarried," 7:8; but cf. 7:19) and his apostolic strategy (9:20-21). Nevertheless, since there was apparently no community with already established norms in Corinth, let alone an institutionalized structure of authority, Paul was desperate to instill some authority in the situation. He had virtually no choice but to resort to devices such as symbolic sanctions, threats, and even psychic coercion.

The established church's later use of Paul's statement about the destruction of the flesh so that the spirit might be saved (5:5) to justify the torture and burning of sinners, heretics, and "witches" vividly illustrates the danger of secular and ecclesial rulers arrogating to themselves the power of community discipline in order to suppress doctrinal dissent and social difference.

On Handling Disputes Within the Assembly (6:1-11)

In 6:1-11 Paul continues his shocked tone, interspersed with sarcasm, accusation, and threat, in a series of rhetorical questions. He addresses these rhetorical questions initially to the man who was taking a "brother" to civil court in 6:2, but quickly turns to the whole assembly, which itself should be dealing with internal disputes in 6:3-6. In 6:7-8 he again addresses the disputants, but there should be no paragraph break, with 6:7 continuing the discussion of the lawsuit mentioned in 6:6. The declaration in 6:9-11, connected to 6:8 with an "or" (in Greek), makes the transition from "wrongdoers" in 6:1-8 back to the subject of "immorality," introduced in 5:1-13 and continued in 6:12-20.

◊ ◊ ◊ ◊

Apparently having heard a report about one "brother" taking another "brother" to a civil court, Paul registers his horror in 6:1: "*Dare* one of you take a case against a brother for judgment before the unrighteous instead of before the saints?" (AT). Paul views those who run the civil courts (and perhaps people "in the world" more generally) as unjust. Because the unrighteous violate the divine principles of justice, they will not inherit the kingdom of God (cf. 6:9). Opposite the "unrighteous" outside the movement are the "saints" inside, those who have been set apart as citizens of the new age. According to Paul's Jewish apocalyptic worldview, those "saints," as the citizens of the eschatological society, "will judge the world" (6:2). As part of the final events—judgment against oppressive rulers and vindication of the suffering faithful—"God will judge all the nations by the hand of his elect" (1QpHab 5:4; *1 Enoch* 1:9; 95:3; Dan 7:22 LXX; Rev 20:4). Drawing on a motif found in more elaborate apocalyptic visions (*1 Enoch* 67–69; cf. 2 Pet 2:4; Jude 6), Paul even claims that "we are to judge angels" (6:3), seeking to jolt the Corinthians into recognizing that they should handle their own disputes, the "trivial" matters of ordinary mundane life (6:2*b*, 3*b*).

The next rhetorical question, found in 6:4, then seems to ask, "If you have ordinary cases (which you should be handling within the assembly), do you (by going to the civil court, in effect) appoint as judges those who have no standing in the assembly?" Implying that the Corinthians do indeed appoint others as judges, he responds with sharp accusation and biting sarcasm in 6:5-6. Having hesitated to shame them in his long opening argument (4:14), he now does so bluntly for not acting as an autonomous community set apart from the world. The sarcastic rhetorical question in 6:5 ("Can it be that there is no one among you [who is] *wise*?" [emphasis added]) mocks the claims by several Corinthians of having become "wise" (cf. 1:26 and so forth). The problem, repeated from 6:1, is not just that "brother goes to court against brother" (the NRSV substitutes inclusive for androcentric language), but that he does so "before unbelievers" (the unrighteous). This is far more than merely wanting members of the assembly to live quietly and not air their dirty linen in public. As indicated in 6:2-3, Paul's concern here is that the assembly, as the eschatological people of God, stands over against "the world," which stands under God's judgment. Just as the Qumran community governed itself as the community of the new age over against the government of the "Wicked Priest" in Jerusalem, so (in Paul's mind) the assembly of saints should exercise authority over its affairs, over against the dominant imperial society.

Continuing the point of the last rhetorical question (6:6), only now ostensibly addressing the litigant, Paul explains in the strong language of 6:7, "Already [regardless of the outcome of the lawsuit] it is completely a *defeat* for you that you have [civil] lawsuits with one another!" (AT). He supplements with two further rhetorical questions: "Why not rather be wronged? Why not rather be defrauded?" "Do not repay evil for evil" is standard in Paul's ethical exhortation (Rom 12:17; 1 Thess 5:15). These rhetorical questions are more pointed to the Corinthians because of their claim to be "wise," already alluded to in 6:5. That the wise person would rather be wronged than wrong had been a standard point in ancient philosophy since Plato's portrayal of Socrates in the *Apology* (30C-D; cf. *Gorg.* 469B, 473A, 474B; 475C-E). The rhetorical questions of 6:7 are clear allusions to this standard topic in philosophy: The truly wise person cannot be harmed by insult or injury. Seeking redress is an admission of having been harmed, already a defeat for a wise person. In 6:8 Paul then addresses not the brother being taken to civil court, but, by implication, his accuser and others: "But you yourselves wrong and defraud." The parallel construction at the end of the two "but . . ." clauses in 6:5-6, 7-8 invites a comparison, perhaps even equation, between the litigating "brothers" and the "unbelievers."

Paul's focus on economic wrongdoing such as "fraud," along with the "ordinary" or "civil" cases previously mentioned (6:3-4), indicates that the litigant was pursuing precisely an economic matter. The context of this paragraph, sandwiched between two discussions of "(sexual) immorality," suggests that the case had to do with marital relations, perhaps in some economic way such as inheritance. The courts in provincial cities as well as in Rome itself operated for the advantage of the wealthy and powerful (e.g., a patron could sue his freedman's heirs for his share of his former slave's estate). Thus only someone with connections (i.e., involved in some patronage network) was likely to have taken a case to an official court.

Paul delivers a stern warning in 6:9-10, holding out his vision of "the kingdom of God" as an eschatological goal that is imminent but still to be attained (cf. 4:20). With "wrongdoers" picking up the "wrongdoing" of verse 8, Paul insinuates that they are in danger of being in the same situation of those "in the world" that are to be judged, rather than that of the eschatological judges. To drive his point home Paul recites the same list of wrongdoers that he had already cited in 5:10-11, adding four more to the list. Heading the list are the two kinds of offenders he is focusing on in chapters 5–6 and 8–10 respectively: "fornicators" and "idolaters." Of the four additions, "thieves" (which occurs only here in Paul's "catalogues of vices") refers directly to the problem of defrauding on which 6:1-11 focuses. In 5:10-11 he stacked the list of wrongdoers with economic offenders ("the greedy and robbers") in anticipation of the fraud and theft he was about to discuss in 6:1-11. In 6:9-10, while retaining the economic offenders ("thieves, the greedy, . . . robbers"), he expands the list of sexual offenders, presumably in anticipation of the discussion of "immorality" in 6:12-20 and chapter 7. Again the Decalogue is not far under the surface, with the focus on the three commandments regarding idolatry, adultery, and theft.

The meaning of the Greek terms in 6:9 translated "male prostitutes" (malakoi) and "sodomites" (arsenokoitai = more literally, "male intercourse") is disputed. This is the earliest known use of the latter term, and post-Pauline authors rarely use it with reference to what could be called "homosexual" relations. One possibility is that the words refer, respectively, to the "passive" and the "active" partners in male intercourse. It is more likely however that they refer to "masturbators" and "male prostitutes" (Countryman 1988, 118-20, 127-28).

Giving the Corinthians the benefit of the doubt in 6:11, Paul reminds them that "this is what some of [them] used to be." In Greek the next sentence has a strong "but" before each of the three verbs. In reference to what they used to be, these three primary metaphors of salvation declare them "washed" from the degradation of their former practices, "set apart" for ethical life according to God's will, and "justified." Thus, despite their former lives, they can now inherit the kingdom from which they would have been excluded because of their former lives.

◊ ◊ ◊ ◊

Like his instructions about the incestuous man (5:1-13), Paul's adamant reaction to one Corinthian brother taking another to civil court in 6:1-11 vividly illustrates how he understood the relation between the movement he was building and the dominant society. On the one hand, since the point of this whole mission was to bring as many people as possible into the movement, the assemblies he was establishing were to be open to and interactive with outsiders (5:9-10). On the other hand, not only were the assemblies to maintain group solidarity and discipline, they were to conduct their own affairs autonomously, in separation from "the world." For Paul this is not simply a carryover of the concern of Jewish diaspora communities to maintain self-government insofar as possible over against the government of the city in which they lived. Paul understood the independence of his assemblies as an integral part of the eschatological drama inaugurated by God in Christ's crucifixion and resurrection.

The subsequent institutionalized separation of religion and politics ("church" and "state") in the West blocks recognition of the political implications of a section such as 6:1-11. The apocalyptic orientation of Paul's mission was rooted in the experience of a subject people dominated by the Seleucid and Roman imperial regimes. The very purpose of Jewish apocalyptic literature was to bolster the resolve of Jewish communities to persist in their traditional way of life and maintain their independence of the dominant imperial society. Those who persisted in the just, covenantal way of life anticipated vindication as "saints," even participation in the final judgment of the (oppressive) nations. Like other apocalyptic Jewish visionaries, Paul viewed the dominant order and the people in it as practitioners of injustice (6:1, 10). By contrast, the assemblies he was establishing were supposedly communities of justice ("saints") separated from "the world" in anticipation of "inheriting the kingdom of God."

Thus, for Paul to insist that his assemblies be self-governing, handling their own internal disputes and so forth, was indeed a rejection of the civil courts (*contra* Conzelmann 1975, 105; Fee 1987, 232). The latter belonged to "the world" that stood under condemnation by God and was about to be "judged." The law and the courts in the Roman Empire were forms of social control, a vested interest of the wealthy and powerful (Garnsey 1970). Courts in the provinces, as well as in Rome, gave preferential treatment to people of higher status and usually worked to the disadvantage of those of lesser status. Paul's insistence that the Corinthian assembly handle internally its own disputes was hardly an innovation. It is likely that Jewish diaspora communities had their own mechanisms for handling internal conflicts. More explicit cases of communities of subject peoples constituting their own courts, over against those maintained by the high priests or kings (client rulers for the Romans) come from the Qumran community and the Jesus movement in Palestine (1 QS 5:25–6:1; CD 9:2-8; Matt 18:15-17 // Luke 17:2-4; cf. Luke 12:57-59 // Matt 5:25-26). In Paul's mind, while it was still in the world, the assembly should constitute virtually an alternative, self-governing society.

The list of vices in 6:9 has been used as a proof-text in arguments condemning homosexual relations. As noted earlier, it is conceivable that Paul was referring to the passive and active partners in male intercourse, respectively, thus rejecting the sexual humiliation imposed by powerful men on subordinates such as slaves. As noted, however, the terms in question probably referred to "masturbators" and "male prostitutes." Certainly the terms Paul uses here were not references to an ancient equivalent of modern homosexual relations. The list in 6:9 thus provides no indication that Paul considered such a relationship to be sinful.

Argument Against Immorality (6:12-20)

It is difficult at first to discern the argument, perhaps even the issue in this paragraph. Two terms dominate, "fornication/ prostitute" *(porneia/pornē/porneuo)* and "body" (found eight times in 6:13-20). Statements relating the two in 6:13, 18 may be the keys: "the body is meant not for fornication," and "the fornicator sins against the body itself." As he does again in 7:1*b*-2 and 8:1, Paul proceeds first by restating and qualifying principles held by the Corinthians in 6:12-13, then states his own main point in 6:14, which he explains in 6:15-17. "Flee immorality" (NRSV: "Shun fornication!") in 6:18*a* may be the imperative conclusion to 6:12-17 or an exhortation explained and developed by 6:18*b*-20, or both.

◊ ◊ ◊ ◊

That "all things are lawful (authorized) for me" in 6:12 is a Corinthian principle is confirmed by its citation and virtual negation again in 10:23. The sense of the term *exestin/exousia* is stronger than the English words "lawful" (NRSV) or "permissible." The Corinthians addressed here seem to have a sense of individual empowerment and authority (cf. 7:4; 8:9) that has something to do with enlightenment (see discussion on "knowledge" in 8:1, 4). Paul's response, "*But, not* all things are *beneficial*" (emphasis added) is framed initially to counter excitement about individual authority with the question about what is beneficial or advantageous—that is, for the whole assembly, as becomes evident in 6:15, 19 (you plural). Both key terms, "authority/power" *(exousia)* and "interest/the beneficial" *(sympherein)* had currency in Stoic and other philosophical discussion, particularly of individual (inner) freedom. Yet they both belonged more widely to a long tradition of political rhetoric (M. Mitchell 1992, 33-35). As becomes increasingly evident in the ensuing arguments of the letter, Paul is pressing the broader political sense of what is in the interest of the whole community against certain Corinthians' excitement over their newly gained individual enlightenment. Paul's counter to his repetition of the Corinthians' slogan in 6:12*b* involves a play on the verb "authorize/empower" that is difficult to replicate in English—literally, "I am empowered for everything, but I will not be overpowered by anything."

The first of the three statements in 6:13, "Food is meant for the stomach and the stomach for food," is, like 6:12*a*, almost certainly another citation from the Corinthians. The second statement in verse 13 also appears to fit the worldview of the Corinthians, whereby the stomach (and its food), like the body in general, is perishable and irrelevant, if not a hindrance, to spiritual salvation (cf. the denial of the resurrection of "the dead" in 15:12). Such a statement hardly serves Paul's argument, but it would be intelligible in relation to the Corinthians' freedom to eat "food sacrificed to idols" (chap. 8, especially 8:8). If we understand it as the second half of the Corinthians' principle, then the otherwise baffling sequence of statements in verses 13*abc*, 14, including the pointless "the Lord [is] for the body," become intelligible. Paul is countering the Corinthians' principle in verse 13*ab* with his own in verses 13*b*-14, which he constructs on the same pattern (except that Paul adds the pointed phrase, "not for fornication" in 6:13*b*). Thus:

"Food is meant for the stomach and the stomach for food,"
and God will destroy both one and the other.

But

The body is meant . . . for the Lord, and the Lord for the body.
And God raised the Lord and will also raise us. . . .

The awkward "the Lord for the body" is merely necessary to complete the parallel structure (not all rhetorical phrases may have theological significance). The parallel future verbs, which stand in last place in the respective principles and have similar sounds (*katargēsei* and *exegerei*), have parallel objects, the "stomach" and "us." But they form a striking contrast, "destroy" versus "resurrect." Paul affirms what the Corinthians' principle denies (anticipating the discussion of the resurrection of the dead/body in chap. 15).

Paul's addition of "not for fornication" and "by his power" not only breaks the pattern but gets to his principal concern, "immorality," by also inserting a reminder of God as the power of eschatological action. Verse 13*c* thus states the point that verses 15-17 develop and explain, with verse 15 as an explanation of verse 13*c* and verses 16-17 as an explanation of verse 15. From verses 15-20 Paul's argument centers on "body" in several connections and permutations. It may help in following the various twists of his argument to understand that the Corinthians apparently view the body as belonging to a separate, inferior level of existence from the true self (soul or spirit), while Paul thinks in terms of embodied selves in virtual corporate relations with others. The metaphor of verse 15, with the bodies of the Corinthians as the bodily "members" of Christ, suggests that they have some relation to each other, but focuses on the connection with Christ, in explanation of verse 13*c*. This image anticipates, but is not the same as that of "the body of Christ" in chapter 12, which focuses on the interrelationship between the "members." It also suggests some connection with the resurrection, but is focused on being "members" of Christ in the present. The rhetorical question about making the members of Christ into members of a prostitute suggests both rending the bodily members of Christ and defiling the "body" of Christ. Unthinkable!

In 6:16, shifting from the metaphor of the body to that of sexual union, Paul appeals to "the two shall be one flesh" (see Gen 2:24) as proof-text for the sex partner of a prostitute being "one body with her." It would obviously be impossible to become "one body" with a prostitute and remain a bodily "member" of Christ. In the counterpart to "becomes one body with [the prostitute]" in verse 16, Paul shifts the image to "becomes one *spirit* with [the Lord]" in verse 17. He softens the impact of the mutual exclusivity of being "united in one *body*" with the one or the other in an attempt to counter a viewpoint that separates body from soul, perishable mundane life from immortal spiritual life. In asserting his view of embodied selves involved in corporate social unions, he is not only mixing up what they separate, but claiming the spirit and spiritual for his own position. There is an implied continuity or identity between the "bodies" who are members of Christ in verse 15 and the person(s) united to the Lord who becomes one "spirit" with him.

With "Shun fornication!" in 6:18 Paul finally exclaims what he has been driving toward. The rest of the paragraph, 6:18-20, gives further explanation and argument. Taken at face value as Paul's statement, 6:18*bc* is a puzzle. That fornication is "against the body itself" (v. 18*c*) appears to contradict "every sin . . . is outside the body" (v. 18*b*). Either Paul is again citing a Corinthian claim (note the form: an abstract principle) and countering it, or he is simulating their position in order to highlight his counterposition. Against the view that the body has nothing to do with any sin, he insists that, to the contrary, fornication in particular is a sin against the body. Two readings of verse 18*c* are possible. Either Paul is addressing primarily the split between body and sinning, using this particular case ("the fornicator sins against the body itself"), or he is countering the excitement over individual empowerment ("he who fornicates sins against his own body").

The rhetorical question in verse 19 provides explanation for verse 18c as well as further reason to "flee fornication." Far from being separate from the spiritual realm, the body is in fact a "temple of the Holy Spirit within you, which you have from God" (6:19). The second-person plural suggests that they are collectively, as an assembly, the "temple" of the Spirit, as does the previous use of the temple metaphor in 3:16. The emphasis here, however, falls on their respective personal bodies. The final phrase, "and that you are not your own," makes unavoidably clear that Paul is here countering certain Corinthians' enlightened and empowered individualism by persistently calling attention to the relationships with God, Christ, the Spirit, and one another in the assembly that constitutes their new life (cf. 3:21b, 23).

Paul's concern in this paragraph as throughout the letter focuses on the new historical situation created by the Christ events and the coming of the Spirit. In the short statement of verse 20a Paul reminds the readers of the effect of Christ's crucifixion before he drives home the point of the whole paragraph in the final exhortation in verse 20b. We know the allusion of "bought with a price" only because of Paul's statements elsewhere that through Christ's crucifixion God has "redeemed us" (e.g., Gal 3:13; 4:4-5), with the emphasis on liberation from bondage (to the Law/elemental spirits of the universe). The metaphor here also highlights the liberation accomplished by Christ's crucifixion. Paul's point is to check what he sees as a self-centered empowerment of certain Corinthians, not to present the new life as "slavery" to God (*pace* Fee 1987, 265). The final imperative, the positive counterpart to the negative "shun fornication" in verse 18a, pulls together the whole paragraph in an exhortation stating what he sees as the proper relationship between the embodied self and God.

◊ ◊ ◊ ◊

First Corinthians 6:12-20 offers us a glimpse of the ethical aspect of the Corinthian pneumatics' spiritual transcendence, something that will become clearer in chapters 8 and 10. Emerging from a hellenistic or hellenistic-Jewish worldview in which the soul, as the true self, was distinct from the body, the Corinthians' sense of spiritual transcendence in relation with *Sophia* had apparently consigned the body and its needs to a separate level of life. Illuminated by *Sophia* and empowered by the Spirit, the Corinthian pneumatic believed that "all things" were authorized for the now wise, mature, reigning individual self. Just as the soul was meant for *Sophia* and *Sophia* for the soul, so the body, with its needs, had it own level of existence. This is not exactly a blatant "libertinism." The Corinthians did not lack a sense of sin. Rather, sin was more a matter of the integrity of the enlightened self in self-consistency with its knowledge or consciousness (see reading on chap. 8 below). Thus sin was a matter utterly "outside the body."

Paul knew just enough of the Corinthians' principles to get the gist of their position. Anxious about its implications, he fired back a preemptive warning focused on fornication. Since there is no indication that he had heard of some particular case, he must have been speaking hypothetically about being "united to a prostitute." He was shocked at the potential implications of their self-understanding, not simply because he was rooted in a more parochial society in which sexual relations were confined to patriarchal marriage. His worldview, his orientation to reality, was fundamentally different. For Paul, the self was embodied and life was fundamentally social, relational, and historical. Thus "salvation" consisted not in individual transcendence of the bodily social life, but in the fulfillment of history effected by God in the Christ events. That made possible the transformation of bodily social life in the solidarity of the corporate community in which the members' "bodies" were the bodily "members" of Christ. Paul was apparently deeply anxious about the threat of "fornication." In his adamant argument against potential indulgence as the implication of transcendent individual enlightenment we can discern the basis of his own more restrictive ethics in a less enlightened, parochial sense of corporate solidarity with the new society (assembly) he was busily "building."

CONCERNING MARRIAGE AND SEXUAL RELATIONS
(7:1-40)

The opening phrase of 7:1, "Now concerning the matters about which you wrote," indicates both a new topic, and that Paul is responding to a letter from the Corinthians. The similar "formulaic" phrase, "now concerning," at the beginning of his discussions of several other topics later in the letter (7:25; 8:1; 12:1; 16:1, 12) may indicate that Paul is again responding to the Corinthians' letter. The obvious link between the argument on marriage and sexual relations in chapter 7 and that in chapters 5–6 is sexual immorality. Paul begins his argument in chapter 7 by seemingly agreeing to a Corinthian principle ("It is well for a man not to touch a woman.") only to qualify it immediately because of the threat of immorality. In a series of arguments advocating sexual relations instead of sexual abstinence, "because of immorality," the persuasiveness of his case depends on immorality appearing as a serious threat. That is why he placed discussion of two blatant cases of immorality just prior to discussion of sex and marriage (Wire 1990, 73).

The reflective, measured, at points almost humble, argument in chapter 7, however, marks a dramatic change in tone from the shock expressed in chapters 5–6. This is the least combative argument in the letter, and perhaps the least authoritarian. Phrases such as "this I say by way of concession, not of command" (7:6); "it is well for them" (7:8; see also v. 26); and "I have no command . . . but I give my opinion" (7:25) are unusual for Paul (cf. Phlm 8-9). Also utterly unusual for Paul or any writer in antiquity, is the fact that Paul repeatedly makes a point of addressing alternatively the women and men, wives and husbands—in contrast with the usual address using the masculine form only, even if meant as inclusive of women. He shifts to this highly unusual gender-inclusive and reciprocal rhetoric here evidently to influence the women who were asserting the principle that "it is well for a man not to touch a woman" (7:1).

The argument proceeds in three steps. In 7:1-16 Paul urges the Corinthians to remain in their marital (and sexual) relations. In 7:17-24 the principle of "remaining in the calling in which you were called," is presented with an illustration and a significant exception.

In 7:25-38 Paul presents options to men engaged to "virgins," followed by a brief final recapitulation of the first step in 7:39-40. The principle of not seeking a change in status presented in 7:17-24 persists throughout the argument (7:2, 8, 10, 11, 12-16, 26-27, 37, 40). Within 7:1-16, after a general introduction focused on the question of sexual abstention (or separating from partners) within marriage, Paul addresses successively the particular situations of "the unmarried, the married, the rest," in 7:8-9, 10-11, 12-16. Within 7:25-38, verses 26-28 present the two options that are repeated more explicitly in verses 36-38, and verses 29-35 are a two-step explanation of perspective and motives. On virtually every subtopic of his discussion, Paul offers an exception or qualification of his command or opinion.

To the Married and Unmarried/Widows (7:1-16)

Judging from how Paul elsewhere in the letter cites a Corinthian principle and immediately qualifies or counters it (e.g., 6:12-13; 8:1, 4-6; 15:12), he must be doing the same here. "Touching a woman" was a euphemism for sexual intercourse in hellenistic culture (e.g., Plutarch, *Alex.* 21.9). Thus "it is well for a man not to touch a woman" must have been a principle of sexual asceticism, apparently spiritually motivated. Then the whole series of statements Paul makes in chapter 7 makes sense as his response. The Therapeutics near Alexandria, described by Philo, provide a strikingly similar example of women and men who leave their spouses and become "elderly virgins." Their motivation for spurning the pleasures of the body, moreover, is their devotion to *Sophia,* whom they consider to be their spiritual life-mate. This makes the comparison all the more compelling, considering the importance of *Sophia* to the Corinthian spirituals addressed in chapters 1–4.

The sequence of balanced statements in 7:2-4 is Paul's basic counter to the Corinthians' principle. He is concerned about "cases of sexual immorality," as illustrated in the "cases" in 5:1-13 and 6:15-19. That "each man/woman" should have his/her "own" wife/husband does not state a universal obligation of marriage. It means that each person already married should have or possess his or her partner (cf. the Greek use of "has" in 5:1). In terms of sexual relations that means that each one gives the partner her or his "due," the obligation owed in terms of "conjugal (sexual) rights" (7:3). The basis for this is their mutual "authority" over each other's bodies (7:4).

It would be pointless in a patriarchal society to assert that the husband had authority over his own body. Thus in 7:4 Paul must be responding to a Corinthian principle that "[a woman had] authority over her own body." After reversing that principle, Paul sweetens his denial of authority over her own body with the reciprocal wife's authority over her husband's body. This is certainly a break with patriarchal marriage patterns, at least rhetorically. "Authority" appears to be the principal ethical principle of the Corinthians. In 6:12 and again in 10:23 Paul cites their slogan, "All things are possible/authorized (NRSV: "lawful") for me." Such a principle, however, need not be taken in a negative, libertine way. Among the Corinthians it could have been an expression of empowerment, whether in liberation from parochial taboos such as dietary restrictions (eating food offered to idols, in chaps. 8–10) or old-fashioned customs such as patriarchal property rights (the man "having" his father's wife, in chap. 5). Those who, in relation with *Sophia,* had transcended matters of the body could also have been empowered with "authority" over the body and its relations.

Paul's statement in 7:5 of a limited exception to the rule just enunciated explains more precisely what is bothering him in the Corinthians' behavior. Some of them have been abstaining from sexual relations, thereby not giving each other (what he sees as) conjugal obligations. Paul places clear restrictions on their asceticism: only by "agreement" with the spouse, only for a "set time," and only for the purpose of devotion "to prayer," with the final purpose of "[coming] together again." Temporary separation from intercourse with one's wife for purpose of prayer is known from contemporary Jewish piety (*T. Naph.* 8:8). Permanent abstention from sexual relations is often associated with women in prophetic or other religious roles in other New Testament cases and in the general hellenistic-Roman culture (see Wire 1990, 83, 240-45, 260, 267). Hence it is tempting to see here a reference to yet another aspect of the spiritual transcendence of certain Corinthians. The same women who have received the spiritual gifts of prophecy and glossolalia are also abstaining from sexual relations as part of their consecration to *Sophia* (or ecstacy in the Spirit; see discussion on chaps. 12–14). Grammatically, "so that Satan may not tempt you" modifies "do not deprive one another." "Because of your *lack of self-control*" (emphasis added) raises again the specter of immorality with which his whole counter to the Corinthians' ascetic principle began in 7:2*a*. (On Satan as a *provocateur*, not a personification of evil in a dualistic worldview, see discussion on 5:5.)

Paul's "concession" in 7:6 refers to the qualification in 7:5, "except perhaps by agreement for a set time." It is a concession with regard to the immediately preceding command to "not deprive one another." This reading illuminates the sense of the whole paragraph, 7:1-7. After introducing the issue with a quotation of the Corinthians' principle in 7:1*b*, Paul gives his commands, which counter that principle in 7:2-3: Because of the threat of immorality, husbands and wives should give each other conjugal rights. He bases his argument, in 7:4, in the reciprocal authority each has over the other's body. Paul, in 7:5, applies his command of 7:3 even more precisely to the issue of withdrawal from sexual relations in marriage, yet allows an exception as a concession. In 7:7 then, aware that they may be appealing to his own celibacy as a paradigm, he explains that, although he wishes all were as he is, his celibacy is "a particular gift from God."

The actual or potential appeal to his own celibacy perhaps leads to focusing next (7:8-9) on the cases for which he is willing to make his own unmarried status a model: "the unmarried and the widows." "Practicing self-control" is likely a specific reference to the Corinthians' sexual celibacy, not a general or hypothetical reference. Paul's qualification—and memorable maxim: "It is better to marry than to burn (with desire; NRSV: be aflame with passion)"— in 7:9 indicates just how seriously he took the sex drive.

"To the married" in 7:10-11 Paul has a command from "the Lord": in effect, the prohibition of divorce (cf. Mark 10:2-9, 11-12; Luke/Q 16:18). That Paul so rarely refers or alludes to the sayings of Jesus suggests that he had little interest in or acquaintance with them. In Gal 1:11-20 he proudly insists that he did not receive his gospel from people, that is, did not spend time learning from those who had been with Jesus. When he explicitly cites "the word of the Lord" in 1 Thess 4:15-17, he is referring to a revelation he himself received from the exalted Christ. That his two clear references to particular sayings of Jesus are both in 1 Corinthians (here and in 9:14) suggests, however, that by the time he wrote 1 Corinthians there was some knowledge of Jesus' sayings in the Corinthian assembly. Paul's interruption in 7:11 of his procedure of gender-inclusive alternation between husband and wife with a serious exception makes the address to the husband seem a mere after-thought and suggests that he is addressing primarily certain women here and throughout 7:1-16. Expecting that the Corinthian women will not necessarily follow the command not to divorce, he insists that at least a divorced woman must not marry some other man (i.e., and thus commit adultery; cf. Mark 10:12). As in 7:1-7 Paul is not citing a universal rule (prohibition of divorce), but addressing the particular situation in Corinth.

"To the rest" in 7:12-16 addresses those in marriages with nonbelievers, again proceeding in repeated gender-balanced state-ments, suggesting that Paul is appealing specifically to certain women. Although Paul declares pointedly, "I say—I and not the Lord," his instructions in 7:12-13 apply the Lord's command against divorce in 7:10-11 to these special cases. The believing partner is not to initiate divorce. Thus 7:15ab offers the exception to maintaining such marriages: only "if the unbelieving partner separates," then "the brother or sister is not bound (enslaved)" to maintain the marriage.

For Paul, holiness—the reason given in 7:14 for believers main-taining their marriages—is a matter, not of a magically transferable quality (contra Conzelmann 1975, 121-22), but of social relations, of ethical behavior according to the will of God (1 Cor 7:34; 1 Thess 4:1-7). "Holy" can also characterize those who have been baptized into the ranks of believers or who have come to believe in Christ (1:30; 3:18; 6:11). The principal connotation here is that they are separated from the world and sin into the new community of Christ. Paul thinks of corporal-sexual relations as a mutually engaging bond (cf. 6:12-20) in which the holy would be more powerful than the unholy. The holy part would affect the whole, as in the case of the "first fruits" making the whole batch of dough holy or the root making the branches holy (Rom 11:16). Thus in 7:14 the unbeliever is made holy through her or his relationship with the believer (and might even be "saved," 7:16). Similarly, through the (mother's) continuation in the marriage and household the children are acceptable to God. After stating the exception to his instruction to maintain marriages with nonbelieving partners (v. 15ab), Paul expands on the reason for staying in such marriages (vv. 15c-16): "For all you know, you might save your [partner]."

If we review this difficult reference to holiness in the context of the whole argument of chapter 7 and the whole Corinthian situation, another possibility emerges for understanding Paul's statements in 7:14. It seems likely from his argument in 7:25-38 that "holy" (v. 34) was yet another term used by the Corinthian pneumatics to characterize their spiritual status, apparently in specific connection with their sexual asceticism. Thus Paul may be directing the Corinthian (women) ascetics' own term for their own transcendent holiness back toward them with a very different twist. Assuming they are concerned about "holiness," what about extending it, within marital-familial relations, to their partners and children?

General Rule with Illustrations and Exception (7:17-24)

With 7:17-24 Paul enunciates a general principle for marital status and provides a rationale for the principle with two illustrations, "circumcised-uncircumcised" and "slave-free." In the assemblies he was founding as communities in a kind of alternative society, Paul was attempting to overcome the basic social-economic power relations that were integral to the Roman imperial social order. The Pauline assemblies symbolized their transcendence of these traditional social-economic relations in the baptismal rite of entry into the movement: "There is no longer Jew or Greek, there is no longer slave or free, there is no longer male and female" (Gal 3:28). Paul has this triad of social relations in mind as he moves to illustrate a principle pertinent to the one, marriage relations, from the other two, Jew-Gentile and slave-free. The three sets of relations, however, are not symmetrical and analogical, and Paul must make an exception to his "rule in all the assemblies" (NRSV: "churches").

The NRSV translation of this section is seriously misleading and must be corrected on two important points that affect the meaning of his argument. (1) That each should lead "the life . . . to which God called you" in 7:17, apparently perpetuating Luther's translation of God's "call" as one's occupation or station in life, is anachronistic. The translation "to which" fits neither illustration, "slave-free," nor "circumcised (Jew)-uncircumcised (Gentile)." Elsewhere Paul consistently uses "call/called" *(klēsis)* for his own or others' call into the movement or toward salvation (Jones 1984, 32-43). In 7:17, however, Paul is apparently referring to one's life circumstances at the time of one's call, as can be seen in the parallel articulations of the same "rule" in 7:20, 24. In the context, this fits both the broader subject he is addressing in 7:1-16 and one of his illustrations of the rule, that is, whether at the time of one's call a person was married or unmarried, circumcised or uncircumcised. Indeed, the only case for which Paul offers no exception to a general rule in the whole argument of 7:1-24 is that of circumcision or uncircumcision. Probably nearly all members of the Corinthian assembly were "uncircumcised." Since "Judaizing" apostles had not yet come into the Corinthian community, circumcision was not an issue there as it had become in the Galatian assemblies. While perhaps shocking to some of Paul's Jewish compatriots, his statement that circumcision (or uncircumcision) is "nothing" would have been unexceptionable to the Corinthians. His comment that "obeying the commandments of God is everything," moreover, indicates that for Paul "the Law" was still valid as an ethical code to guide community life and social relations.

(2) In another important misreading, the NRSV inserts "your present condition" into the somewhat vague last clause of 7:21. This is utterly unwarranted both rhetorically and in terms of Greco-Roman slavery. Ironically, this widespread misreading of 7:21 (17-24) serves as the sole "proof-text" on which most interpreters still base their view that Paul was socially conservative, that is, that he opposed any change in the established social order. Illustration of this "rule" of "[remaining] in the condition in which

you were called" (7:17, 20, 24) works well in the case of circum-cised-uncircumcised, but turns out to be problematic in the case of slave-free. This may lie at the root of the perennial difficulties of understanding Paul's formulation and meaning in 7:21(23). The last (elliptical), imperative clause of 7:21, "rather use (it)," requires completion from the context. The most obvious completion gram-matically would be from the nearest substantive term, "freedom," with which the previous clause ends, and not "slave(ry)" from three clauses earlier in verse 21 or "call" from verse 20. In addition, the aorist tense of the verb "use (it)" suggests a single action (even if in the future), rather than the continuous action of "make use of." Thus, 7:21*b* should be read: "But if you are able to become free, rather use it" (cf. the NRSV footnote "avail yourself of the oppor-tunity"). Historical social realities confirm this completion of the sentence (i.e., "use the opportunity to become free"). The social relationships of slave-free were not analogous to those of married-single or circumcised-uncircumcised. People in the latter circum-stances had at least some possibility of changing their status. Slaves, however, had little power to affect their status. Their potential emancipation was strictly in the hands of their master. There would have been little point in instructing slaves about to be freed by their master to "make use of your present condition (i.e., slavery) now more than ever" since they had no choice in the matter.

Such considerations enable us to see that in 7:21(23) Paul is making another exception to another general principle, as he does throughout his argument. Through most of his argument in chapter 7, in the four paragraphs prior and one immediately after 7:17-24, Paul follows the same general pattern of argumentation. He first enunciates a general rule (vv. 2-3, 8, 10, 12-13, 26-27) and then makes exceptions (set off by "but") for particular contingencies (vv. 5, 9, 11*a*, 15, 28), occasionally offering reasons for the rule or the exception. The wording of 7:17-24 can be seen to follow the same pattern of general rule, now a broader general principle, in 7:17, 20, 24 and illustrated in verse 18, with explanation in verse 19. However, 7:21 does not provide a second illustration of the principle, but an exception to it, with explanation given in verses 22-23.

In his first illustration of his general principle, from circumcision and uncircumcision in 7:18, Paul follows a definite rhetorical pattern, repeated in 7:27, of two pairs of circumstantial questions followed immediately by imperatives that forbid seeking the alternative condition. When he moves to his second illustration of the general principle, from slave and free in 7:21, Paul breaks that rhetorical pattern in two ways, with a variation on the imperative and then with an additional clause. We would have expected "You were called a slave? Do not become free. You were called free? Do not become a slave." Instead we read: "You were called a slave? Do not be concerned. But if you are able to become free, rather use (the opportunity)" (AT). By adding the statement in verse 21*b* "But if (indeed)" (NRSV: "even if"), Paul thus contradicts the "rule" articulated in 7:17, 20, 24. Moreover, the justification given in verses 22-23 only makes sense if verse 21 reads that the slave should take the opportunity of freedom: "Whoever was called in the Lord as a slave is [already!] a freed person belonging to the Lord." In verse 22*b* Paul finally mentions the second of the pair, "slave-free," except that he moves directly to the reason why a free person cannot become a slave: "Whoever was free when called is a slave of Christ," hence the person cannot possibly become the slave of another master. Both cases are finally covered in 7:23: since they were "bought with a price," neither a slave nor a free person can become "slaves of human masters."

Paul's exception to his rule with regard to slaves would have had direct resonance with members of the Corinthian community, even if no particular cases of slavery were currently in dispute among them. From the mention elsewhere of households, we can deduce that some members of the community must have (perhaps previously) been slaves and others must have been slaveholders. The particular reference to "Lucky" (NRSV: "Fortunatus") and "the Achaian" (NRSV: "Achaicus") in connection with Stephanas's household (16:17) indicates that they were most likely either the latter's slaves or freedmen still connected with him. It may be puzzling why Paul bothered to illustrate his general rule in all the assemblies with "circumcised-uncircumcised" and "slave-free," insofar as the first was so clear-cut that it offered no analogy for the exceptions so important in the rest of chapter 7 while the latter turned out to be nothing but an exception to the rule it might have illustrated. Perhaps it is just this combination of illustration and exception that he was after. Or perhaps he inserted this subsection of his argument precisely in order to address the slave-free issue in passing just to reinforce the ideal of the movement.

Concerning Virgins (7:25-40)

The opening phrase of 7:25, "now concerning virgins," signals the discussion of a new but related issue. Abstention from sexual relations, which is only an exception for the married, becomes the rule for "the virgins." It is not, however, a simple matter of applying the rule to remain as you were when called. "Virgins" in this passage evidently refers to young women who are betrothed, but eager themselves or encouraged by others to remain virgins (see just below). The question is which way to move, and in this case Paul's own preference for celibacy in view of the imminent "appointed time" comes through clearly. Now Paul shifts the tone of his argument. In contrast with the arguments in chapters 1–4 and 5–6, he no longer appeals to his apostleship. He almost makes a point of not having a "command of the Lord." In contrast with his usual authoritative pronouncement, he tenders his "opinion" and his "wish," speaking mainly of the context in which they are to make their own decision on the basis of their own particular relationship. Yet here, in contrast with 7:1-16, he writes in gender-balanced statements about men *and* women only in 7:32-34. Most of 7:25-38 is addressed not to the "virgins" themselves, but to the men betrothed to "virgins."

Traditionally, because of the reference to "his virgin" (NRSV: fiancée) in verse 36 and the verb "cause to marry" in verse 38, the passage has been understood as addressed to fathers about their virgin daughters. It is clear from the phrase "the unmarried woman *and* the virgin" (emphasis added), in verse 34, however, that "virgins" has a more specific (or different) reference than young unmarried women. That verses 36-37 are addressed to men about their (potential) sexual disposition toward the(ir) "virgins" indicates that the latter must refer throughout the passage to *betrothed* young women. Further, that Paul pointedly reassures the engaged men that "you/she does not sin" if you marry suggests that they or someone in the Corinthian assembly had the sense that it was wrong for "virgins" to marry. Finally, the opening statement in Paul's argument, "it is well for you to remain as you are" (7:26b), which is formulated exactly like the quotation in 7:1b (introduced awkwardly by Paul in v. 26a), must be another principle of the Corinthian spirituals' ascetics ideal.

Paul agrees with the Corinthians' position as he has cited it, but offers his own reason: "in view of the present crisis" (v. 26a NRSV footnote). Both "crisis" *(anagkē)* here and "distress" *(thlipsis)* in verse 28 have been taken eschatologically, partly because of what Paul says later in verses 29-31 and partly because elsewhere in the New Testament these terms refer to eschatological woes that will precede or accompany the *parousia* (Luke 21:23; Rev 7:14). However, considering that Paul himself uses both of these terms with regard to present sufferings (2 Cor 6:4; 1 Thess 3:7), his reference here is more likely to "the *present* crisis." Perhaps he means simply the "crisis" of whether to pursue the ideal of "virginity." In 7:26-27, as in 7:36-38, Paul is addressing the particular situation of those engaged (previously obligated) to "virgins," not repeating his instructions to the unmarried and married in 7:8-9, 10-11. Paul does use "bound to a woman" elsewhere for the marriage bond (7:39; Rom 7:2). But the Greek term for "woman" (*gynē,* translated "wife" in the NRSV) is more ambiguous than the English, usually but not always meaning "wife"; and the Greek term "free from" *(lysis),* which would be strange in reference to divorce, is commonly used in ancient papyri for release from an obligation or contract. In 7:36-38 Paul is clearly addressing men engaged to be married, and the whole argument in 7:25-38 begins and ends with a focus on "virgins."

As in each of the previous paragraphs, Paul again has an exception or, in this case, a qualification (v. 28a): To marry would not be a sin. It is remarkable that a first-century Jew such as Paul would write this. Far from not being a sin, marriage was virtually an obligation in ancient Jewish circles. Paul appears to be working out of precisely such an understanding of life throughout the first several steps in his argument above, 7:1-7, 8-9, 10-11, 12-16. Thus in verse 28 he must be addressing a Corinthian ascetic position that holds that it would be wrong to violate the "virginity" of young betrothed women by proceeding with the previously arranged marriage. Paul immediately adds a qualification to his qualification: He would spare them the troubles that those who marry will experience in this life. That is, although proceeding with marriage to the betrothed woman who is a "virgin" is no sin, it is better not to marry.

Framed by "I mean" at the beginning and "I say this" at the end, 7:29-35 constitutes a lengthy explanation of the preceding advice, in two steps. In 7:29-31 Paul presents his own understanding of the appropriate stance toward "the world" in which his counsel about marriage is rooted. With "the appointed time has grown short" and "the present form of this world is passing away" (vv. 29a, 31b), he states in stark form the temporal-historical and social-political implications of the plan for the fulfillment of history that God has now implemented in the crucifixion and resurrection of Christ, and which is soon to be consummated at Christ's *parousia* (4:5; 11:26; 15:23). Paul is not battling a realized eschatology in Corinth, but pressing his own eschatological orientation on those who do not think in the same way. The climactic events of history are already underway; their completion is imminent. Since the institutionalized "form" of society as we know it is "passing away" (v. 31b; cf. Rom 8:18-25), the appropriate stance toward the world is "as though . . . [not]." In 7:29a-31a Paul offers five illustrations that make clear that the economic system (private property, slavery, commerce, and so forth) and basic social forms (patriarchal marriage, and so forth), as well as the emotional aspects of life rooted in them, are about to disappear. His stance here has been compared with Stoicism. However, having no sense that "the . . . form of this world is passing away," the Stoics withdrew into the security of the inner life of the mind/soul, in detachment from the dominant social forms and cultural values (cf. Epictetus, *Diss.* 2.16.8; 3.22.67-76; 4.7.5.). Paul envisions freedom from the forms and values of the dominant society even while continuing to interact with nonbelievers (cf. 5:9-13).

In 7:32-35 Paul applies the "as though . . . [not]" stance to the question of marriage between "virgins" and their intended. "I want you to be free from anxieties"—presumably about marrying or not. Yet the gist of the following pairs of statements in verses 32b-34 is not clear. We should read the verb "is anxious about" consistently in these sentences. If it is to be taken pejoratively, then Paul would apparently be addressing the asceticism of certain Corinthians. The ascetics' anxieties about their spiritual transcendence (which he restates in his own preferred terms, oriented toward "the affairs of the Lord") are comparable to those of married people, which they are supposedly transcending. If, on the other hand, the phrases are taken more positively, then Paul appears to want the Corinthians to be free of anxiety both about the affairs of the Lord and about pleasing a spouse, that is, along the lines of the "as thought . . . [not]" principle in verses 29-31. The only difference then between married and unmarried would be that the married person "[is] divided" (v. 34a), indicating that the unmarried condition is the better one (as stated in vv. 26-28, and stated again explicitly in v. 38).

On either reading of "is anxious about," there are two discrepancies here between the portrayal of men and that of women. First, Paul refers to two categories of women, "the unmarried woman *and* the virgin" (v. 34b). Second, the case of women includes a purpose clause, "so that they may be holy in both body and spirit" (v. 34a; cf. "how to please the Lord," v. 32b). This clause shows that the purpose of "virginity" was "holiness." The phrase "in both body and spirit" is then either a direct reflection of the Corinthian ascetics' concern for bodily purity for the sake of their spiritual transcendence, or else Paul's expression of his own concern that the body as well as the spirit should be kept holy.

The explanatory digression is concluded in verse 35. "For your (pl.) own benefit" looks to the good of the whole assembly (as in 6:12; 10:23; 12:7). Paul genuinely does not want to restrain them by his preceding explanation. The clause following "but" reads literally "for what is appropriate and constant to the Lord without distraction." The NRSV translation "unhindered devotion to the Lord" should not be construed in the direction of an ascetic piety similar to what Paul is opposing. Paul's concern in 7:32-35 is the alleviation of anxiety about sexuality and marriage in the stance toward "the world" (7:29-31).

Paul concludes the discussion of "virgins" in 7:36-38 by restating more explicitly the two options already suggested in 7:27-28*a*. Again he is writing directly to men engaged to "virgins." Translating "his *virgin*" instead of "his fiancée" (see NRSV footnote to v. 36) indicates far more clearly that spiritually motivated "virginity" is at issue. In the conditional clauses addressing the contingencies of the decision in 7:36, Paul expresses his concern about potential immorality rooted in the male sex drives. The resolution, "let him do as he wishes" (NRSV: "let them marry") suggests that the issue in the Corinthian assembly involved an engaged man eager to marry (or at least in a quandary about it), with "his virgin" and/or others defending her continuing "virginity." Paul's explicit, repeated emphasis that it is not a sin to marry must be directed against a Corinthian position that it was wrong for a "virgin" to marry.

Preceding his statement of the second (better) option (v. 37), Paul sets forth an even lengthier series of conditions. In encouraging a man to follow the Corinthian spirituals' ascetic ideal, Paul goes to great lengths to encourage him to do it for his own reasons, to reach an autonomous decision. The NRSV translation, "having his own desire under control," focuses the issue on the man's struggle with his own sexual desire. The Greek says, literally, "(whoever/if he) has authority *[exousia]* with regard to his will." That is surely an allusion to the Corinthians' principle that "all things are lawful (authorized) for me" (6:12; 10:23). It also alludes to the Corinthian principle that a woman has authority over her own body, which is implied by Paul's formulation in 7:4. One suspects, further, that "necessity" in verse 37 alludes to the worldly constraints that the Corinthian spirituals believe they have transcended in their newfound "authority/freedom" (see further on chaps. 8–9 below). (Alternatively, "necessity" may refer to the constraints of strongly held positions among the Corinthians.) Finally, "has determined in his own mind" must also be read in the context of the Corinthian spirituals' ideal of virginity. Verse 37 should thus be translated more literally and contextually: "But he who stands firm in his heart, having no necessity, but having authority with regard to his will, and (who) has decided in his own heart to keep his own virgin, (he) will do well." Summarizing in 7:38 Paul suggests that there are really two good options. A man can pursue either one without doing wrong, although refraining from marrying the virgin is the better of the two. It is striking in this whole section of his argument (7:25-38) that, despite the pointedly gender-inclusive formulations in the previous section (7:1-16), Paul utterly ignores the wishes of the "virgins." The issue of whether a "virgin" continues in her "virginity" is left completely up to the strength of her fiancé's sexual desire or his "authority" over his own will. She is even called "his (own) virgin" (vv. 36, 38).

In 7:39-40 Paul returns to what he sees as the major problem among the Corinthians with regard to marriage and sexual relations, that women were separating from their husbands for ascetic motives. He reasserts the traditional Jewish stance on marriage in which he was rooted. "A wife is bound as long as her husband lives," after which she is free to marry again. But Paul qualifies this freedom by specifying that the second marriage must be "in the Lord." His closing comment is closer to what the ascetic Corinthian women probably want to hear: It is more blessed to remain single (v. 40*a*). However, the statement that they are bound to their husbands effectively denies them that potential celibacy for the present. Paul's insistence on his own authority (v. 40*b*) is less authoritarian than elsewhere in the letter (cf. 4:14-21; 14:37-38).

◊ ◊ ◊ ◊

A number of things in Paul's discussion of sex and marriage indicate that women were the principal addressees of 7:1-16 and that primarily women in the Corinthian assembly were involved in sexual asceticism. Thus the sequence of marital situations addressed in chapter 7 indicates not only that women of several different marital statuses belonged to the assembly, but also that women in each of those statuses were abstaining from sexual relations or even separating from their husbands, going against social customs and expectations. This suggests there were many women ascetics within the assembly. That previously married women could remain single indicates, furthermore, that some sort of mutual support network had emerged among the ascetics within the Corinthian assembly.

Collation of several bits of information from this chapter and related passages in 1 Corinthians provides a profile of the Corinthian women ascetics' position and behavior. With regard to sexual relations and marriage they believed "it is well for a man not to touch a woman" (7:1*b*). Convinced that "all things are lawful (authorized) for me" (6:12; 10:23), they maintained over against traditional patriarchal sexual and marital relations that a woman has authority over her own body (7:4). The women who, empowered by *Sophia* (or the Spirit), had transcended the mundane realities of bodily-sexual life were now "holy," set apart and dedicated to their new life in the Spirit (7:34). In their spiritual transcendence (as "wise, mature, of noble birth, rich, and *pneumatikoi*," 1:26-28; 2:6-16; 4:8-10) they had (re)gained a (spiritual) "virginity." They held out the ideal that young women, even those already betrothed, should remain "virgins"; it would be wrong for them to marry (7:28, 36). It is noteworthy that the Therapeutrides as portrayed by Philo of Alexandria parallel the Corinthian women ascetics' position and behavior in all of these respects (see introduction).

The asceticism of the Corinthian women was not an otherworldly spiritual ideology with no relation to their life situation. Indeed, it would appear to have been liberating for them in direct relationship to key aspects of the generally debilitating situation of women in antiquity (Wire 1990, 63-64, 74-75). With life expectancy at around thirty-four years for women (forty for men) and a general shortage of women because of the exposure of female babies (the principal means of birth control), women were expected to marry young (soon after puberty), usually to men many years older, and to remarry quickly if widowed or divorced. Because of the shortage of free women, free men often married their own slaves or freedwomen. But free women were also dependent on their husbands (or fathers) in all civil and judicial as well as economic matters, having no place in society except in a patriarchal household. The patriarchal marriage-and-family was reinforced culturally-politically, moreover, as the foundation of the civil and imperial order. Social custom, further, confined women to the household, while men interacted in public life. Far from leading to self-negation and isolation, the Corinthian women's asceticism meant a transcendence of debilitating dependence on their husbands and of subordination to their authority, as well as an unprecedented wider participation in social life (Wire 1990, 93, 97). The concern of these women was not to avoid evil, but to participate in divine gifts of liberating enlightenment and devotion to the divine *Sophia,* who was instrumental in freeing them from sexual subordination and domestic confinement. God did not call these Corinthian women to remain as they were when called, but transformed their personal lives and empowered them with new social possibilities. Of course such departures from social norms and practices would have been disturbing to those deeply rooted in the traditional social-cultural patterns, according to which women were expected to be confined to their households and subordinate to their husbands.

The Corinthian women ascetics may well have built on or appealed to a central theme of Paul's preaching, the baptismal formula that seems to inform his choice of analogies to the marriage issue in 7:17-24. Insofar as the formula cited in Gal 3:28 is a guide to the ideals symbolized in the baptismal rite by which people were formally incorporated into the assembly, in their new life there was no longer "male and female." One of the ways this could have been understood was that patriarchal marriage was now transcended (Schüssler Fiorenza 1983, 211). Judging from his commands in chapter 7, Paul understands the traditional marriage (including sexual) relationship as relativized by the eschatological events now underway (7:29-31), but by no means transcended in practice. As can be seen elsewhere in this letter as well (especially in 1–4; 11:17-34; 12–14; 15), Paul has a strong sense of corporate-communal life for which the marriage bond, family, and community, as well as the embodiment of the person, are especially important. Because his own understanding of life was so deeply rooted in the traditional social forms, he could not imagine transcending such structures in which persons were embedded except by individuals who had special "gifts" or roles such as his own (7:7).

Besides the sexual politics involved in the marital relations in Corinth, sexual politics was also involved in the way Paul addressed those marital relations. He must have designed the pointedly gender-inclusive formulations here, so unusual in Greek and Roman antiquity, to appeal to women. But he did this in order to demand more from them. He appealed to the women to provide legitimate sexual relations for the men in order that the (threat of) men's drive toward immorality could be controlled. In doing that, however, he demanded virtually nothing from the men, while asking the women to sacrifice their newly gained freedom and empowerment (Wire 1990, 80-86). If we take the text at face value, it seems that Paul was conceding their principle in order to persuade them into behavior that went against that principle. Of course, his acceptance of their principle may have been only a rhetorical ploy. In that case, he was only pretending to agree with their ideal precisely in order to induce them to act against it. Then, moreover, once readers lost sight of the original, conflictual rhetorical situation, Paul himself was read as espousing what was originally the Corinthians' principle and qualifying it only for certain contingencies.

Paul's argument on sexual relations is also noteworthy for what it discloses about his basic approach to ethical issues. Paul became far more exercised over arrogance and disputes within the assembly (chapters 1–4) than he did about marriage and sexual relations. Instead of laying down universal laws, he focused on particular life situations such as the significant differences between marriages or between marriage and engagement. Even when he had a "command of the Lord" he was under no illusion that it would necessarily be obeyed. He applied general rules or commands flexibly, allowing for individual needs or desires. Striking, against the background of ancient moral instruction, is his suggestion of working out differences and making mutual agreements. He did articulate the general principle (not a law or all-inclusive command) that one should remain in the situation in which one was called (7:17, 21, 24). But he then made explicit exceptions based on the relative oppression experienced in one's particular life situations.

Far more important as the source and grounding of his ethical positions than commands (even of the Lord) or general principles were traditional (Jewish) social forms (which he did not articulate but which we can discern) and his understanding of the particular historical situation in which he and the Corinthians stood. In the old cliché, he was "in but not of the world." He was free from the dominant social-political-economic institutions ("the form of this world" that is "passing away"), yet he continued to work within and interact with people in the dominant society. The key to understanding Paul's response to the Corinthians on the issues in chapter 7 is to discern what social forms he thought should be continued, however changed, even though he expected the imminent disappearance of the dominant political order.

Paul has often been construed as socially conservative on the basis of 1 Cor 7:17-24. The legacy of Paul the social conservative is closely interrelated with the long-standing misreading of 7:21, along with several Deutero-Pauline passages exhorting slaves to be obedient to their masters (e.g., Eph 6:5; Col 3:22; 1 Tim 6:1-2; Titus 2:9-10), and the use of these passages to legitimate slavery. This understanding of Paul, particularly of his stance with regard to slavery, has been part and parcel of the idealization of Greco-Roman civilization (which was based on slave labor) by culturally dominant circles in Western Europe and the Americas—as exhibited, for example, in public architecture and elite educational curricula. A closer reading of this passage in its literary and historical context, however, indicates no basis for this widespread and long-standing interpretation of Paul. He was by no means delineating a believer's religious or spiritual status in isolation from the social situation. Precisely the opposite! He had been proclaiming that, for those who believed that in Christ's crucifixion and resurrection God had inaugurated the eschatological events of the imminent kingdom of God, the principal social-economic divisions of "this world" that are "passing away"—slave-free, Jew-Gentile, and patriarchal marriage—had been broken through. This had been articulated in the baptismal formula cited at the baptismal ceremony in which they had joined the movement, the assembly of the new society.

It had become apparent, however, that living out that ideal entailed different problems in the contingencies of the concrete formal and informal power-relations of "the world" in which Paul's assemblies still lived. Unless or until emissaries came from Jerusalem who believed that Gentiles had to join Israel in order to inherit the blessings to Abraham, it was a simple matter to insist that the uncircumcised need not become circumcised, since neither status was now of any significance in the new society of those who were now heirs of those blessings. With regard to slaves, the possibilities depended on particular concrete situations. As established in the exegesis above, however, Paul was clear that slaves should seize any opportunity to become free. This was a pointed exception to his general principle stated in 7:17, 20, 24. His stance with regard to slavery is articulated unambiguously in verse 23: "You were bought with a price; do not become slaves of human masters."

Only with regard to sex and marriage could Paul be described as conservative. In that regard his anxiety about men's ability to control their lust led him to appeal to women to continue giving men their conjugal rights, in a perpetuation of traditional patriarchal marriage relations. Ironically, while manipulating the Corinthian women in this direction with his rhetoric of equality, Paul did state that a woman has authority over her husband's body. This was at least a minimal bit of equality in a patriarchal society in which the only thing that mattered was the husband's authority over his wife's body.

In terms of his stance toward "the world" Paul could be characterized not as conservative but as revolutionary, insofar as he anticipated the imminent end of the whole old order of Roman imperial society. The established "rulers of this age" had finally sealed their own doom when they "crucified the Lord of Glory" (2:8). Although Paul did not advocate an active challenge to the established order, he also did not want his communities to escape from "this world." Since "the appointed time [had] grown short," this world was already "passing away." Meanwhile his project was the systematic formation of new communities of "saints" among the peoples in the major towns and cities of the empire, assemblies that would persevere in solidarity while working out appropriate solutions to emergent contingencies.

ARGUMENT CONCERNING FOOD OFFERED TO IDOLS (8:1–11:1)

"Now concerning . . ." opens discussion of another issue, "foods sacrificed to idols," about which the Corinthians may have inquired in their letter (cf. 7:1; 12:1; 16:1). In chapters 8–10, more than in any other section of the letter, it is possible to discern both sides of the argument. Paul indicates at points that he is citing certain slogans of the Corinthians (e.g., 8:1, 4). We can often detect from his argument other points at which he cites Corinthian opinions. For example, the warning about "this liberty of yours" in 8:9 clearly indicates that the preceding statement in verse 8 about idol-food being a matter of indifference represents the Corinthians' position, not his own. The phrase "accustomed to idols until now" in 8:7 indicates that the "weak" for whom Paul is concerned are Gentiles, not "Jewish Christians" or Jews. Nothing in chapters 8–10 suggests that there are concrete factions of strong and weak. The word *strong* does not even occur here (only in 1:27 and 4:10, referring to high spiritual status), and *weak* (8:7, 10), which refers specifically to the consciousness of "others," is probably Paul's term, with the word "others" (Gk. "someone," 8:10) being rhetorical-hypothetical, not a reference to particular persons.

Most decisive for how the structure and meaning of Paul's argument can be understood, 8:1-13 addresses the same situation as 10:14-22, that is, "eating in the temple of an idol," as indicated explicitly in 8:10 and 10:20-21. In fact, 10:14-22 is the climax and main point of the argument, not a digression, while 10:23–11:1 appears to be almost an afterthought, dealing with a related matter of lesser importance, not Paul's agreement with the "strong." Paul's argument in this section of the letter can thus be seen as proceeding in five steps. He introduces the issue and begins the argument against eating idol-food in a temple, ending with a fundamental principle in verse 13. He illustrates that principle biographically in a defense of his own refusal to accept financial support in 9:1-27. In 10:1-13 he warns the Corinthians who were eating idol-food that they are risking the wrath of God. Then in 10:14-22 he states in clear terms his prohibition of such a risky practice. His recapitulation of the argument in 10:23–11:1 includes a concession to the enlightened ones, apparently to soften the impact of the blunt prohibition of "idolatry" he has just pronounced.

On Not Using Ethical Authority Rooted in *Gnōsis* (8:1-13)

Paul's strategy here in chapters 8–10, as in 1:10–4:21, is to discuss the beliefs in which he thinks the Corinthians' behavior is rooted before he focuses on the behavior itself. As he eventually makes clear in 8:9-10, the practice of some Corinthians "eating in the temple of an idol" was an exercise of their authority or "liberty" (NRSV; *exousia*), which in turn was rooted in their "knowledge" *(gnōsis)*. Thus Paul first deals with the *gnōsis* in 8:1-6 before directly addressing their liberty of eating food offered to idols directly in 8:7-13. As he proceeds, moreover, he quotes—and qualifies—several principles of the Corinthians, which accounts for some of the twists and turns in his argument.

◊ ◊ ◊ ◊

The issue of "food sacrificed to idols" involved whether those who had joined the Jesus movement(s) should still participate in the most constitutive social relations of Greco-Roman society. The word *eidōlothyton* ("food sacrificed to idols; 8:1, 4, and so on) does not appear in Jewish literature prior to Paul (the next earliest occurrences in are 4 Macc 5:2 and *Sib Or* 2:96), who uses it only in this letter. It almost always refers to food sacrificed in the presence of an idol and eaten in the temple precincts. Judging from 8:10, it must have the same meaning in 8:1-13 as in 10:19-21 (and in other early Christian literature), where it clearly means eating in a temple in the presence of the idol. Paul picks a different term, "sacred food" (*hierothyton*; NRSV: "offered in sascrifice"), when he refers to eating dinner at a friend's house (10:27-28). For Paul, eating food sacrificed to idols must have been virtually the same as idolatry (cf. "worship of dead gods," *Did.* 6:3). He saw idolatry and fornication as *the* major issues for the assembly still living "in the world" (see above, on chaps. 5, 6, and 7; cf. Acts 15:29; 21:25; Rev 2:14, 20). In every social dimension—from extended families to guilds and associations—and city celebrations to the imperial cult, sacrifice and banqueting were integral to, indeed constitutive of, community life (Stowers 1995). Participation in banquets held in temples was important in establishing the social connections and cultivating patronal relations, particularly for anyone wanting to curry the favor of social-economic superiors. Meat offered for sale in the market posed a less serious problem, although much of the meat in the market would have been brought from temple sacrifices. Whether to buy it was a problem only for those who had attained a certain economic level, since most people in antiquity were too poor to afford meat on a regular basis. Distribution of sacrificial meat at the Imperial or Isthmian Games would have been one of the few opportunities for the poor to enjoy meat.

Immediately after announcing the new topic in 8:1a Paul cites, with seeming approval, a principle of the Corinthians: "all of us possess knowledge [gnōsis]." Clearly another prized possession of some of the Corinthians, gnōsis dominates this step in Paul's argument (8:1, 7, 10, 11; the verb appears three times in 8:2-3; cf. 1:5; 12:8). Hellenistic-Jewish literature provides a complete contemporary parallel to the Corinthians' gnōsis, especially as it connects with other aspects of the distinctive Corinthian religiosity to which Paul is apparently responding throughout this letter. Most significantly, gnōsis was closely associated with sophia, sometimes as a virtual synonym, sometimes as the content that Sophia provided to her devotees (e.g., Wis 10:10). Thus the wise person dwelling in Sophia possessed "knowledge of God" (Philo Leg. All. 3.46-48). Gnōsis thus referred to a content possessed, as well as to the act of knowing, and was sometimes the theological content of sophia.

Paul at first seems to approve, but then, immediately denigrates the Corinthians' gnōsis as to its effects (8:1b-3). Knowledge "puffs up"—presumably the knowers ("puffed up" in their high spiritual status, cf. 4:6, 18); "but love builds up"—presumably the community (cf. chap. 13). In verses 2-3 Paul directly challenges the Corinthian claim to possess knowledge (cf. his counter to "wise" in 3:18, and to "spiritual" in 14:37). Verse 2a begins with "if anyone claims to have already attained full knowledge" (the word translated "something" in the NRSV was almost certainly absent from the original text). The irony is unmistakable. The pretentious claim of having attained knowledge indicates that the person does not yet in fact understand much. The words "God" and "by him" (v. 3) were almost certainly missing in Paul's text, and are both redundant with regard to the Corinthians' *gnōsis* and diversionary with regard to Paul's point. The simple but subtle statement in verse 3 fits perfectly with the contrast Paul drew in verse 1c: But if someone loves, he or she is known (Paul means that if someone acts with love toward others in a way that builds up the community, one is known, i.e., appreciated in the community).

As becomes clear in 12:8 and 14:26, *gnōsis* can also refer to a particular teaching *(logos)* or principle. Almost certainly, therefore, the statements Paul cites in verse 4 are particular principles of the Corinthians' *gnōsis,* that is, their theological knowledge: "We know that 'no idol in the world really exists,' and that 'there is no God but one.' " For hellenistic Jews such as Philo, *gnōsis* (or its synonym) is primarily "knowledge of God" as reached by way of *Sophia* (*Quod Deus* 143), and that "God is One" (or "the truly existing One") is the lesson Moses continually teaches in the Laws (e.g., *Spec. Leg.* 1.30). The corollary principle of *gnōsis* for enlightened hellenistic Jews such as Philo, as for the Corinthians, was that "no idol in the world really exists." In the Wisdom of Solomon, as in Philo's works, the critique of false gods contrasts ignorance of God, the supposition that idols and certain things *in the world* such as natural forces or heavenly bodies are gods, with knowledge of God, which means righteousness and immortality (Wis 13:1; 14:22; 15:2-3). Only the mind enraptured by the beauty of *Sophia,* writes Philo, is able to know the One alone, which means true "wealth and kingship for the wise" person (*Migr. Abr.* 197; cf. Wis 6:15-21; 7:11-17; 1 Cor 1:26; 4:8). Such hellenistic-Jewish enlightenment theology makes sense not only of the Corinthian principles cited in verses 1 and 4, but also of their connection with other aspects of the Corinthians' devotion to *Sophia* and their apparent claim of immortality (cf. Wis 15:2-3). Knowledge of the One God was also often connected with a mission to Gentiles, whose conversion, like Abraham's, was a transition from ignorance (the worship of things in the world), to knowledge of the One, which brought kingship, perfection, and nobility (*Virt.* 212-19; cf. 1 Cor 1:26; 2:6; 4:8).

The complexity of conjunctions with which the long and awkward sentence in 8:5-6 begins suggests that Paul is here further elaborating on, as if in agreement with, the Corinthians' principles just cited in 8:4. The "even though" clause (v. *5a*) sets up the long concluding "yet for us" statement in verse 6. In between, however, Paul inserts a parenthetical statement (v. *5b*) that asserts precisely the opposite of the Corinthians' principles of *gnōsis*. His correction of the Corinthian theology, while seeming to concede to the Corinthians' dismissal of other gods as "so-called," bluntly asserts the reality of "many gods and many lords." Even though he also used the polemical term "idols," he knew that the Thessalonians and others among whom he worked had to turn from their previous serving of other gods, even if the latter were not "living" or "true" (1 Thess 1:9). With this parenthetical comment in verse *5b* Paul sets up his later prohibition of eating in temples in 10:14-22, where it is evident just how seriously he takes the reality of people's service to and fellowship with other gods and lords.

First Corinthians 8:6 is a major statement of faith. Yet it does not follow from 8:5 and generally fits poorly in its context. The combination "one God, the Father" does not appear anywhere else in Paul's own letters. Elsewhere Paul refers not to Christ's mediating "all things" but to his subjecting all things to himself (15:25-28; Phil 3:21). Most unusual in Paul's letters are the formal prepositional predications about God, "from whom are all things and for whom we exist," and about Christ, "through whom are all things and through whom we exist." The most striking parallels appear in hellenistic philosophical reflection about the causes or primal principles of the universe (the source, "from which"; the cause, "by which"; the form, "according to which"; the instrument, "through which"; and the final cause, "for which"). Hellenistic-Jewish wisdom speculation, such as that represented by the Wisdom of Solomon and Philo, had long since appropriated these forms (Philo, *Cher.* 127; *Quaes. Gen* 1.58; cf. Seneca, *Ep.* 65.4.8). Most notably, *Sophia/Logos* was that "through which/whom" all things had been created (e.g., Wis 8:1, 6; Philo, *Det.* 54; cf. *Fuga* 190; *Leg. All.* 3.96) and also had a revelatory or soteriological role. In a formulation close to the one in verse 6, Philo writes that Moses "is translated 'through the Word' of the Cause, *through which* also the whole world was formed. This is in order that you may learn that God values the wise person as the world, for by the same *Logos* he makes the universe and leads the perfect person from earthly matters to himself" (*Sacr.* 8; cf. Wis 7:27, and for the whole Corinthian position as reflected in 1 Cor 8:1-6, see Wis 9:10-18).

First Corinthians 8:6, which is such a foreign body in the midst of a genuine Pauline letter, is thus explainable as Paul's attempt to replace *Sophia*, the source of the Corinthians' *gnōsis*, with Christ. In 1:24, in an attempt to displace the Corinthians' focus on heavenly *Sophia* and the high spiritual status she provided her devotees, he had asserted that the real *sophia* of God was the crucified Christ. Now in 8:6 Paul borrows one of the particular forms of their enlightenment theology. While leaving intact their affirmation of God as the source and final cause of all things, he replaces *Sophia* with Christ, applying to him the predicates of the instrument of creation ("through whom are all things") and the instrument of salvation ("through whom we"; the NRSV inserts "exist"). In three successive steps Paul thus challenges the enlightened Corinthians' *gnōsis* (vv. 1b-3), contradicts their radical monotheistic principle (vv. 4-5), and finally attempts to replace *Sophia*, the source of their *gnōsis*, with Christ (v. 6), before finally focusing on their liberty to eat food sacrificed to idols.

In 8:7-13, moving from gentle observation in verse 7 to more ominous warning in verse 12, Paul appeals to the enlightened Corinthians to discontinue their practice of eating food offered to idols. He now counters what he ostensibly accepted in 8:1b. In fact, *not* everyone has knowledge, that is, some do not realize that "no idol in the world really exists" (v. 7a). Paul draws out the implication in 8:7b-12. In order to understand what he is arguing, we need some sense of the key terms on the Corinthians' side of the argument, particularly of the term translated in the NRSV as "conscience" in 8:7, 10, 12, and 10:25-27, of the closely related term "liberty/authority" in 8:9, and of the extent of the quotation in verse 8.

Consciousness would far better render the sense of the Greek term *syneidēsis* (NRSV: "conscience"), both here and elsewhere in Paul's letters. Its heavy concentration in chapters 8–10 (and its absence from the parallel discussion of "eating" in Rom 14) suggests that it must have been yet another key concept of the enlightened Corinthians. That a "weak consciousness" stems from a lack of *gnōsis* (8:7) suggests that those of "weak" consciousness were weak mainly in the eyes of those who, by possessing *gnōsis*, had a strong consciousness. "Weak" (and by implication "strong") in chapter 8 does not refer to parties of people (the "divisions" of 1:10-12), but to the "consciousness" of individual Corinthians.

Both here and in 9:4-6, 12, 18, the Greek word *exousia* (NRSV: "liberty") has the sense of personal "authority," "right," or "liberty" (NRSV), which is very different from Pauline usage elsewhere (e.g., Rom 13:1-3; 1 Cor 15:24; 2 Cor 10:8; 13:10). *Exousia* is the concept corresponding to the Corinthian principle that "all things are lawful [possible; (Gr. *exestin*)] for me," cited earlier in 6:12 and again later in 10:23, in connection with eating idol-food. The word "free/freedom" (in an absolute sense) in 9:1, 19; 10:29, moreover, is probably almost synonymous in the vocabulary of the Corinthians who possess *gnōsis*. Philo, typical of Jewish intellectuals who had taken over certain Stoic and Cynic teachings (e.g., Diogenes Laertius 7.121; Epictetus 3.1.23, 25), again provides an illuminating parallel (Horsley 1978b, 580-81). "[The wise] will have the power *(exousia)* to do anything and to live as he wishes; the one for whom these things are lawful [possible; *exestin*] must be free *[eleutheros]*" (*Quod Omnis* 59).

The terms "authority/liberty" and "[strong] consciousness" provide the link between the Corinthians' *gnōsis* (vv. 1*b*-6) and their "eating food offered to idols" (vv. 1*a*, 7-13). As can be seen again from parallels in Philo (e.g., *Praem.* 162-63), the Corinthians' *gnōsis* of the *One God* versus many gods, and of *Sophia* as the *instrument of creation, strengthened* their *consciousness*, making it pure and secure in its moral *authority* (or power; Gk. *exousia*) or *freedom* (Gk. *eleutheria*). Thus strengthened in their consciousness, nothing they could do in the realm of the body, which was utterly separate from the spiritual world, could impinge on the security of their immortal soul. The "strong consciousness" of the Corinthians who possessed *gnōsis* gave them the individual authority/liberty to participate in feasts on "food sacrificed to idols.".

Paul's sharp warning in verse 9, "but take care . . ." about using "this liberty of yours," indicates that the whole of verse 8 must be quoted or paraphrased statements of the enlightened Corinthians' individual "authority." This also best explains the origin of the variations in the manuscript traditions. Thus in verse 8*b* the reading "We are no better off if we do not eat and we are no worse off if we eat," which fits best with verse 8*a*, should be substituted for the NRSV translation. ("We are no worse off if we do not eat, and no better off if we do.") If the whole of verse 8 is taken as the Corinthians' position, it also fits well with the separation of the spiritual from the worldly realm articulated in the Corinthian principle of *gnōsis,* cited in 6:13 ("Food is meant for the stomach and the stomach for food.").

In verses 7-9, Paul thus couches his warning in the Corinthians' own terms of "authority" and "consciousness," even appealing to their sense of maturity or superiority as enlightened ones. He in effect acknowledges that their own possession of *gnōsis* that "no idol in the world really exists" makes their "consciousness" strong and therefore enables them to exercise their "authority" to eat food offered to idols without fear of defilement. In verse 7, however, he appeals to them to recognize that others in the community are *not* possessed of such *gnōsis,* and that at least hypothetically their "consciousness," still "weak" since they only recently converted from their previous devotion to various false gods, will be "defiled."

To illustrate his point in verse 7, he cites their arguments for their own "liberty/authority" to eat idol-food in verse 8, and then counters with what he sees as the possible effect of their behavior in verses 9-12. They focus on their own "authority"; he focuses on its effects in relations to others, which he portrays as ominous. As elsewhere in the New Testament, *proskomma* in verse 9 means an occasion or cause for falling, not merely an occasion for moral offense, or "stumbling block." In verse 10, finally referring directly to what he sees as the concrete problem—their daring practice of reclining at sacred banquets in temples—Paul raises the likelihood that others in the assembly will see them. His concern about these others is not that they will be morally offended in their "conscience" (NRSV), but that their "consciousness" will be "built up" to the point that they will regard such practices as harmless and will themselves join in temple banquets.

That such a "brother" (NRSV: "believers") could be "destroyed" by dining in a temple because he has only a "weak consciousness" (v. 11), is rooted in the importance of sacrificial meals for constituting the social structure at its various levels. Paul is insisting that the enlightened Corinthians recognize the social bonds celebrated and constituted in rituals such as corporate religious meals. Their brothers and sisters who, in their lack of enlightenment, did take such meals seriously could be placed in extreme conflict and jeopardy. Indeed, later in this section of the letter, Paul declares that the enlightened themselves are in danger of destruction by participating in meals focused on idols (10:14-22). Paul's statement is thus a most serious one, heavy with irony in its juxtaposition of causative prepositional phrases: "For *by your gnōsis* the weak one is destroyed, the brother *for whom Christ* died" (AT). Just as he replaced the Corinthians' heavenly *Sophia* with the crucified Christ—the real *sophia* of God—in 1:24 and just as he literally went out of his way to substitute Christ for *Sophia* as the agent of creation and salvation, so here he pointedly contrasts the potentially destructive effects of their *gnōsis* and the salvific effects of Christ's death. Finally in verse 12 Paul comes to his point, the warning that in the potential harmful effects on their "brothers" of their temple banqueting, they are sinning against Christ. In the parallel participial phrases he uses first his own language of "sinning against brothers" (see NRSV footnote) and then their language of consciousness. The enlightened ones may have thought that their participation in idol banquets would have the effect of "building up" others' consciousness. Paul says the effect is just the opposite, "striking blows against their consciousness" (*vs.* NRSV: "wound[ing] their conscience").

To conclude this step in his argument (v. 3), Paul formulates a principle of behavior keyed to its effects on others, and articulates in the first person (to fit the autobiographical illustration he will offer in chap. 9). He broadens the reference from eating idol-food to eating food generally, partly because he himself would not have been participating in temple banquets and partly to enunciate a more general ethical principle: consideration of other persons rather than individual authority should be the guide for behavior.

Illustration: Paul's Nonuse of Apostolic Rights (9:1-27)

In the structure of the argument of chapters 8–10 as a whole, chapter 9 is an autobiographical illustration of the principle set forth in 8:13, that, for the sake of others, one should not make use of one's liberty/authority. Yet Paul is far more defensive and goes to far greater lengths to justify his rights than would be necessary simply for a personal illustration. His posing of one rhetorical question after another (nineteen in all) indicates a clearly defensive strategy. The heavy concentration of explanatory clauses, particularly in 9:15-25, further intensifies the defensive tone. His explanation in 9:15-18 of why he does not make use of his rights is too emotionally charged to be very functional as an illustration of the principle in 8:13. As he indicates in 9:3, this is as much or more his *defense* written to those who were examining and judging him as it is an illustration from his own practice of how the Corinthians should act with regard to food sacrificed to idols.

◊ ◊ ◊ ◊

Paul's first move is to establish his freedom as an "apostle." In a series of four rhetorical questions he elicits a positive recognition (v. 1). His own commissioning as an apostle had happened in a transcendent revelatory experience (literally, an "apocalypse") of "Jesus our Lord" (thus also 1 Cor 15:8; 2 Cor 12:1-5; Gal 1:13-17). In verse 2 he then addresses an apparent challenge to his apostleship by "others," claiming that the very existence of the Corinthian community is the legally valid attestation, "the seal" of his apostleship. The "others" here may be the same as the "others" mentioned in verse 12 as "sharing in your authority/right" (NRSV: "this rightful claim on you"). In response, he declares in verse 3 that what follows is his "defense *(apologia)* to those who are examining me" (*vs.* "would examine me," in NRSV; cf. 4:3-4, for those sitting in judgment of him).

In the first step of his "defense" in 9:4-12*a* Paul establishes his "right" as an apostle, continuing the device of rhetorical questions that evoke a recognition of those rights. He purposely uses the word *exousia,* the same one the enlightened Corinthians use for their "authority" or "liberty" (8:9). "Right" best renders its sense in the context of this "defense" in chapter 9. "Authority/liberty/right," moreover, is virtually synonymous with "free/freedom" in the enlightened Corinthians' theology (9:1, 19; 10:29). Thus Paul's pointed use of *exousia* in 9:4-6, 18, and particularly his reference to "your *exousia*" in 9:12 provide a substantive link between 8:7-13 and chapter 9. This strengthens the rhetorical link whereby the "apology" in chapter 9 is the illustration of the concluding principle in 8:7-13.

"Food and drink" in 9:4, another link with 8:7-13, refer not to Paul's right to eat any and every food, but to his rights and freedom as an apostle, as indicated in verse 1 and again in verses 5-6. Paul is insisting that he has the same right to economic support from the communities of the movement as do Cephas and other apostles. When they do not have to work for their sustenance, they are free to pursue their respective missions. The second question (v. 5) focuses less on the right to be married than on the right to receive support for "a believing wife" who accompanied the apostle on mission. The mention of Barnabas with himself as the only ones supposedly with "no right to refrain from working for a living" (v. 6) discloses two important related bits of information: that his working for a living and refusal of support was at the root of the accusations to which he is responding, and that his own peculiar practice in this regard goes back (at least) to the time he was working with Barnabas in a mission based in Antioch.

In 9:7-10 Paul offers several particular arguments for why apostles have a right to support from the communities. Continuing the sequence of rhetorical questions in verse 7, he gives analogies from military service and agriculture. By analogy with the latter, apostles have a right to be supported from the products of their particular kind of labor. Divine, scriptural authority, "the Law," confirms this apostolic right (vv. 8-10). Paul engages in a little scribal *halakhah* (making of legal rulings in application to particular issues), in this case on the basis of Deut 25:4: "You shall not muzzle an ox while it is treading out the grain." Paul is probably citing from memory. Scriptural knowledge, like other forms of knowledge, was largely oral in diaspora as well as in Palestinian Jewish culture. In the ancient world such concretely formulated principles functioned as examples to be applied to analogous human relationships, such as Paul indicates with "whoever plows" and "whoever threshes" in verse 10. The rhetorical question, "Is it for oxen that God is concerned?" (along with the following one) simply anticipates the desired conclusion: "It was indeed written for our sake." Only after thus establishing the general application of "not muzzling the ox" to human relations is he ready to narrow the "for our sake" of verse 10 to the apostles, and particularly to himself in 9:11-12*a*.

By his choice of terms in verse 11, Paul may in part be mocking the Corinthian spirituals. *Pneumatika* and *sarkika* ("spiritual" and "material," NRSV) can simply refer to "religious" versus "material" matters (as in Rom 15:27). In 2:14–3:1 Paul used this dichotomy in his heavily sarcastic put-down of the Corinthians' claim that they were spirituals who had transcended even the intermediate status of "infants." Here Paul is apparently including his ministry within the Corinthians' category of spiritual things, and leaving the material support to which he had a right in the category of "fleshly things," which they were denigrating anyhow. The NRSV translation of verse 12 ("this rightful claim on you") hides the key term around which this whole argument revolves: "(your) *exousia*." That "others" share in "your authority/liberty" must be an allusion to Apollos as the one who had introduced the enlightened Corinthians to *gnōsis* and the "authority" it provided them. The rather clear implication is that Apollos had accepted support (his "right" as an apostle) from the Corinthians. Thus since Paul had been the founder of the assembly in Corinth (see 3:10!) and Apollos had only built on the foundation Paul had laid, Paul surely has even more of a claim ("authority/right") on the Corinthians than those "others."

In 9:12*b*-15*a*, suddenly breaking away from his argument by rhetorical questions, Paul comes to the main point of his autobiographical illustration of his principle with regard to eating idol-food. Despite having the "right/authority" *(exousia)* of getting his living from the gospel, Paul did not make use of it. He then explains this in verses 15*b*-18 and 19-23 (-27). The past tense in verse 12, "we did not make use of this right" (AT) probably refers specifically to his practice during his earlier mission in Corinth (*vs.* the generalizing "we have not made use of" in the NRSV). "Endure anything" refers in this context to working for a living while preaching the gospel; to charge for the latter, he believes, would have placed an "obstacle" in its way (picking up on the "stumbling block" of 8:9). Although verses 13-14 present, in effect, a further analogy and authorization for the rights of an apostle, they are part of the new step in the argument. The distinction made in verse 11 between religious and material things is still in mind. The example that those who work in the temple eat temple foods (v. 13) suggests that Paul and other apostles also have a right to specially sacred foods—a pointed implication in the middle of an argument about the "food sacrificed to idols" that is eaten in temples.

In verse 14, returning to the matter of his own rights (of which he makes no use), Paul appeals to what "the Lord commanded." Paul is not citing a saying of Jesus here. Judging by what we know of Jesus' teachings from the synoptic Gospel tradition and noncanonical literature, Paul is referring not to a command but to a proverb ("the laborer deserves his wages/food"). It was applied in various contexts to Jesus' disciples sent out on mission or to traveling prophets and teachers (Matt 10:10; Luke 10:7, *Didache* 13:1-2). Thus Paul apparently knows at least the gist of the tradition of Jesus' sayings regarding the support of those on a mission. He gives little or no indication in his letters of having known the larger tradition of Jesus' sayings, however. Except for the words of institution of the Lord's Supper in 11:23-25, the only places where he refers to, but without actually quoting, traditions of Jesus' sayings are here in 9:14 and earlier in 7:10.

If this teaching of Jesus was known to the Corinthians, then Apollos was the likely transmitter. He could well have justified his own acceptance of support from (some) Corinthians by reciting this Jesus saying (i.e., in a form such as in Luke 10:7). The most persuasive evidence of this is Paul's failure specifically to quote Jesus' words, even though a laborer's "reward" or "wages" (the Greek term in the versions of the saying in both Luke 10:7 and 1 Tim 5:18) is precisely the issue in this context (vv. 17, 18) just as it was the issue also in the parallel discussion of laborers in 3:8, 14. That is, Paul does not actually recite the saying here because Apollos had appealed to it, and because Paul himself was not observing it. Instead, Paul purposely formulates the Lord's command to suit his continuing explanation of why he does not make use of his rights: "[he] commanded those who proclaim the gospel to *live* by the gospel" (AT; the NRSV paraphrase, "get their living by," is too limiting). Again, as after 9:4-12*a*, however, no sooner does Paul solidify his right to support from the gospel than he insists, with the emphatic "I" that begins verse 15, that he has not made use of any such rights. In verse 15*a* the perfect tense verb in, "I have made no use of," suggests a more general practice in his mission, and leads him to the explanation that follows.

In 9:15*b*-18 Paul immediately plays on his formulation of the Lord's command in his explanation of why he does not make use of his rights. He feels strongly about the issue: "Indeed I would rather *die* than that!" (emphasis added). "My ground for boasting," judging from the immediate context, probably refers specifically to not making use of the right to support that was his as an apostle proclaiming the gospel (vv. 12*a*, 15*a*, 16; see also 2 Cor 11:7-10, "this boast of mine"). Declining this right had also been his practice in Thessalonica (1 Thess 2:7-9), and he had probably made a point of his practice, which was different from that of the other apostles during his initial mission in Corinth. This was an integral part of his whole sense of prophetic calling as an apostle, as he now explains in terms that allude both to his prophetic commissioning and to the Corinthians' focus on freedom and authority.

Preaching the gospel is not his ground for boasting (v. 16). He does that because "[a] necessity is laid upon me" (NRSV's "obligation" is too weak). "Necessity" referred to the constraints of ordinary human affairs that the enlightened Corinthians (like the Stoics) believed they had transcended in their "liberty/authority" and "freedom." But Paul refers to his own sense of having been commissioned, like the prophets, to a God-ordained destiny like Isaiah and Jeremiah before him, having been set apart and called when still in his mother's womb (Gal 1:15; Isa 49:1; Jer 1:5). This sense of vocation is confirmed by the ensuing statement, "woe to me," a (biblical) prophetic form of calling woe upon one who is obligated by a covenant or commission.

In verse 17 Paul moves back into the enlightened Corinthians' language of "liberty/authority," and alludes to the Jesus-saying that he had paraphrased in verse 14 legitimating wages/reward for apostles. According to the enlightened viewpoint such as that of Philo, and presumably of Apollos and the Corinthians addressed here (also of Stoic-Cynic philosophers), only the wise person is not compelled by necessity, and is able to act willingly, not unwillingly—in other words, possessing the "liberty/authority" to do all things and live as one pleases (Philo, *Quod Deus* 47-48; *Quod Omnis* 61, and also, especially, 13-14, 21-22, 35-36, 42-43, 51, 57, 59-61). Paul uses precisely these concepts in verse 17, but portrays his own calling as the opposite of such an enlightened person. Only if he preached of his "own [free] will" would he receive wages. But if (in the dichotomous thinking of the Corinthians) he did not preach of his "own will" (which was precisely the case, given the "necessity" laid on him in his calling), then he had been "entrusted with a commission."

The term *commission* (*oikonomia*; literally "household administration") that Paul uses with reference to the necessity laid on him (his prophetic calling as an apostle, v. 16) has a range of possible meanings. Most obvious in this context, where Paul is incorporating and countering concepts of the enlightened Corinthians such as "freedom from necessity," would be the notion that the wise person is charged with the administration or guidance of the universal household. Given Paul's background in the Jerusalem temple-state, Paul probably also knew the term with reference to a high-ranking officer or servant of a ruler. It was also used for the steward of an estate, who was often a high-ranking slave. Although the latter reference is unlikely here, because of the rhetorical context, the historical reality of ancient slavery clearly hovered in the background of discussions of freedom versus necessity. Paul is probably implying that he has been assigned a place in the divine economy, and is no mere house-philosopher of some Corinthian patron. His principal meaning, however, is that he is serving in the cause of divine authority, and precisely *not* willingly. With this he is countering the Corinthians' claim to possess an authority that enabled them to act with complete free will. We might also take note of the analogy set up by this concept: The royal officer or estate steward who has a commission does not get wages from the people he manages, or from the fields and laborers he supervises, but from the ruler or master he serves. Precisely that relationship comes into view at the end of this illustration and defense, 9:24-27, where Paul's extended athletic metaphor has eschatological overtones.

Instead of explaining his alternative source of support, since he did not accept wages, Paul poses the rhetorical question: What then is my "reward/pay"? (v. 18). He provides an utterly paradoxical answer: His "pay" is to make the gospel "free of charge." The latter term suggests the opposite of expensive or extravagant, and the opposite of being supported by a patron. Paul appears to be saying that his "pay" is to make the gospel free of patronage, because he does not wish to use up (or perhaps "use as one likes," or even "abuse") his "right/authority/liberty" in the gospel. His formulation of this last clause purposely replaces "use" (vv. 12*b*, 15) and the "right (liberty)" *of an apostle* (vv. 4-12*a*) with "using up/abuse" and "liberty (right) *in the gospel*" (from which he lives by a necessity and calling [vv. 14, 16]). The sense could be that he not misuse his right in the gospel by using it to make a living or that he not use in any way he likes the liberty in the gospel which, paradoxically, he has by necessity.

In verses 19-23 Paul then picks up directly on this "right/liberty" in further explanation of the freedom he has in the gospel. The paradox from verse 18 continues not in any opaque abstract (non)sense of "freedom is slavery and slavery is freedom," but in reference to certain concrete types of missionary situations. Continuing to engage, but setting his mission diametrically against the enlightened Corinthians' claim of freedom, Paul states: "For though I am free with respect to all [continuously], I have made myself a slave to all [as part of his mission strategy], so that I might win more of them." Although he speaks of himself as a "servant of Christ" in the opening of three letters, only here and once later in the Corinthian correspondence (2 Cor 4:5) does he refer to himself as a slave of the people among whom he works. His "self-enslavement" would thus appear to be specific to this argument against the enlightened Corinthians' "liberty," not a general understanding of Christian life and discipleship.

To illustrate his paradoxical self-enslavement as an expression of his freedom, Paul quickly leaves those images behind in a series of statements about his missionary tactics, repeating the purpose with each one: "so that I might win . . ." (vv. 20-22). The NRSV translation, "for though," at the outset of verse 19 may blunt the paradox, which is that precisely in (because of) his freedom he is able to adapt his own behavior to the particular needs of given missionary situations. He is still holding up his own behavior as a paradigm for how the enlightened Corinthians should act in their newfound "liberty/authority" (8:9-13). In Greek texts the term *ioudaioi* ("Jews," v. 20) is always potentially ambiguous. Thus "Jews" and "those under the law" in verse 20 may be the same group; or if the first term means "Judeans" in particular (as it may at some points in Paul's letters), then "those under the law" could mean other, diaspora Jews. The parenthetical "though I myself am not under the law" is a defensive aside, warding off the impression that his argument is rooted in the sort of parochialism the enlightened Corinthians claim to have transcended. "Those outside the law" (v. 21; literally "the lawless") would be Greeks as distinct from Jews—that is, not people who do "unlawful" things, but people who are not committed to the law of the Jews. A second parenthetical comment ("though I am not free from God's law," v. 21) is less defensive, probably simply a play on words in which Paul can say to those who know that there is "no God but one" that even though he became as a lawless person to the lawless people, he is not therefore lawless with respect to God but "enlawed" with respect to Christ (NRSV: "under Christ's law"). With his statement, "to the weak I became weak," in verse 22 Paul brings the argument back around to those whom the enlightened Corinthians' behavior might destroy, as he had warned in 8:7-11. Moreover, whereas in other cases he had merely become "as [if] a Jew" and so on, to the weak he actually "became weak" (without the "as").

In verses 19-22 Paul is still speaking about "liberty/rights." At the end of verse 22 he claims that the purpose of his nonuse of his apostolic rights is the exact opposite of the potential result of the idol-food eaters' insistence on theirs. They are destroying the weak, while he aims to save people. In the last of the many purpose clauses of this paragraph (v. 23), Paul claims to "do all for the sake of the gospel, so that [he] might become a sharer in it" (AT; the NRSV's "blessings" is not in the Greek). Only indirectly and by implication could this be read as a continuation of the question in verse 18 about what his pay is. Rather, verse 23 (like v. 27) continues the discussion of getting one's living from the gospel (see v. 14). Paul uses the term "sharer" in connection with the process of eschatological fulfillment of history now underway (in his mission; cf. Rom 11:17; Phil 1:7). The eschatological implications of sharing in the gospel then continue in the agonistic metaphor of verses 24-27.

Paul brings his autobiographical model of behavior to completion with an exhortation that goes well beyond the principle (8:13) he is purportedly illustrating. In verses 24-27 he offers an extended athletic metaphor, some aspects of which can be misleading. The exhortation at the end of verse 24 and the example at the beginning of verse 25 articulate his point: Run in such a way that you reach the goal! And that requires self-control! Paul's metaphor is full of allusions to the Corinthian situation, to the enlightened Corinthians, and to additional terms in which they may have been articulating their "liberty/authority." The entire extended metaphor, beginning with "in a race" (more likely "in the stadium"), alludes to the Isthmian and Imperial Games that dominated the highly competitive culture of Roman Corinth. Besides the many athletic and rhetorical contests that composed the Games themselves, the presidency of the Games was the highest honor that any of the high-ranking patrons in the city could attain.

Although the emphasis in verse 24 is not on competition, or that only one receives the prize, Paul is undoubtedly appealing to the Corinthians' competitive concern for attaining high status. It is even possible that he here is giving a different twist to another of the enlightened Corinthians' images of how their *gnōsis* of the one true God makes their consciousness strong and authorizes their liberty to eat meat sacrificed to idols. The Jewish philosopher Philo, who uses so many terms that seem to have been current among the Corinthians, too, writes of how, in contrast to the "slave," who is passively subject to the "blows" of the senses, the person possessed of "knowledge," "strengthened" like a fine "athlete," simply regards sense-perceptible matters with "indifference" (*Leg. All.* 3.201-202). Thus the theological "athlete" does not leave the sacred "contest" without a "wreath," but wins the "prize" of victory, which enables the soul to "know God" clearly (*Nom.* 81-82). Paul, however, has the struggle taking place precisely *in* the sense-perceptible social world that Philo and the enlightened Corinthians believe is transcended in their knowledge of God.

The contrasting terms "perishable" and "imperishable" with which Paul describes the "wreaths" (v. 25) are distinctive to 1 Corinthians (especially 15:42, 50-55), and were probably a way the Corinthians contrasted the immortality and security of their spiritual status with the social-material world. Paul, of course, is referring to the eschatological goal, which he repeatedly asserts in his arguments to the Corinthians, especially in chapter 15. The parallel illustrations in verse 26 illustrate this same concern, that the enlightened Corinthians not "run aimlessly," without a clear sense of the goal, or engage in mere shadowboxing.

The boxing illustration leads Paul to a final comment about punishing and enslaving his own body (v. 27; cf. the reference to "self-control" in v. 25). The final clause repeats the warning about attaining the eschatological goal: "so that after proclaiming to others I myself should not be disqualified," that is, by failing to meet the test (cf. 2 Cor 13:5-7). Insofar as verses 24-27 function as a warning about not keeping their eye on the eschatological goal, it is also a transition to the further warning in 10:1-13 (in which the Israelites did not reach the goal) and to the stern prohibition of idolatry in 10:14-22.

Warning That the Corinthians Are Risking God's Wrath
(10:1-13)

Although Paul carefully structures this step of his argument, he makes abrupt breaks in the repetitive patterns within the structure. Initially Paul agrees with the Corinthians that "our ancestors" received "the same spiritual food . . . drink," and so forth (10:3-4; cf. 8:1-6). Parallel to the structure in 8:1-13, Paul here initially agrees that "all our fathers" (NRSV: ancestors) enjoyed certain salvific contents in 10:1-4 only then to insist that "most" or "some of them" were destroyed in 10:5-11. He begins with what is supposedly common ground with the Corinthians only then to disagree sharply "nevertheless" (v. 5). Within the fivefold pattern ("and all . . . ," 10:1-4) establishing the common ground, moreover, he adds a structurally awkward explanatory clause in 10:4*b* that is interrupted by the interjection "and the rock was Christ." Again in 10:6-10, as in 10:1-4, Paul structures his argument into five statements (the repeated exhortations "[and] we must not/do not . . . , as some of them did"), followed by a blunt warning and a reassurance about God's wrath. First Corinthians 10:1-13 is not a "midrash" in form: its point of departure is not a scriptural text, it is not set in the context of the scriptural text, and it is not presented for the sake of the scriptural text. Nor is there any reason to view this passage as an independently composed piece of scriptural interpretation that Paul merely inserted at this point. While skillfully composed, 10:1-13 is integrally connected with the whole argument of chapters 8–10 and is directed specifically to the Corinthians who were devoted to and possessed of *gnōsis.*

◊ ◊ ◊ ◊

"I do not want you to be ignorant" (NRSV: unaware; v. 1) is ironic, because Paul is about to correct the Corinthian spirituals on some point about which they claim full knowledge! It is clear from the context that "our fathers" (the NRSV has the inclusive "ancestors") includes the Corinthians. Paul thinks of the Gentiles who had joined the assemblies as a "wild olive shoot" grafted into Israel (Rom 11:17), not by having been circumcised (Gal 3–4!), but by having been brought into the history of Israel, which is now being fulfilled in the delivery of the Abrahamic promise to all peoples. Paul saw a fundamental continuity between "us, on whom the ends of the ages have come" (v. 11) and the historical Israelites. The Corinthians also identified with the Israelites, but understood them as spiritual ancestors in relation to key symbols of transcendent salvation.

First Corinthians 10:1-3 is full of allusions to incidents from stories of Israel's Exodus and wilderness experiences, yet only once, and briefly, does Paul actually cite Scripture (Exod 32:6b in v. 7). Paul, Apollos, and the Corinthians were living in an essentially oral culture, so seldom would anyone actually have been quoting from an actual text. Over the generations, multiple modes of telling the centrally important stories of God's deliverance of the people from Egyptian bondage and guidance in the wilderness had developed. Two standard modes of reciting those foundational events are pertinent to 10:1-13 (-22). In one, attention focuses on a few key wilderness incidents or symbols of deliverance, such as "a cloud for a covering, . . . food from heaven," and "the rock [from which] water gushed out" (Ps 105:37-41), or "bread from heaven, . . . a well of water following them, . . . and a pillar of cloud" (the *Biblical Antiquities* of Pseudo-Philo 10:7 [first century CE]). Another standard recitation also mentioned those key incidents of deliverance, but juxtaposed them with Israel's idolatry, apostasy, and "fall" in the wilderness (such incidents as the golden calf, apostasy to Baal Peor), to serve either as a confession of sin or as an exhortation urging renewed commitment to God (cf. Pss 78, 106; Neh 9; and the "Song of Moses," Deut 32). Paul stands in the latter tradition in 1 Cor 10:1-13 (-22).

Paul's sudden shift of tone in verse 5, however, suggests that in 10:1-4 he is echoing language of the Corinthian spirituals. It seems likely that their emphasis on the exclusively positive soteriological symbols of cloud, rock, and spiritual food and drink drew on the other standard summary of wilderness symbols. The Corinthians, moreover, presuppose a highly significant further development of that summary of wilderness stories. In the hellenistic-Jewish religiosity represented by Wis 10–19 and Philo, those key symbols of deliverance from the Exodus and wilderness stories had been spiritualized. Both the protective "cloud" and the "rock" that provided water had become symbols of divine *Sophia* (Wis 10:17-18; 19:7), with the manna and water as symbols of the spiritual food and drink that God or *Sophia* provided for souls hungering and thirsting for immortality and imperishability. Strikingly similar to the symbolism Paul cites in 10:1-2, in Wis 10:17-18 (cf. 19:7) *Sophia* both covers the holy ones and brings them through the sea. Similar to the symbols in 10:3-4 are the spiritualized water from the rock and the heavenly bread or food of angels in Wis 11:4; 16:20-22. Even more suggestive for our understanding of the Corinthians' spirituality, Philo frequently dwells on the "rock," the "divine spring" and the "heavenly food" as three of the most prominent images for *Sophia/Logos* nourishing the "wise" and "mature" with imperishable "wisdom" and salvific "knowledge" (see esp. *Leg. All.* 2.86; *Det.* 115-17; *Fuga* 19, 137-39, 177-202; *Heres* 79, 191; *Somn.* 1:47-51, 198-200; 2.221-22, 249; *Quaes. Gen.* 4.8). Although Philo does not recite these key soteriological symbols in sequence in the same way as Wisdom of Solomon, it is clear from how he interweaves the various terms that they belonged together as a standard set of soteriological symbols in the tradition that Apollos must have introduced into the Corinthian community.

The notions of spiritual people and spiritual things are distinctively Corinthian (see on 2:6–3:4; 12:1; 14:37; 15:44-49). Thus the "spiritual food" and "spiritual drink" and the parallel references to being "under the cloud" and "[passing] through the sea" in 10:1-4 must all be symbols of the saving *sophia* or *gnōsis* acquired by the enlightened Corinthians from their meditation on Exodus and wilderness symbols, spiritually understood. The benefits gained by being under the cloud, passing through the sea, and banqueting on spiritual food were the security and indelibility of transcendent salvation. Considering that Paul downplays baptism in 1:14-17 and is incredulous at certain Corinthians' "baptism for the dead" in 15:29, it is almost certain that the ancestors' baptism in the cloud and in the sea (10:1-2) was also a Corinthian symbol of immortality afforded by *Sophia*. Paul himself may have inserted "into Moses" (v. 2) on the analogy of "into Christ" as a rhetorical dig (cf. "in the name of Paul," 1:13). That "the rock was Christ" (and not *Sophia;*

v. 4) is Paul's third attempt in this letter to replace the Corinthians' *"Sophia"* with his own "Christ" as the agent of salvation (see 1:24 and 8:6). It is doubtful that Paul was alluding to God as the rock of Israel's salvation from the Song of Moses (Deut 32:4, 15, 18, 30-31). In the context here the reference is clearly and explicitly to the rock from which Israel drew water in the desert (cf. Num 20:7-11; Ps 105:41; Wis 11:7), which Philo understood as *Sophia*. In any case, and however important for Paul himself, in the flow of his argument "the rock was Christ" is an aside, a parenthetical comment, and not a major doctrinal statement.

Paul's dramatic counter to the spiritual Corinthians' focus on key symbols of *Sophia*, the source of their enlightenment and security, is abrupt and blunt, and it shifts the focus from the "ancestors" to God: "Nevertheless, God was not pleased with most of them, and [literally: for] they were struck down in the wilderness" (v. 5). In his historical understanding of the Exodus and wilderness stories, Paul has in mind the failure of most of the Israelites to reach the promised land, despite all of God's miraculous saving efforts. As in 9:24-27; 10:11, and elsewhere in the letter, Paul's eschatological orientation is never far from the surface of his rhetoric.

Paul develops this warning in 10:6-11 with five successive exhortations of "we must not/do not . . . as some of them did"). He frames the exhortation in 10:6, 11 with parallel statements that what happened to the ancient Israelites "occurred as *typoi* of us." The term *typos* almost certainly did not yet have a standard meaning in Greco-Roman rhetoric. The English terms "model," "paradigm," or "example" (NRSV) would render this sense both here and in Rom 5:14, where Adam is presented as a *typos* of Christ. Paul's intention here, obviously, is to indicate what the Corinthians should not do by reciting as negative paradigms what happened to "some of them (their 'ancestors')" in the Exodus-wilderness stories.

While Paul stands in a long Israelite-Jewish tradition of exhortation based on such incidents of faithlessness by the people in the wilderness, he selects the examples of what happened to "some of them" precisely to address certain aspects of what bothered him about the Corinthians' views and practices. The general warning not to "desire evil" alludes to the Israelites' craving for meat as they remembered the fleshpots of Egypt (cf. Num 11:4, 34). The tone is surely ironic. We may presume that the Corinthian spirituals would also have understood "desire" (for meat) as the counterpart of their transcendent spiritual life in the material-social realm (as suggested by their principles cited by Paul in 6:13). That Paul actually cites Scripture only in connection with idolatry in verse 7 indicates that this is his major concern, and the call in verse 14 to "flee from the worship of idols" confirms this. The incident that Paul recites, that of the golden calf (Exod 32:6), in which the people were sacrificing to and banqueting in the presence of the idol, was the classic example of Israel's idolatry. "Sexual immorality" (v. 8), which was Paul's principal concern in chapters 5, 6, 7, was regularly tied to idolatry. The "twenty-three thousand" would be those who coupled with the daughters of Moab (Num 25:1-9), although Paul has somehow reduced the number of those who fell by a thousand. Putting "the Lord to the test" in 10:9 (v. 9; NRSV footnote) is what Paul thinks the enlightened Corinthians are doing when they eat food sacrificed to idols, which is the overall topic of argument in chapters 8–10. This was precisely what the one tradition of exhortation portrayed the Israelites as having done when they clamored for food and drink in the wilderness, and for doing this were destroyed by serpents (Exod 16:2-3; 17:1-7; Num 21:4-9; especially Ps 78:18). The main NRSV translation represents a text in which "Christ" has been substituted for "the Lord" on the basis of the reference to Christ in verse 4. When Paul asks for no complaining (v. 10), he may be thinking of Corinthian complaints about himself. "Grumbling" is a frequent motif in the wilderness narratives (Exod 16:7; 17:3; Num 11:1; 14:27, 29; 16:41; 17:5). It is unclear who "the destroyer" is (the expression occurs only here in biblical Greek; but cf. Exod 12:23; Wis 18:25), whether some avenging angel or Satan. After the rebellion of Korah (Num 16:49; cf. the "craving" incident in Num 11:33), the destruction came by plague.

In verse 11, where he again refers to Israel's experiences as exemplary for "us," Paul also articulates a particular understanding of the purpose of Scripture. Scripture tells of events that happened to the ancient Israelites. Yet since those events had a paradigmatic purpose, they were "written down (i.e., became "Scripture") to instruct us." The comment that "the ends of the ages have come" indicates clearly that Paul understood both Scripture and the events it narrated eschatologically, directed to the fulfillment of God's ultimate purpose that was now being realized in the Christ events and in his own mission among Corinthians and others. That he and the addressees are living at the crucial turn of the ages makes all the more poignant the warning to which he has been leading: "So if you think you are standing, watch out that you do not fall" (v. 12), which is similar to the warning in 9:24-27. The Corinthians who are so confident of their spiritual salvation must practice self-discipline in order to reach the kingdom of God or they will end up like the Israelites who failed to reach the promised land because, presuming on their salvation, they practiced idolatry and provoked God's wrath.

The reassurance in verse 13 appears to interrupt the flow of the argument from 10:1-13 to 10:14-22; we would expect the command to flee idolatry in verse 14 to follow directly upon the warning in verse 12. That Paul is prompted to insert this mitigating reassurance of God's faithfulness shows that he himself is sensitive to the severity of his criticism of the enlightened Corinthians. Yet even in reassuring them that God will not let them be tested beyond their strength to persevere, he is not relieving them of responsibility. He is interpreting their eating of idol-food as a test out of which they must quickly find their way.

Prohibition of Eating with Idols/Demons (10:14-22)

With a blunt warning about the consequences of banqueting in temples (v. 21), Paul completes the argument begun in chapter 8. He had set up this conclusion to his argument on the Corinthians' *gnōsis* in 8:5 and his reference by his words of caution about an enlightened one banqueting at a temple in 8:10. Now he explicitly counters the enlightened Corinthians' belief that idols (gods) have no reality by pointing out the real *communal relations* that are involved when one dines in their temples, and counters their claims about individual *authority* with a call for group *solidarity* in the new community centered on Christ.

◊ ◊ ◊ ◊

In 10:14 Paul finally makes clear that idolatry and idolaters (yet another theme distinctive to 1 Corinthians: see 5:10-11; 6:9; 10:7, 14) focus specifically on the enlightened Corinthians' eating of food sacrificed to idols (banqueting at temples; 8:1, 4, 7, 10; 10:19). He views this as idolatry, which for an ancient Jew meant compromising one's exclusive loyalty to God. After sharply admonishing the Corinthians to *"flee from idolatry"* (v. 14 AT), he appeals to them as "sensible people" who claim to have wisdom (v. 15). In preparing for the prohibition of banqueting in temples (v. 21), he focuses on the communal sharing expressed in the Lord's Supper (vv. 16-17). The crux of his argument is "sharing" *(koinōnia)* in the sense of communal participation and solidarity. According to the tradition cited in 11:25, the "sharing in the blood of Christ" made possible by "the cup of blessing" means solidarity in the new covenant God made with the people in Christ's death, which is renewed in every "sharing" of the cup at celebrations of the Lord's Supper. The "sharing in the body of Christ" made possible by "the bread that we break" means both identifying with Christ's crucifixion and experiencing solidarity with the community that Paul elsewhere calls "the body of Christ" (see especially 12:27).

Paul's interpretation of the bread in the sense of communal sharing (v. 17; chap. 12) is unique in the New Testament (cf. *Did.* 9). In what is clearly the main point of his argument, he combines "the body of Christ," represented by the bread, with "body," as a standard political symbol of how a people of a city-state, though many, are united. This creative combination has a political-communal thrust. The community members had become one "body" initially through their baptism in the Spirit (cf. 12:13). Their "sharing in the body of Christ" is the expression of their continuing solidarity with one another and with Christ. Comparison with a somewhat similar understanding of the bread in *Did.* 9 is also instructive. There the (eschatological?) gathering together of the people is likened to the grain *being gathered together* to make the bread, whereas Paul emphasizes the *active* participation of the people who "partake."

The phrase "Israel according to the flesh" (v. 18; NRSV footnote), which occurs only here in the New Testament, and was perhaps evoked by the enlightened Corinthians' "spiritual" reading of the Scriptures (cf. vv. 1-4), refers to the historical Israel (as does "Israel of God" in Gal 6:16). Specifically, Paul is referring to the Israelites' eating their tithes of grain and wine and oil "in the presence of the LORD your God" (Deut 14:22-27), a historical example of the "fathers" (NRSV: "people") having been "sharers (NRSV: "partners") in the altar," that is, with God (for whom "the altar" was a standard circumlocution). What seems to us an abrupt shift of topic in verse 19 (back to 8:1, 4) merely indicates that the argument all along has been "food sacrificed to idols" and the enlightened Corinthians' *gnōsis* in which their eating was grounded. The context here, which is about eating a meal with a god, confirms that Paul's concern throughout chapters 8–10 is banqueting in temples (not food that is sold in the public market).

In verses 19-20 Paul states the conclusion toward which his argument has been moving. Drawing an analogy, especially, with the historical Israel, where, by sacrificing to God the people became sharers with God, Paul claims that those who "sacrifice to demons and not to God" become "sharers with demons." The phrase "sacrifice to demons" (v. 20) comes from Deut 32:17, a text from which developed the Jewish apocalyptic view of other "gods" or "idols" as demonic powers opposed to the purposes of God. This was a tradition in which Paul was firmly rooted, and contrasts with the enlightened Corinthians' view that idols were nothing (8:4). The Song of Moses (Deut 32), from which Paul takes this key phrase, portrays Israel in the desert having rejected its "Rock" for alien gods, precisely the behavior that the Corinthians have been warned about in verses 1-13.

Paul is finally ready to pronounce his prohibition in 10:21. He formulates it in terms of a diametric opposition and mutual exclusivity of solidarity with the Lord and solidarity with demons. It is not a matter of permission ("cannot"), but of ability or possibility (power): It is not possible to partake in the table of the Lord *and* in the table of demons. The addition of two rhetorical questions (v. 22) are reminders about the historical examples given in verses 1-13, and serve as a warning. Watch out lest you provoke the Lord and end up being struck down like some of "our ancestors" in the wilderness! The first rhetorical question alludes once more to the Song of Moses: "They made me jealous with what is no god, provoked me with their idols" (Deut 32:21). The second rhetorical question also makes a not-so-subtle criticism of the enlightened Corinthians who thought of themselves as "strong" in their spiritual status (1:25-27; 4:10), nourished by the spiritual food and drink they derived from spiritually understood Scripture (cf. 10:1-4). The first rhetorical question alludes pointedly again to the Song of Moses: "They made me jealous with what is no god, provoked me with their idols" (Deut 32:21).

Recapitulation of the Argument, with Exceptions (10:23–11:1)

Paul begins and ends this final step of the argument about "food sacrificed to idols" by restating his main point that one must show consideration for the other, as he himself has tried to do (10:23-24, 31–11:1). In between he concedes to the enlightened Corinthians' ethical "liberty" on two matters that he views as relatively unimportant (10:25-27), although he qualifies the second (10:28-29*a*). The rhetorical questions in 10:29*b*-30 are an anticipation of possible objections, not an explanation of the preceding qualification in 10:28-29*a*. While summarizing the whole argument of chapters 8–10, the section 10:31–11:1 also focuses attention on Paul's own practice as laid out in chapter 9.

◊ ◊ ◊ ◊

Paul's counters to the Corinthian slogan that he cites in 10:23 (the same as in 6:12) recapitulate his sharp critique of individual freedom of action, and do not simply qualify it. His demand in 10:24 to "not seek your own advantage, but that of the other" is more than a qualification of their principle. Paul is no champion of the liberty of consciousness in 1 Corinthians (see 8:7 for "consciousness"). He insists that they proceed on the principle of the common good and edification of the community, rather than on the principle of absolute liberty generated by their *gnōsis*.

In a striking shift from his adamant prohibition of "eating food sacrificed to idols" in the temples of "demons" (10:14-22), he next concedes to the individual ethical "liberty/authority" of the enlightened Corinthians in two hypothetical cases (10:25-27) that he considers matters of relative unimportance. He allows them to "eat whatever is sold in the meat market" (where few people in antiquity could afford to make purchases anyway), "without raising any question on the ground of consciousness" (10:25; NRSV: "conscience"). The latter phrase has a double meaning. To people who believed that their "consciousness," strengthened by their possession of *gnōsis* and close relationship with *Sophia,* gave them freedom to act as they wished, Paul is saying that consciousness is irrelevant in this matter. Paul's more straightforward meaning can be discerned from comparison with later rabbinic reasoning that it was not the food in itself but the intention of the eater that was decisive (Tomson 1990, 208-16). Paul is saying not to worry about your own or another's intention in the case of marketplace food. His citation of Ps 24:1 [LXX 23:1] in 10:26 may well be another allusion to principles of the Corinthians. In their enlightened reasoning they could well have made deductions from such scriptural statements as this to prove that any and all food was permitted since God was its creator. The appeal to Ps 24:1, of course, may be Paul's own. In either case, behind the appeal may be a Jewish use of this verse to support the practice of saying blessing over every meal.

The second illustration (10:27), accepting a dinner invitation from an unbeliever, concedes the same freedom with regard to eating. The qualification (10:28-29a) attached to the second illustration applies, in effect, to both illustrations or any similar situation of eating. The hypothetical informant ("someone") in 10:28 is apparently an unbeliever/outsider because the term "offered in sacrifice" is the standard hellenistic word for ritual sacrifices, not the polemized "food sacrificed to idols" (see 8:1). Paul urges concern for this "someone," just as he had urged regard for the "brother" or "other" in 8:10-13; 10:24. His reference again to "consciousness" (10:28b; NRSV: "conscience") and especially his apparent afterthought, "I mean the other's consciousness, not your own" (v. 29a), aimed at the Corinthians' obsession with their own individual *gnōsis* and consciousness.

Verses 29b-30 is not an explanation of 10:28-29a. Rhetorical questions can be used either in deliberative rhetoric to recapitulate an argument or to anticipate opposing arguments. The rhetorical questions in 10:29b-30 can be understood as doing both. In his recapitulation of the Corinthians' *gnōsis* and his counterargument, Paul anticipates their objections to his principle of consideration for the other person who directly opposes their principle of freedom grounded in strong consciousness. This sets up the concluding statement of his principle (10:31–11:1), which summarizes the overall argument in chapters 8–10, focusing again on his own practice (alluding especially to 9:20-22). Finally, he grounds his own practice in the example of Christ, whose concern for others led him to the cross (cf. 1:17-25; 2:8-9).

◊ ◊ ◊ ◊

The theology and the ethics of the Corinthian spirituals become more discernible through Paul's argument in chapters 8–10, particularly through his quotation of their principles. As is already evident in 1:18–2:8, they focused on personal transcendence of worldly affairs through possession of heavenly *Sophia* and the benefits she conferred. Paul's citation of their slogans in 8:1-6 reveals that the fundamental content of their individual salvation was *gnōsis* of the true essence of things. Such *gnōsis*, particularly theological knowledge, rooted in the rich tradition of hellenistic-Jewish wisdom, evidently mediated to Corinth by the eloquent Alexandrian Jew Apollos, was stated in simple statements of being or nonbeing, such as "there is no God but one" and "no idol in the world really exists" (8:4). By deploying the metaphysical doctrine of the principal causes of existence, they maintained the transcendence of God as the ultimate source and final cause of what exists ("from whom" and "for whom," 8:6), while giving *Sophia* the central mediating role as the instrument of both creation and individual salvation ("through whom," 8:6). These Corinthians stand near the beginning of a long tradition of philosophical theology that runs through Clement of Alexandria (c. 150-215) and Origen (c. 185-254) to modern theologians such as Paul Tillich, in which God or the divine is conceived in terms of being itself and other realities are understood in terms of essences or definitions.

The Corinthians addressed in chapters 8–10 did not withdraw from the world, unlike the Therapeutics near Alexandria. Rather, they understood the ordinary social "world" as a neutral or indifferent sphere in which those who possessed *gnōsis* had absolute ethical "authority" or "liberty." By virtue of their individual consciousness having become strengthened by *Sophia*, they were enlightened about reality and possessed absolute authority to act in the world out of that knowledge. All things were possible for them. Since the other so-called gods did not really exist, there was no reason to stay away from banquets that ostensibly honored them. To the Corinthians, traditional prohibitions such as Jewish food laws would have been merely ethnic taboos, unnecessary for people with a strong consciousness to observe. Their views about individual freedom were similar to those of modern enlightenment liberalism. In both cases ethical liberty involves an almost absolute individualism and an abstract understanding of freedom, the point of which is precisely to transcend the contingencies of concrete social life or "necessity." Thus the effects of one's free actions on other people or on society as a whole receive little attention.

Paul was responding to such a view from a radically different orientation. He focused not on individual enlightenment and liberty but on the countersociety he was helping to build in his assemblies, which was struggling to reach the goal of the kingdom of God. His God was the ultimate agent of that historical project. Theology was not a matter of existence and nonexistence, but of God's engagement with human relations, attachments, and strivings. While the enlightened Corinthians (like modern liberal theologians) knew that idolatry was merely foolish superstition of the unenlightened, Paul (like many other ancient Jews) took idolatry seriously. Many gods and many lords played important roles in human affairs. For Paul, sacrifice involved a real interaction between human and divine. The people participating in the feast of a god were sharing in a fellowship focused on that god. His God was a jealous Lord who demanded exclusive loyalty, as in the passage from the Song of Moses that he cites in 10:22. Such loyalty required individual and group discipline that avoided idolatry. Modern functional analysis has shown how the many sacrificial feasts at various social levels held the whole complex network of kinship, tribe, city, and imperial society together in a ritual constitution of power relations. Paul, of course, did not have the tools for such analysis, but he took seriously the networks of religiously cemented political-economic relations that were established and perpetuated by the feasts where "food [was] offered to idols." Like other Jewish leaders, he resorted to repeating the prohibition of idolatry as a way of maintaining the solidarity of his communities as an alternative society over against "the world," which was permeated with idolatry. In this respect Paul stands in Israel's biblical tradition, which continues both in rabbinic Jewish literature (e.g., the tractate, *Abodah Zarah*, ["idolatry"] in the Mishnah) and in Christian communities, where the prohibition of idol-food was common (e.g., Acts 15:20; Rev 2:14, 20; *Did.* 6:3 and throughout the East and West at the end of the second century).

For Paul the sharing of food offered to idols was not an issue of "ethics," but of the integrity and survival of his assemblies as an alternative society. In 8:1-13 Paul clearly criticized the enlightened Corinthians' ethics of individual liberty. But that was only the first main step in a complex argument, in which Paul placed the effects of their behavior on other members of the assembly in the broad context of God's "political" action in the world and the struggle of the new movement to maintain discipline and attain its goal (10:1-22). Paul's concerns in chapters 8–10, as elsewhere in the letter, cannot be reduced to separate discussions of theology and ethics. His principal concern was for the integrity and solidarity of the alternative society he was attempting to build up over against the networks of power relations by which the imperial society was constituted.

Recognition of Paul's broader political concern expressed in 10:1-22 may help illuminate why he launched such an intense defense of his own peculiar behavior as an apostle (9:1-27) simply to illustrate the principle articulated in 8:13. As he moved from the ethics of the effect of the enlightened ones' behavior on others (8:1-13) to insistence on political solidarity over against the dominant society (10:14-22), he engaged in an extended discussion of the economics involved in building up the movement as an alternative society.

Prior to his calling, Paul had apparently been supported economically in the tributary system of the Jerusalem temple-state. If we take seriously his comment that he had been a Pharisee (Phil 3:5), then as a scribal retainer he would presumably have received economic support from the high priestly rulers out of the revenues (tithes, offerings, dues) they received from the Judean and other villagers. By contrast with the tributary system that redistributed the products of the peasantry upward to their rulers, the early Jesus movement(s) adapted the economic reciprocity of village communities rooted in the traditional egalitarian ideal of maintaining the subsistence of all members of the community (Acts 2:44; 4:32-37). Just as villagers shared their own meager resources with their destitute neighbors, so the early communities of the Jesus movement(s) provided for the economic subsistence of the apostles and prophets who moved from place to place building and consolidating the movement, as indicated in the mission discourses in the synoptic Gospels (Mark 6:8-10; Luke 10:2-9). First Corinthians 9:4-11 offers further rationalization of this means of supporting apostolic labor by drawing on agrarian lore that was traditional in Israel and among other ancient peoples.

Paul's refusal to accept support from the communities in which he worked dated from well before his Corinthian mission, indeed from at least the time of his collaboration with Barnabas in "the regions of Syria and Cilicia" (9:6; Gal 1:21). Perhaps his peculiar practice was rooted in his peculiar background as an apostle. Because Peter, James (the brother of the Lord), and most of the other original apostles came from the peasantry, they were used to sharing in the poverty of village life, the subsistence living from which all were somehow supported. Paul, however, as a former retainer who had lived from revenues taken from poverty-stricken peasants, may have been sensitive about continuing to live off of the poor once he identified with them in the Jesus movement(s). Paying his own way by working with his own hands, considered demeaning by the dominant culture, was yet another way he could identify with the humiliation of the crucified Christ, who was now his Lord and commissioner (cf. 1 Cor 4:12).

In his "defense" in chapter 9 Paul is using his own refusal of support to oppose yet another economic system that he found highly problematic. He responds specifically to the charge of not having accepted economic support from certain Corinthians. Those who were examining or judging him on this matter may well have been those who were still operating according to the values of the patronage system that was in place in most provincial cities during the early empire. Perhaps one (or more) of the Corinthians who had sufficient means was eager to enhance his own prestige and honor by serving as Paul's patrons. Apollos had apparently accepted such patronage. According to the protocol of the patronage system, Paul's refusal would have been an offensive repudiation of their friendship, and his working with his hands would have been a further threat to their pride, as potential patrons (Furnish 1984, 507-8; Marshall 1987, 244-51). His personal concern was to avoid becoming a "house apostle" to some Corinthian patron. His broader concern was to avoid having the alternative society he was building in the assemblies, in Corinth and elsewhere, simply replicate the controlling and exploitative political-economic power relations that structured the imperial society, from the emperor down to freedpeople and slaves (cf. Judge 1984, 11-13).

This was likely a driving motive in the intensity of his defense in chapter 9. The enlightened ones who were participating in such feasts were probably eager to cultivate or maintain connections in the larger society. For ancient Greeks and Romans, participation in feasts of sacrificed food was one of the principal ways that political-economic power relations were constituted. It would have been extremely difficult for anyone in ancient Corinth, particularly anyone dependent on a kinship or patronage network constituted in sacrificial feasts, to cut off and be cut off from such a network. But that is precisely what Paul was insisting upon in 1 Cor 10:14-22, although he mitigates his demand somewhat by allowing acceptance of dinner invitations to private houses where idol-food may be served (10:27). Paul was by no means suggesting curtailment of all contact with the "immoral" of the world (5:9-10). Yet he was expecting the members of his assemblies to discontinue participation in the associations and celebrations by which the networks of "this world [that] is passing away" were constituted, whether the official courts of law or feasts where idol-food was eaten.

It is important to note, however, that Paul had not developed any vision of an alternative political economy for his alternative society in the making. This is evident from his use of imagery drawn from household administration ("commission," 9:17), which implied a picture of God as the divine estate-owner and Paul himself as the steward. Such imagery goes together with other controlling metaphors in this letter, such as God as a monarch, Christ as the alternative emperor (see on chap. 15), and Paul as the Lord's servant (Gk. "slave"). These prominent images suggest that his rejection of the patronage system in favor of an egalitarian ideal of reciprocity was made possible by, yet remained within, an overall controlling vision of the "monarchy" of God. In this he was firmly rooted in the biblical tradition.

Both Paul and the Corinthian spirituals based their views on the Jewish Scripture, but they understood Scripture in very different ways. Like the Therapeutics near Alexandria, the enlightened Corinthians seem to have gained their *sophia* from Scripture spiritually interpreted—"by taking it allegorically, since they think that the words of the literal text are symbols of something whose hidden nature is revealed by studying the underlying meaning" (Philo, *Vita Cont.* 28; cf. 78). As noted in the exegesis above, this kind of spiritual interpretation understood key figures and incidents of the Exodus-wilderness stories as symbols of divine *Sophia* and the salvation she provided to souls hungering and thirsting after immortality. Insofar as Wis 10 and Philo afford helpful comparisons, Apollos and the Corinthian spirituals understood the Scriptures not as an account of *Sophia*'s activity in Israel's history, but as a series of stories and symbols of the ways in which *Sophia* provided salvation for her devotees. Secure in the immortality attained through partaking of the "spiritual food" and "spiritual drink" supplied by *Sophia*, who was the "spiritual rock," the enlightened Corinthians possessed the "liberty/authority" to do "all things" in the mundane world without fear.

By contrast, Paul understood the Scripture as narratives of events in the history of the ancient Israelites. In 10:6-11 he focused on the events of Israel's struggle to remain faithful to the God who had both delivered the people and demanded the community's disciplined and exclusive loyalty to the purpose of its deliverance. For Paul those events also had a paradigmatic purpose and had therefore been "written down [i.e., as "Scripture"] to instruct us." The key to Paul's understanding of the events narrated in Scripture is his belief that the purpose of the plan that God was implementing in the history of Israel was finally revealed in the Christ events and now known to those "on whom the ends of the ages have come" (10:11). In this respect Paul stood in the same apocalyptic tradition as those other dissident Judean scribes who wrote the Dead Sea Scrolls and who believed that the Scriptures were written to illuminate events of their own community and its historical experiences and context. Paul's application of the scriptural narratives as paradigmatic for his own time was also rooted in that Jewish apocalyptic tradition.

Quite apart from Paul's own intention in his argument against participation in feasts on "food sacrificed to idols," his use of certain formulations deriving from the Corinthian spirituals' resulted in christological concepts that took on a life of their own in subsequent generations. The statements in 8:6 and 10:4 are often taken as expressions of a "wisdom Christology." Because such a *Sophia*-Christ is unique to the Corinthian correspondence (cf. 2 Cor 4:4) and not easily reconcilable with Paul's primary emphasis on the death, resurrection, and *parousia* of Christ, this wisdom Christology has been attributed to the Corinthians. Yet a close examination of Paul's arguments suggests that it was Paul himself who, in effect, identified Christ with *Sophia* as part of his rhetorical strategy. In his attempt to displace *Sophia* as the focus of Corinthians' spirituality, he argued that the true *sophia of God* was the crucified Christ in 1:24, 30. Similarly he placed the crucifixion of the "Lord of glory" at the center of "the wisdom of God in a mystery" (NRSV:

"God's wisdom, secret and hidden") in 2:7-8. Confronting the most basic of the Corinthians' affirmations regarding *Sophia* he took an even bolder step, replacing *Sophia* with Christ. As a result, however, predications that originally applied to *Sophia* now applied to Christ, who thus became the preexistent divine mediator of creation and salvation and the "spiritual rock" from which the "fathers" drank in the wilderness. These predications were far more operative in the worldview of the Corinthians and other people in hellenistic-Roman cities than the preaching of a crucified and exalted eschatological Lord. Later hellenistic Christians simply assimilated Christ into the figure of *Sophia,* only now on the authority of the apostle Paul. The result can be seen in the Christ-*Sophia* hymn in Col 1:15-20.

First Corinthians 10:1-4 has been the focus of a great deal of subsequent Christian theological reflection, particularly about Christ, the sacraments, and scriptural interpretation. In this connection, it is important to note what Paul himself does not say here. His simple substitution of Christ for *Sophia* as the "spiritual rock" (v. 4) does not suggest that Christ was the agent of Israel's history of salvation. Nor was Paul suggesting that there was something sacramental about the baptism "into Moses in the cloud and in the sea" or the spiritual food and spiritual drink. Neither baptism nor the Lord's Supper had yet become sacraments in the later Christian sense. As noted above, baptism "into Moses" was probably simply Paul's rhetorical twist. He was not insinuating that the spiritual food and drink were prefigurations of the Lord's Supper. The Corinthian spirituals surely must have found great value in the *Sophia*-banquet of spiritual food and drink through which they became immortal and secure in their transcendence of worldly troubles and corruptibility. However, nothing in 1 Corinthians suggests that the spiritual people celebrated an actual meal as the symbol of their spiritual banquet. The concept of spiritual food and drink, nonetheless, may well be symptomatic of the prevailing cultural ethos in which the elements of the Eucharist or Lord's Supper later became more "the medicine of immortality" (Ign. *Eph.* 20:2) than the community's proclamation of "the Lord's death until he comes" (11:26).

ARGUMENT CONCERNING HAIRSTYLES (11:2-16)

The discussion in 11:3-16 fits so poorly into the context that recently some have judged it a later interpolation into Paul's letter (e.g., Walker 1989; Trompf 1980). Without this paragraph the letter flows smoothly from 8:1–11:2 on to 11:17-34. The discussion of food sacrificed to idols comes to its climax in the mutually exclusive opposition between banqueting in pagan temples and sharing in the Lord's Supper. After a brief comment on market food and private invitations to dinner in 10:23–11:1, Paul then moves to a discussion of the Lord's Supper itself in 11:17-34. To set up his sharply corrective comments on conduct of the Lord's Supper he first commends the Corinthians in 11:2 for maintenance of the traditions he handed on to them, then in 11:17 he introduces their behavior at the Lord's Supper as an exception. What Paul recites in 11:23-25 (cf. 15:3-5) and discusses in 11:17-34 is precisely such a tradition mentioned in 11:2, whereas the custom or practice discussed in 11:3-16 is not. Also, the term "to begin with" in 11:18 suggests that what follows in 11:18-34 is the first instance he has in mind among the "traditions" in 11:2. The discussion of hairstyle in 11:3-16 interrupts the otherwise easy movement from 11:2 to 11:17, displacing the division at the Lord's Supper in 11:18-34 as the first exception to their faithfully maintaining the traditions. This makes nonsense of the "first/to begin with" in 11:18. At the end of 11:3-16, moreover, no transition is made into (as it were) yet another matter that he must correct. There is simply the abrupt switch from "we" in 11:16 to the more personally direct "I" in 11:17 (as in 11:2). In addition to its poor fit into the literary context, the vocabulary and content of the passage are strange for Paul. Much of the vocabulary and phrasing in 11:3-16 are more typical of the Deutero-Pauline letters (e.g., Colossians, Ephesians, 1 Timothy, 2 Timothy).

Most interpreters, however, have considered the discussion of hairstyles in 11:3-16 to be an original part of 1 Corinthians (e.g., Murphy-O'Connor 1988). In that case, Paul is interrupting his series of lengthy arguments on issues raised in the Corinthians' letter (7:1-40; 8:1–11:1; 12–14) with brief discussions of hairstyles in worship and of conduct at the Lord's Supper. The reason for placing the discussion here is probably that both topics pertain to the gatherings of the whole assembly, which is the context of the use of spiritual gifts that he discusses in the next section, chapters 12–14.

◊ ◊ ◊ ◊

The opening statements (11:3) are difficult to understand. The standard reading of "head" in the metaphorical sense of "authority over" is rarely attested in Greek. The best alternative meaning for "head" appears to be "source" (cf. "head" for progenitor of a clan; Philo, *Congr.* 61). This statement about the man being the "head" (source) of woman is clarified by the reference in 11:8 to the creation story in Gen 2, where the woman is taken out of the man. That God is the source of Christ (v. 3) is also immediately intelligible in this reading. That "head" does not mean "authority over" is confirmed by the only appearance of the term for "authority" *(exousia)* in the passage at 11:10 (as noted in the NRSV footnote, "symbol of" is not in the Greek text): "the woman ought to have authority on the head," that is, over her own head (reading "having authority" parallel to John 10:18 and Acts 9:14). Although some relationship of subordination is entailed in the statements of verse 3, the meaning of "head" hardly indicates a subordination inherent in the nature of the universe (an ontological "chain of being"). But even if verse 3 is not taken in this ontological sense, it stands out as a unique statement in Pauline letters, very different from Paul's formulations of relations between God and Christ or between Christ and people or between women and men elsewhere in 1 Corinthians (cf. e.g., 3:18; 8:6; 15:20-28, 49).

The phrase "down the head" in 11:4 (NRSV: "with something on his head"), vague in the extreme, must be determined from the rest of the passage. Contrary to the NRSV translation and numerous interpretations, the passage focuses on hairstyles, not head-covering or veils. Verbs for "having one's hair cut off" and "letting one's hair grow long" appear in verses 6-7 and 14-15 respectively. The terms the NRSV translates by "veiled" and "unveiled" (vv. 5, 6, 7, 13) mean, rather, loosening a person's head-covering or hair (e.g., as in Lev 13:45; Num 5:18; Philo, *Spec. Leg.* 3.60). That these terms in verses 5-7, 13 refer to unbound *hair* is confirmed by the "long hair" and especially by the term "wrapping" (NRSV: "covering") in verses 14-15. In both Greek and Roman society, men normally had short hair and women long hair braided or otherwise wound up around their heads (thus portrayed on coins and statues). Women let their hair down only for mourning or for some religious rites. It was also standard social custom for women as well as men to have their head uncovered, as can be seen in portraits of women, including Roman women in Corinth. It seems highly unlikely that 11:3-16 would have been lining up with Greek practice of men praying with head uncovered and against both Roman and Jewish practice of men praying with head covered. By contrast, if the issue was hair length and arrangement, this passage fits standard Greek and Roman as well as Jewish practice. Thus "down the head" in verse 4 is best taken as a reference to long hair, which would have been considered disgraceful for a man, particularly when praying or prophesying.

After the brief reference to man's hair in 11:4, the discussion focuses more extensively on a woman's hair in 11:5-6. This pattern continues throughout the passage. The references first to a man (vv. 3, 4, 7, 14) set up and legitimate what is written about a woman's situation and behavior (vv. 5-6, 8-10, 15). The argument in verses 5-6 that it is "disgraceful" for a woman to "have her hair cut off or to be shaved" is hypothetical. It does not presume that some women were cutting off their hair. As becomes clear in 11:15 the issue addressed in verses 5 and 13 is the arrangement of a woman's long hair, whether it should be let down or remain tied up (the standard custom) when she is praying or prophesying. The problem was apparently that some women were letting their hair loose in an inspirational situation of prayer or ecstatic prophecy, as was done by the devotees of gods and goddesses such as Dionysus and Cybele, the Great Mother (Schüssler Fiorenza 1983, 227).

Verses 11:4-6 should thus be translated (without the NRSV assumption that the issue is veils or other artificial head-covering): "Any man . . . with hair down (around his) head . . . , but any woman . . . with head uncovered (by her bound-up hair), it is one and the same thing as having her head shaved. For if a woman will not be covered (with her bound-up hair), let her cut her hair off; but if it is shameful for a woman to have her hair cut off, she should cover her head (with hair bound-up)." Verses 5-6a are sarcastic, as verse 6b indicates in asserting the main point.

Verses 7-12 present a new argument. The contrast begun in verse 7 is not completed until verse 10. In between, verses 8-9 give a lengthy explanation, and then verses 11-12 qualify the statements made in verses 8-9. Ostensibly, verses 7-10 (beginning with "For . . .") explain verses 3-6, yet make no reference back to the statements in verse 3 that supposedly ground the whole discussion. "Reflection" or "glory" (man as God's and woman as man's) in verse 7 must have the sense of honor, which in Greek and Roman culture had to be reflected in subordinate others. (Verse 15 finally indicates that woman's glory = honor is her long hair, properly wrapped around her head.) Verses 8-9 register two points derived from the creation story in Gen 2 in order to demonstrate that woman is the reflected glory of man: she was made from him, and for his sake (cf. Gen 2:23 and 18–20). Woman, given authority over her own head, is thereby expected to maintain her subordinate and glory-reflecting position—by keeping her hair properly arranged. Verses 11-12 appear to have been added to mitigate the severity of verses 8-9 as a statement of the derivative, subordinate, and subservient role of woman. Yet, even as verses 11-12 remind men that they are interdependent with women "in the Lord," they also reinforce the argument that women should remain in their traditional subordinate position that reflects honor on men.

"Because of the angels" at the end of verse 10 appears as an afterthought or throwaway phrase. The view that the angels are the "sons of God" who lusted after the daughters of men (Gen 6:2), should be rejected along with the unjustified "veils" reading of the passage with which it fits. If we consider the angels along with the "authority" woman has on her (own) head, then these passages may be an allusion to a claim by certain women that they have "authority" to be uncovered because in their prophetic inspiration they were already like the angels (cf. "speak in the tongues of . . . angels," 13:1).

In the concluding step of this passage (11:13-16), the decisive argument that makes the issue clear is from "nature." The appeal to nature as having decisive authority is uncharacteristic of Paul. It is puzzling that the author of this paragraph ignores the well-known deviations with regard to Greek and Roman customs whereby, among men, philosophers, peasants, and "barbarians" wore their hair long (and were not subject to odium or ridicule; Dio Chrysostom, Or. 35.11). "Nature" was hardly universal in the case of men's hair. We can catch the sense of the clause at the end of verse 15 either way it could be read: Either "For her long hair is given to her in the place (instead) of a (cloth) wrapping" or "For her long hair is given to her as a (hair) wrapping." While the appeal to the other "churches" is superficially similar to other such appeals in 1 Corinthians (4:17; 7:17; 14:33), the phrase "the churches of God" diverges from Paul's usual formulations.

◊ ◊ ◊ ◊

This passage came to be understood as an absolute subordination of woman to man rooted in the nature of the universe, a hierarchy descending from God through Christ and man to woman. The subordination is clear. The principal argument is that woman is derived from man in the creation story in Gen 2. Not surprisingly 11:2-16, particularly 11:3, became one of the principal scriptural bases for the subordination of women in Christian culture.

If Paul wrote this paragraph as part of 1 Corinthians, he would appear to have been concerned about the behavior of women caught up in ecstatic prophesying, somewhat as he was about the madness of speaking in tongues in 14:23. In the latter case, however, he was concerned about the negative impressions of outsiders, whereas 11:3-16 aims only to reinforce a custom that maintains the traditional social order. If this paragraph is taken as an integral part of Paul's arguments to the Corinthian spirituals, then their views reflected here may be correlated with the rest of their self-understanding: In their baptism (into *Sophia*, 10:3-4) they have been newly transformed into *Sophia*, the "image of God," and have transcended the distinctions of "male and female." Hence, they enjoy their gifts of prophecy without the traditional distinctions of gender, thereby reflecting God's glory (cf. Wis 7:25-27!; cf. Wire 1990, 126-27).

However, this paragraph differs significantly from the other exhortations in 1 Corinthians. In contrast with every other section of the letter, where Paul refers to the imminence of final events and the continuation of the historical circumstances of life, or both, this paragraph has no eschatological perspective. The argument in 11:3-16 differs strikingly from that of chapter 7, which also deals with central issues in the relations between men and women. There, clearly convinced that men's and women's sex roles have been relativized and are about to change decisively with the "end," he works around that carefully, in gender-balanced rhetoric addressed to both men and women. In chapter 7, moreover, he does not advocate any hard and fast general norm, but adjusts to particular people's circumstances. On the much less central issue of hair arrangement, however, the paragraph in 11:3-16 presents an established practice or custom grounded in creation and nature.

Finally, we can easily imagine that this paragraph, whether by Paul or a later interpolator, was motivated by anxiety among the heads of the churches. Prophetic inspiration was regarded in Greek culture as madness or as possession by a deity. A typical manifestation among women was tossing the head and the hair in disarray. To the male heads of society, however, the women's loose hair symbolized that the women themselves were loose from social constraints. This male anxiety was surely well-grounded. Many women must have been attracted to ecstatic forms of religion because of their confinement within the highly authoritarian patriarchal Greco-Roman social order. Possession by a god provided a certain legitimation for their rebellious behavior.

ARGUMENT CONCERNING DIVISIONS AT THE LORD'S SUPPER (11:17-34)

If the preceding discussion of the arrangement of a woman's hair when prophesying was originally missing in 1 Corinthians, then 11:17-34 would fit readily after 11:2. As was common in deliberative rhetoric designed to persuade the listeners to change their behavior, Paul would then be using commendation or praise in 11:2 apparently to soften the Corinthians' receptivity to the criticism in verses 17-22 of their procedure at the Lord's Supper. The argument of 11:17-34 proceeds in four steps: after rebuking them for their procedure at the Lord's Supper (vv. 17-22), Paul repeats the tradition of the words of institution (vv. 23-26), applies that tradition to their situation (vv. 27-32), and finally gives instructions for how they should proceed thereafter (vv. 33-34).

Verse 18 has formed the basis of virtually all scholarly hypotheses that 1 Corinthians is a composite of two or more letters. Here Paul seems unaware of the factions he addressed in chapters 1–4, and in 11:19 views as a divine necessity what he condemned in that earlier argument. Such theories, however, preceded the recognition both that "to some extent I believe it" is a standard rhetorical device of mock (dis)belief and that verse 19 may not be appropriately understood as a theological motif of necessary eschatological divisions. Moreover, the phrases "when you come together . . ." in verses 18 and 20 indicate that these divisions are specific to the times when they "come together in assembly" (AT).

◊ ◊ ◊ ◊

It is hardly by coincidence that Paul uses the term "to come together" *(synerchesthai)* repeatedly in this context (vv. 17, 18, 20, 33, 34 and 14:23, 26; but nowhere else). The term had strong connotations of a people joining together to form a society (as in Aristotle's political theory, *Pol.* 3.4.3; 3.5.10; 3.6.7; 6.5.2), or of factions being reunited (e.g., Aelius Aristides, *Or.* 24.49). Moreover, "when you come together in assembly" (AT) in 11:18 is precisely paralleled by "when you come together *in the same place*" (AT) in 11:20, the latter phrase (left untranslated in the NRSV; cf. 14:23) meaning both "in the same place" and "together." Thus with the phrase "for the worse" in verse 17, and by innuendo in verse 20, Paul is saying that when they come together they are anything but "together."

If 11:19 appears to be a puzzling "theological aside" (e.g., Fee 1987, 537), that is only because it has been read in terms of the prophetic-apocalyptic motif of "end-time divisions" (e.g., Matt 10:35-37 // Luke 12:52-53). Thus *haireseis* is often translated as "factions" and taken as synonymous with "divisions" (*schismata*, v. 18), and the term *dokimoi* is often translated as "genuine" (as in the NRSV). In the Corinthian context, however, "genuine" would more appropriately be translated "esteemed" or "distinguished," while *haireseis* (faction), rare in Paul's letters, could have a connotation as weak as "choices" or "discriminations." Thus Paul's comment in verse 19 should be taken as irony, even sarcasm, continuing the mock belief at the end of verse 18: "For of course there must be 'discriminations' among you so that it will become clear who among you are the 'distinguished ones' " (AT).

Given the sharp rhetorical tone of the context (vv. 17-20, 22), verse 21 should also be read as rhetorical accusation, not as a precise explanation of what is bothering Paul. To explain how they are not eating "the *Lord's* supper" he accuses "each" of eating "your *own* supper." The verb translated "goes ahead with" in the NRSV has rather the intensive, not temporal, sense of "devours." It should therefore not be taken in connection with the verb in verse 33 that the NRSV translates "wait for," but which means, rather, "receive one another." Paul's concern is that the communal character of the Lord's Supper is neglected because of individual agendas ("one goes hungry and another becomes drunk," v. 21). His angry response, in verse 22, is in the form of rhetorical questions. Those obsessed with their own dinner can banquet in their own houses some other time! The wording of the rhetorical questions finally indicates whom he is addressing: those who have enough means to "have [i.e., own] houses [NRSV: "homes"]" and who, in their insensitivity, both "show contempt for the [assembly] of God and humiliate those who have nothing."

If the problem, as Paul sees it, lies with those who "own houses," then Greco-Roman dining practices may shed some light on the situation, particularly in connection with where the assembly's celebration of the Lord's Supper was taking place. As explained in the introduction, the assembly in Corinth apparently consisted of several subgroups or "house-assemblies" based in certain households. When "the whole [assembly]" met for the Lord's Supper and other matters (14:23), presumably they met in one of those house-holds. (If Romans 16 was written from Corinth, then one such household was that of Gaius, Rom 16:23.) That would have placed a householder in the role of host to the "Lord's Supper" as well as head of a constituent household subassembly. Those prominent householders, moreover, may have set a certain tone at the communal meals of the assembly simply by following standard Greco-Roman patterns of hosting and dining, such as assigning places by social rank and providing those of higher status with better and larger portions of food and wine. Women, children, and slaves, of course, were only rarely included in such dinners at all. Although we cannot take the terms of Paul's rhetoric literally as references to a simple conflict between "rich" and "poor," the hellenistic-Roman obsession with social status (probably especially intense in Corinth) that carried over into dining patterns must have affected celebrations of the Lord's Supper in the ways Paul found objectionable.

Paul's antidote is to remind the Corinthians of the standard tradition of the founding of the communal meal. "Received" and "handed on" in 11:23 (cf. 15:1-3) were virtually technical terms in Jewish culture for the transmission of important traditions such as customs, rituals, and ethical teachings (cf. *m. Abot* 1:1). Hellenistic philosophies used the same terms in transmitting their standard doctrines. To emphasize the authority of this central community tradition Paul identifies it as having come "from the Lord," the ultimate founder and source of the celebration of the Lord's Supper. For Paul and the tradition in which he stood, this celebration was regarded as a continuing observance of the Last Supper ("on the night when he was betrayed," 11:23*b*), and it was therefore focused on Jesus' death.

While Mark (14:12-25), followed by both Matthew and Luke, sets the Last Supper into the context of a Passover meal, Paul's tradition, along with the context in chapter 11, suggests no connection with a Passover meal (the notion of Christ as the Passover lamb in 5:7 was apparently not connected with the Lord's Supper). Besides separating the cup from the bread with "after supper" and making no mention of all drinking from it, Paul's version has thanksgiving instead of a blessing over the bread and no thanksgiving over the cup (cf. Mark 14:22-24). In Paul's tradition, the body, symbolized by the bread, is "for you," whereas in Mark, the blood, symbolized by the cup, is "poured out for many." Both of these phrases symbolize a vicarious sacrifice or martyrdom (on behalf of, in place of). Paul uses just such phrases at several other points in his letters, probably from creedal formulas or homiletic slogans (cf. Rom 5:6, 8; 1 Cor 15:3; 2 Cor 5:15, 21; Gal 2:20; 3:13). The principal emphasis in Paul's tradition as in Mark's is on the new covenant symbolized by the cup. This is sharpened somewhat in Paul's version where the cup alone, separated somewhat from the bread, stands for the covenant, whereas Mark has a close parallel of bread, standing for body, and cup, standing for blood. While Mark's words have the more explicit citation of "blood of the covenant" from Exod 24:8, Paul's "new covenant in my blood" suggests more that "the Lord Jesus" constituted the sacrifice that generated the blood by which God and the people were bound, by analogy with the covenant ceremony in Exod 24:5-8.

Paul's tradition, finally, includes after both the bread and the cup sayings the instruction to "do this in remembrance of me." Mark may have eliminated this command because it did not suit his historical narrative. The repeated "doing" in "remembrance" sanctions the ritual reenactment by which the covenant community was created. Although Paul's tradition does not view the Lord's Supper as a new Passover, the biblical tradition of such memorials as ritual reenactments of Israel's founding events is surely the background from which the celebration of the Lord's Supper as a ritual enactment in remembrance of Jesus' action, in the meal and on the cross, must be understood (cf. Exod 12–13). However, the Corinthians and others socialized into hellenistic culture, and with little acquaintance with the Jewish Scriptures, may well have understood the supper more in terms of Greek memorial feasts for dead heroes.

In verse 26 Paul attempts to drive home the point of the Lord's Supper with a double emphasis. Picking up on the next-to-last phrase of the tradition ("as often as") and including both eating the bread and drinking the cup, he focuses attention both on Jesus' death ("you proclaim the Lord's death"; cf. 1:23; 2:6-8) and on his return (*parousia;* "until he comes"). In the latter Paul is in tune with other traditions of the Lord's Supper/Eucharist (Mark 14:25 and in *Did.* 9:4; 10:5-6, ending with *Maranatha,* "Our Lord, come!") where the orientation is eschatological, toward "the kingdom of God."

When Paul applies the tradition in 11:27-32 he makes immediate use of the eschatological reminder about the (imminent) *parousia.* In a sequence of statements dominated by "judgment," he invites the Corinthians to "examine" themselves and to "discern," in the face of God's "judgment," what behavior is appropriate at the Supper. Traditional interpretations have often lost sight of the social context to which Paul addressed his quotation of the words instituting the Lord's Supper, focusing narrowly on the individual believer receiving the elements of the Eucharist. Even the text was conformed to this narrowing of meaning, with the addition in verse 29 of "in an unworthy manner" (see the NRSV footnote) to "eat and drink" and "of the Lord" to "the body," thus merely repeating rather than applying the warning and admonition in verses 27-28. By translating "answerable for the body and blood" in verse 27, the NRSV has restored the sense of "guilty of" or "liable for," thus moving the focus back to the social-political sphere from the individualistic introspection or obsession with profanation of the sacred to which this passage had long been bound.

What Paul means by the self-examination or "putting oneself to the test" (in the face of God's eschatological "examination"; AT) that he calls for in verse 28 is suggested by his mention of "the body" in verse 29, which is the community, as expressly stated in the earlier reference to the Lord's Supper in 10:16-17 ("we who are many are one body"). The verb "examine" at the opening of verse 28 is cognate with "the distinguished ones" (NRSV: "genuine") in 11:19, alluding to certain Corinthians' sense of their own importance. Those who partake in the Lord's Supper without "discerning the body" of the whole community are in fact causing "judgment" to fall upon themselves in the form of recent sickness and even death of members of the community (vv. 29-30). Repeating the same points in verses 31-32, Paul then gives a positive twist to the interrelated levels of "judging." Had the Corinthians been more discerning about "the body," they would have avoided the present experience of "judgment" (illness and death; v. 31). Nevertheless, the present judgment is to be accepted as disciplinary, and will allow them to be spared the ultimate judgment of God (v. 32).

With "so then" in 11:33-34, Paul pulls this argument together in a final practical instruction. Since there is no good evidence for translating the key verb in verse 21 as "goes ahead with" instead of "devour," the corresponding verb in verse 33 should be taken in its usual meaning of "receive" (as in hospitality), not "wait for" (as in the NRSV). The instruction "If you are hungry (i.e., want a more sumptuous dinner), eat at home" in (v. 34a) thus makes the rhetorical question of verse 22a into an imperative, which is followed by the sanction of potential judgment (v. 34b, recapitulating vv. 27-32). In this passage as a whole, therefore, Paul is pleading with those whom he sees as obsessed with "devouring their own dinner" to "discern the body" of the assembly as a whole and to "receive" the others in the solidarity of the covenant community Christ had founded in the Lord's Supper.

◊ ◊ ◊ ◊

Several dimensions of Paul's vision of "the assembly" he was organizing become clearer in this argument. Both the language he uses for the meetings and the way he draws on the biblical history of Israel indicate that he understood the movement he was building as the divinely inaugurated alternative to the dominant imperial society. The "assembly" that "came together" as a people was to maintain its solidarity by focusing on its founding event in the crucifixion of Jesus. The tradition of the Lord's Supper indicates that "the new covenant" people were the principal social-political reality that had been established in Jesus' death. The founding of the new covenant community, "the body," was what was celebrated in the most fundamental ritual of the movement. "The assembly," finally, was to hold itself together in anticipation of the imminent *parousia* and judgment, when "the world" would be condemned while the assembly itself would be vindicated, apparently as the society of the new age (vv. 26, 32). Paul was under no illusion that the community was some sort of commune or all-encompassing extended family; it consisted of different believer households and members from households in which spouses were not believers. But the coming together of "the whole assembly" for communal meals was especially important in molding some sort of coherence in the community recently established in Corinth. Paul appealed to the founding tradition of the Lord's Supper to press precisely for the discipline he saw necessary to maintain the coherence of the new assembly in Corinth. His recitation of that tradition emphasized both the focus on "the Lord's death" and the orientation toward the Lord's *parousia* that is evident elsewhere in the letter. For Paul at least, the one was the basis of the assembly's solidarity, and the other the sanction and goal of its continuing cohesion.

Judging from Paul's rhetoric, it is impossible to determine just what the schisms at the assembly meals were. We should not assume that there was no bonding among the Corinthians in connection with those meals. Assuming that the problem was not simply some form of spiritual individualism, then there may well have been some mutually supportive bonding among the wise *pneumatikoi* and those who had chosen sexual asceticism (in devotion to Sophia) and those enlightened with *gnōsis* or those possessed of unusual spiritual gifts. Moreover, since the religious experience they shared also distinguished them from those who did not share it, what united them with some may have divided them from others. To Paul it appears that they were not bonding with one another as a whole community and not bonding around (the implications of) the death of Jesus. Yet it would have been difficult for Corinthians who did not share Paul's sense of urgency about the imperial society standing under divine judgment, and his attachment to the new movement as an alternative society, to share his concern about the solidarity of the whole assembly.

What most concerned Paul, apparently, was that the assembly of saints in Corinth, in its social relationships, was beginning to resemble the dominant imperial society to which it was supposedly God's alternative. Ideally the assemblies of the movement were more or less egalitarian communities, intended to embody the tight-knit reciprocal relations and communal solidarity of a village community. In Corinth, by contrast with the much smaller cities of

Thessalonica or Philippi, the assembly was a tiny horizontal association in the midst of an imperial metropolis that was structured hierarchically into patronage networks dominated by the provincial elite. The movement, however, had no alternative but to work more or less within the existing patterns of residence and housing. Thus in Corinth, at least, the movement took the form of house-assemblies that "came together" as "the whole assembly" (see 11:17; 14:23, 26) periodically (weekly?) for celebration of the Lord's Supper, prayers, prophecies, and so forth. Those larger gatherings of the whole assembly had necessarily to be hosted by members who had the largest houses, probably those who were already leaders of the house-assemblies. That set up a situation where it would have been difficult for the few well-off members of the larger assembly to break with the prevailing patterns of social relations that were embodied primarily in banqueting, that is, hierarchical seating and different portions and qualities of food and drink. In this argument, apparently addressed to the well-off members of the assembly, Paul insists that they break with those hierarchical patterns in the social relations symbolically embodied in the Lord's Supper, that they "discern the body" (see v. 29) and that they "receive one another" (v. 33 AT) in more egalitarian relations and solidarity as members of the body.

ARGUMENT CONCERNING SPIRITUAL GIFTS (12–14)

The formulaic "Now concerning . . ." indicates a new argument devoted to "spiritual things" (NRSV: "gifts"), which begins with 12:1 and runs through chapter 14, where it focuses more specifically on "tongues" and "prophecy." As in the previous two arguments (cf. 7:1; 8:1), Paul may be responding to issues raised by the Corinthians in their letter. The introduction (12:1-3) and conclusion (14:36-40) enclose three major steps in the argument: 12:4-30, insisting upon diversity in unity; 12:31–13:13, praising love in contrast with the overvaluation of spiritual gifts that produces divisiveness; and 14:1-33, advocating prophecy that intelligibly edifies the community and devaluing tongues that do not. As in chapters 8–10, these three steps form an aba' structure in which Paul begins the discussion somewhat generally in the first section, offers his own actual or hypothetical action as an example in the second section, and gives more precise (corrective) advice in the third. By comparison with the letter to the Galatians or the "letter of tears" in 2 Cor 10–13, chapters 12–14 are not sharply polemical, although Paul asserts his own apostolic authority explicitly at the very end (14:37-38), just as he does at the end of the argument in chapters 1–4.

Paul's argument concerning "spiritual things" continues with deliberative rhetoric, urging the Corinthians to take a particular course of action in their future community gatherings (summarized in 12:31; 14:1, 39-40). He makes the same appeal to pursue their common advantage or common good in 12:7 as he had in earlier sections of the letter, over against the pursuit of the possibilities enabled by their newfound individual enlightenment (6:12; 10:23). Again, as in earlier sections of the letter (4:[8-]14-17; 8:13–9:27 + 11:1), he presents himself as an example of how (not) to act (13:1-3 and 14:6-7, 11-12). Moreover, a central concern of his argument on "spiritual things," as of his argument on divisiveness (chaps. 1–4), is for the unity of the body politic (chaps. 12 and 13). As one moves from chapter 12 to chapter 14, it is increasingly evident that Paul's argument is corrective, not simply informative: it challenges the Corinthian spirituals' orientation as well as their spiritual practice.

The first two main steps of the argument, chapters 12 and 13, drive toward the specific correctives in chapter 14: (1) that prophecy should be practiced instead of tongues since, because prophecy is intelligible, it can be used to edify the community (14:1-19); and (2) that prophecy and tongues should be practiced to edify the community in deliberately arranged good order, with only two or three speakers, appropriately interpreted and tested, in each meeting (14:26-33). This line of argument helps us discern what the principal issue was regarding "spiritual things." "Tongues" is the only gift included in all of the lists in this section of the letter (12:8-10, 28-30; 13:1-3, 8; 14:6, 26). "Tongues" is pointedly placed at the end of the lists in chapter 12. When Paul finally, in chapter 14, focuses on the particular gifts of tongues and prophecy and denigrates the former in favor of the latter, it becomes evident that he is countering what he considers an overvaluation of "speaking in tongues." Both chapters 12 and 13 are then readily intelligible in this connection. The argument for diversity of spiritual gifts in chapter 12 makes sense as Paul's attempt to counter an overemphasis on tongues. This also explains why he begins the praise of love with reference to the "tongues." In both of these steps of his argument, however, Paul also refers to other key foci of Corinthian excitement, particularly *sophia* and *gnōsis* (12:8; 13:2, 8, 9, 12).

Diversity of Gifts for the Common Good of the Community (12:1-30)

In this first major section of his argument on spiritual gifts, Paul insists on a diversity of manifestations of the Spirit, all of which are integral for the common good of the body politic. After introducing the new topic in 12:1-3, he develops this section of his argument in three steps. In verses 4-11 he insists that there are varieties of gifts from one and the same divine source, all given for the common good. Verses 12-26 comprise a lengthy application of the analogy of the body for the body politic of "Christ," the movement in general. Paul uses this metaphor, common in Greco-Roman antiquity, to argue a distinctive point about the interdependence of the diverse bodily members, all of which are integral and important to the body politic. In verses 27-30 he finally applies the analogy to the members of the Corinthian assembly, now ranking the members by gifts or roles while repeating the main point about diversity.

◊ ◊ ◊ ◊

12:1-3: Paul's reference to *charismata,* "spiritual gifts," in verse 4, used as a synonym for the ambiguous "spirituals" in verse 1, shows that in chapters 12–14 he is focusing on "spiritual things," not "spiritual people." Apparently some of the Corinthians considered themselves "spiritual" (as evident in 2:6-16 and as Paul indicates at the end of this section, 14:37) because they possessed "spiritual things."

At first glance verses 2-3 seem to digress from the topic just raised. The logic does not fit: immediately upon introduction of the topic of spiritual gifts Paul makes seemingly unconnected comments about the Corinthians' former life as pagans and about acclaiming Jesus either as cursed or as Lord. He did something similar, however, at the beginning of chapters 8–10, moving into a discussion of knowledge immediately after introducing the topic of food sacrificed to idols. Here, as there, Paul is obviously framing the subject he is about to discuss. Right at the outset of his argument he both sets Jesus as Lord in authority over spiritual gifts and presents the confession of Jesus as Lord as the criterion of being caught up in the Spirit. This move must be purposely directed at (some of) the Corinthians who, in the free flow of the Spirit into ecstatic unintelligible utterances, would hardly have been focused so narrowly on this confession. This focus on Jesus as Lord fits the discussion of spiritual gifts so poorly, in fact, that it must be yet another attempt by Paul to refocus the Corinthian spirituals on Christ (cf. the Crucified One as God's true wisdom and power in chaps. 1–3; Christ as the instrument of salvation in 8:6; and Christ as the spiritual rock in 10:4).

With the unusual combination of two verbs from the same root, "you were led" and "having been carried away by force (to idols that could not speak)" (v. 2; NRSV: "enticed and led astray"), Paul may be referring to ecstasy the Corinthians had experienced in their former pagan worship. The language also evokes the image of a cultic festival procession led by prominent celebrants through the public area of a city to the sanctuary where sacrifices offered to the god or the cult-image were viewed. In any case, he is offering an analogy: You know from your previous experience that you have no control of your own life when in the power of an overwhelming religious experience (ecstasy or procession). Ecstasy alone, even ecstatic utterance, is no criterion of being led by the Spirit. The real criterion, Paul insists, entails a specific intelligible political content: "Jesus is Lord." Since the reference in verse 2 is to the Corinthians' previous pagan religious experience, the acclamation "Jesus be cursed!" in verse 3 does not refer to an unthinkable curse uttered within a meeting of the assembly, but is a hypothetical construct

Paul creates as a rhetorical antithesis to the distinctive exclamation, "Jesus is Lord!" The latter has the form of a recognition oracle, common in the Greco-Roman world and in Israelite-Jewish prophecy (cf. the demons' recognition of Jesus as "Holy One of God" in Mark 1:24; 5:7). For Paul and his assemblies, exclusive allegiance to Jesus as their ruler was the key criterion of their life in the dawning new age.

12:4-11: As Paul begins discussion of spiritual gifts in 12:4-6 he broadens the focus dramatically. His driving concern throughout chapter 12 is not unity but diversity, or perhaps diversity in unity. Not only are there "varieties of (spiritual) gifts," but varieties of services and varieties of workings as well. Not only are the gifts inspired by the Spirit diverse, but they stand together on a par with and are relativized by the many more secular and mundane activities, the human or "civil" services and the low-status "labors" that are also divinely given. While "the same Spirit," "the same Lord," and "the same God" should not be taken as a nascent Christian doctrine of the trinity, it is interesting that Paul apparently divides the various divine effects among these agents with conscious intent.

In the transitional statement of verse 7, which is a summary of verses 4-6 and an introduction to verses 8-11, Paul works in his other main concern that complements the diversity of gifts: "To each [person] is given the manifestation of the Spirit *for the common good*" (emphasis added). The nine parallel phrases that follow, "to one . . . to another . . . to another," and so on display more precisely what the diversity of "gifts" and workings might be. Clearly Paul is attempting to capture the Corinthians' assent as well as attention by mentioning first the "utterance of wisdom" *(sophia)* and "utterance of knowledge" *(gnōsis)* on which (some of) the Corinthians were so keen (see chaps. 1–4, 8). Paul thus uses their own key "gifts" of wisdom and knowledge, placed first on the list, along with all the other works or labors of the Spirit (v. 11) that the Corinthians do not care about (but which are of basic importance for Paul), to relativize tongues, even as he lists it last and further diminishes it by adding "interpretation of tongues" (v. 10). The Corinthian spirituals probably did not differentiate sharply between gifts in the free flow of the Spirit. Nor, probably, had Paul previously made such precise distinctions. This and other lists of "spiritual gifts" are distinctive to 1 Corinthians within the letters of Paul, being found elsewhere only in Rom 12:6-8, which is dependent on chapter 12. Paul is surely making these elaborate distinctions in order to relativize and downplay tongues.

Beginning in verse 7, however, Paul focuses his discussion on the members of the community and substitutes for the word "gifts" the more general expression, "manifestation of the Spirit." Along with the insistence that all manifestations are "for the common good," his repeated "to one . . . to another" emphasizes both the activities of the Spirit and the members of the community who are to mediate the manifestations to one another. The summarizing statement in 12:11 then pointedly repeats the emphases: "to each [person] individually" and "as the Spirit chooses."

Since Paul elaborates this extended list of manifestations of the Spirit (not "spiritual gifts") in 12:8-10 in order to put tongues in its place, it would go against the gist of his argument to inquire precisely after the nature of the various "gifts." It suffices to note several points: Paul has already downplayed *sophia* and *gnōsis*, on which the Corinthian spirituals themselves were so keen (2:1-5; 8:1-2). The statements he quotes in 8:4 are examples of the Corinthians' "words of *gnōsis*." "Faith" (a "fruit of the Spirit" along with love, peace, et al. in Gal 5:22) must in this context mean something similar to, and therefore overlap with, "gifts of healing" and "working of miracles." Healing characterized not only the ministry of Jesus but the mission of Paul and other apostles. "Gifts of healing" provides a good example of how the gift was given to one for the purpose of healing another, leading to the "common good." Even more do "miracles" (literally "powers") characterize the Pauline mission generally, with Paul reminding his readers joyfully and proudly of the presence in his own ministry of this "sign of an apostle" (Rom 15:19; 2 Cor 12:12; Gal 3:3-5; 1 Thess 1:5). Paul returns to a discussion of the last four manifestations of the spirit—"prophecy," "discernment of spirits," "tongues," and "interpretation of tongues"—in chapter 14.

12:12-26: Paul now uses the well-known analogy between the human body and the body politic to illustrate his argument for diversity of the Spirit's manifestations for the common good of the community. He exploits the analogy between the body and the commonwealth in three steps: He first establishes the analogy and draws the main point about diversity (vv. 12-14), then insists on recognition of the whole body and its diversity (vv. 15-20), and finally illustrates the importance of all the parts of the body and their interdependence (vv. 21-26).

The analogy between the body and the city-state was widely used throughout classical antiquity, usually for conservative purposes, and is known particularly from Stoic political philosophy (e.g., Marcus Aurelius, *Med.* 2.1; 7.13; Epictetus, *Diss.* 2.10.3-4; Seneca, *Ep.* 95.52). According to the Roman historian Livy (*Hist.* 2.32), Menenius Agrippa (fifth century BCE) used a fable about the common emaciation resulting from the other body parts' refusal to feed the stomach in order to persuade the plebs to end their "sedition." But no other ancient writer uses the analogy as Paul does here, to emphasize the diversity and interdependence of the body's members.

"Christ" (v. 12) means the community loyal to Christ, as can be seen from verse 13, and then from where Paul finally refers explicitly to "the body of Christ." Paul draws attention to how both baptism and the Lord's Supper symbolize the unity of the members (v. 13). In transition to fuller development and application of the body analogy, he swings the emphasis back around to diversity (v. 14). In appealing to the rite of baptism, and in the particular phrase "to drink of one Spirit" (v. 13), he again chooses symbols on which the Corinthians were especially keen (see on 1:13-16; 15:29; and also 10:4). The allusion here is to the same baptismal formula that he cites in Gal 3:28 to illustrate that not only Jews, but also Gentiles "in Christ," are now heirs of the promise to Abraham. In chapter 12, by contrast, "Jews or Greeks, slaves or free" illustrates the diversity of people now incorporated into one body.

Paul's omission here of the phrase, "no longer male and female," which is part of the baptismal formula as he cites it in Gal 3:28, may be an attempt to avoid one of the possible bases of the Corinthian spirituals' asceticism and ecstatic prophecy. The Alexandrian Apollos and the Corinthian spirituals may have interpreted this part of the baptismal formula to mean that the sexual differences of the creation (Gen 1:26-27; understood as deficiency in the female) had been overcome in baptism or in one's devotion to *Sophia* or both. Thus empowered, certain Corinthian women apparently believed that they could, or *must,* be free of patriarchal marriage (in sexual asceticism) and that in their spiritual ecstasy they were speaking with the "tongues of angels" (13:1).

Developing and applying the body analogy (vv. 15-20), Paul insists that a separatist or individualistic attitude by one of the members of the body does not "make it any less a part of the body" (v. 15). Body members cannot be reconstituted as independent entities because "God arranged the members in the body, each one of them, as he chose" (v. 18). Paul apparently asserts God's (original) creation (or God's eschatological recreation) of the human (and by implication social) body over against a Corinthian experience of individual spiritual transformation—evidently into immortal souls. (The Corinthians therefore rejected the notion of a "resurrection of the dead" body in 15:12.) For Paul the collective political body was as real in its concrete divine creation as was the embodiment of the person in her or his continuing social relationships. Indeed, as asserted in verse 20, the concrete created reality of the political body necessarily means that it has many members.

In further developing and applying the body analogy (vv. 21-26), Paul emphasizes the importance and the interdependence of all the members of the body. That some high-ranking body parts, such as the eye or the head, could say to lower ranking parts, such as the hand or the feet, "I have no need of you" suggests an attitude of superiority as well as independence. Paul must assume such an attitude on the part of certain Corinthians caught up in their spiritual gifts (presumably tongues). Over against this attitude, Paul applies an extension of the body analogy (v. 23) that both picks up on the Corinthians' excitement about "honor" (see 4:10) and by implication incorporates the supposedly devalued sexual parts (see 7:1) as important: "those members of the body that we think less honorable we clothe with greater honor." He again grounds the analogy in creation: It is God who has given greater honor to the inferior member (v. 24). In 12:21-26 the argument has moved completely away from spiritual gifts to relations among the members of the political body: not only must there be no division (schism; cf. 1:10; 11:18) in the body politic, but there must be an equal concern for one another among the members. In a final step Paul moves in almost the opposite direction from the "honor and shame" values of aristocratic Greek and imperial Roman culture, which were always hierarchical. He insists on the solidarity of the interdependent and equally valued members: "If one member suffers, all suffer together with [her or him]; if one member is honored [literally: glorified], all rejoice together with [her or him]" (v. 26).

12:27-30: The argument begun in 12:4 concludes with two new twists or emphases. First, verse 27 drives home the point already evident, that all the Corinthian addressees collectively (the emphatic "you") are members of the political body of Christ, and that every one of them individually is a member of it (as opposed to separate individual entities in spiritual transcendence). Then, however, in contrast to the earlier listing of manifestations of the Spirit of seemingly equal value, Paul presents a serial list of social roles in the assembly (v. 28). He explicitly ranks the first three, and indicates with "then . . . then" that the rest are of somewhat lesser importance. Listed last are "various kinds of tongues," which he views as problematic, and which are his main interest here. The rest of the list and the ranking are secondary, and should not be taken as an intentionally hierarchical ranking of offices in the church. This explains the unexpected listing of "apostles," and the appearance of this role in the plural—although one effect, whether intended or not, is that Paul has pulled rank on the Corinthian pneumatics. It is not surprising that he lists "prophets" prominently, given his estimate of the importance of this function for the assemblies he has established (e.g., 1 Thess 5:19-20). "Teaching" also appears later in an important role (14:6, 26). By listing ahead of "tongues" the more mundane "helps" and "guidances" (i.e., to other members of the community; NRSV: "forms of assistance, forms of leadership"), which appear only here in the lists, Paul further relativizes the one gift most prized by the Corinthians.

In the second new emphasis, a series of rhetorical questions (v. 29) suggests that (some of) the addressees, besides enjoying their own individual "spiritual things," are also encouraging others to experience speaking in tongues. They may not be oblivious to unity, but theirs would be a unity of all experiencing the ecstasy of tongues, with a corresponding dissolution of embodied difference. The more socially traditional Paul favors embodied difference, and thus the unity of diversely gifted interdependent embodied selves. Paul advocates solidarity in diversity, not uniformity.

Praise of Love (12:31–13:13)

The famous "hymn to love" has sometimes been identified as a digression, or even as an interpolation—perhaps not even written by Paul. However, it is an integral step in a deliberative argument in which Paul shifts into the praise of a virtue as an illustration of his exhortation. It has an exalted style that stands out from its literary context, and should be seen as a brief *encomium*, which in ancient rhetoric was a speech in praise of a hero or, in this case, a virtue. Paul's praise of love *(agapē)* bears similarities to the praise of "love" *(erōs)* by Plato *(Symp.* 197c-e) and to the praise of "Truth" in 2 Esdras 4:34-40. The main divisions, verses 1-3, 4-7, 8-12, 13, correspond respectively to four of the five components of an *encomium:* prologue, (birth and upbringing), acts, comparison, and epilogue, with acts and comparison being the most important parts. The seeming disparity between form and function thus disappears, since *encomia* were used to exhort people to imitate the virtue praised.

This praise of love fits closely into the overall context of 1 Corinthians. For example, most of the verbs used in chapter 13 parallel Paul's characterizations of the Corinthians elsewhere in the letter. To appreciate the way Paul is thinking in response to the Corinthian situation, we might note how the praise of love in chapter 13 elaborates on the thought articulated only in passing in 8:1. There, in his initial reaction to the Corinthians' high valuation of *gnōsis,* he wrote succinctly, "knowledge puffs up, but love builds up." Having urged in chapter 12 that the diverse manifestations of the Spirit be used for "building up" for the common good, in chapter 13 he describes how love comports itself in relation to others. Moreover, the *encomium* ends in a lengthy contrast of love with *gnōsis* (vv. 8-12; cf. 8:1-3), just as it begins with reference to speaking in tongues (v. 1), which is the principal "spiritual gift" at issue in chapters 12 and 14.

◊ ◊ ◊ ◊

First Corinthians 12:31 is transitional, yet it is more an introduction to the praise of love in chapter 13 more than a conclusion to the discussion of the variety of gifts in chapter 12. The positioning of the adverbial Greek idiom *kath' hyperbolēn* makes this transition difficult to translate. The NRSV takes it adjectivally, "a *still more excellent* way." But it would more naturally go with one of the verbs (as in Gal 1:13 or 2 Cor 1:8), either "Strive, *even exceedingly*, for the greater gifts. I will show you a way," or "Strive/be zealous for the greater gifts. And I will demonstrate *even to excess* a way." In any case, 12:31a is an ironic statement; the implicit meaning is the opposite of that ostensibly expressed. Paul has just gone to great rhetorical lengths to downplay "tongues," which the Corinthian spirituals appear to value as the greatest of gifts. Then in what follows (13:1-13) he shows them how ridiculous their pursuit is and insinuates they should abandon it. Further on in the argument (14:12) Paul mockingly repeats the imperative to "strive/be zealous," and then at the end of the whole argument he argues that such zeal be directed to prophecy (14:39).

Part and parcel of the irony here is Paul's sudden shift into the high-blown style of formal, artful praise of a virtue. This is more what we would expect from a rhetorically trained hellenistic-Jewish intellectual from Alexandria, such as Philo or Apollos! We certainly do find such exalted language and style in Philo's flights of spiritual exegesis focused on *Sophia* or the *Logos* ("Word"). However, in contrast with the static, essentialist adjectival, and nominal characterization of *Sophia*, for example, in Wis 7:22-26, Paul's characterization by a verbal construction makes love dynamic and relational. Thus Paul may be imitating the high-blown style in order to parody those who are fond of it.

In verses 1-3, presenting himself as a hypothetical example, Paul first mockingly exaggerates both the Corinthians' favorite spiritual gifts and his own central values and commitment, and then suddenly deflates them. Perhaps by rehearing the words and phrases stacked one upon another, we may sense the exaggeration and excess (in italics): "If I speak with the tongues of men, *and even of angels* . . . ; if I possess prophecy and know *all mysteries* and *all knowledge* and if I have *all faith* so as to remove mountains" and "if I give away all my possessions *and if I hand over my own body*" (AT). Moreover, angels always have a hyperbolic function in Paul's letters (cf. 4:9; Gal 1:8; 4:14), and "to remove mountains" is a grotesque metaphor, and actually giving over one's body in martyrdom did not come into prominence until several generations later. Paul's own tongue is squarely in his cheek as he dictates.

The textual variants in verse 3 may signal yet another aspect of Paul's irony. "Boast" is the oldest and most difficult reading. But the meaning? A possible way of reading the NRSV's primary translation is to understand Paul as mocking his own practice of devoting his whole life and energy to his mission. Another possibility is to read it as an aside: "let me boast just for once." In that case, Paul would be distancing himself from his suddenly high-blown "genre," poking fun at his temporarily grandiloquent style and pretentious offering of sublime ideas.

On the other side of the deflation, "but do not have love," he is clearly mocking his own emphasis on faith and his own poverty and refusal to accept support (see on 9:15) as well as the Corinthians' excitement over tongues and their passion for *gnōsis*. Even if one had *all knowledge* she or he would be nothing (cf. 1:26-29). Even if he sacrifices his very life he gains nothing. These second and third deflations (vv. 2, 3) are in blunt, brief clauses, and form a contrast with the more elaborate first one (v. 1) . In verse 1*b*, the clause should probably be translated "I am a dinging piece of bronze rather than a joyfully sounding cymbal." The word *chalkos* (raw metal, "bronze"?) never occurs with the meaning of a musical instrument (NRSV: "gong"); a cymbal was usually pleasing, even exciting (*alalazon* = "joyous") to the ears of ancient Greeks as well as to Jews/Israelites, and the particle *ē* can be a comparative.

Paul's recitation of the *acts* of love in verses 4-7 shows how truly remarkable love is, but as he praises love, he blames the Corinthians—two sides of the same rhetorical coin. The positive acts of love are the opposite of the Corinthians' behavior. In being "patient" and "kind" (v. 4*a*), love displays the consideration and generosity toward others that Paul has suggested some of the Corinthians lack (cf. 6:1-8; 8–10). What love avoids absolutely are the negative demeanor and behavior Paul sees in (some of) the Corinthians. All of the eight verbs indicating what love does not do (vv. 4*b*-6) refer directly or indirectly to Paul's criticism of them earlier in the letter. The word "envious" recalls the behavior addressed in chapters 1–4, alluding to 3:3 directly and 1:10-17 indirectly; "boastful" (an unusual term, paralleled in hellenistic-Jewish texts) recalls one of Paul's principal criticisms in chapters 1–4; "arrogant" (or "puffed up") is a direct reference to something he sees at the root of their divisiveness (cf. 4:6, 18, 19; 5:2; 8:1; six of the seven occurrences of the term are in 1 Corinthians); "insist on its own way" recalls what Paul rejects in connection with eating idol-meat in 10:24, 33; and "rejoice in wrongdoing" must allude to what Paul criticizes or charges in chapters 5 and 6. The other unusual verbs, translated "rude," "irritable" or "resentful," allude to the divisiveness and jealousy referred to in chapters 1–4 or to the vindictiveness mentioned in 6:1-8, or both. The style of Paul's *encomium* belies its content. He is not really praising love as a reified ethereal quality.

In the last step of the acts section, verse 7, as in the beginning and end of the comparison section, verses 8*a* and 13, Paul does become more purely rhapsodic. Here his tone is no longer ironic, and he seems to be glorifying the qualities that he himself most values. The repeated "all things" creates the effect. The four verbs form a chiasmus, the middle two ("believes" and "hopes") focused on the future in an intense trust and hope that enables endurance and perseverance ("bears" and "endures") in the present.

The comparison section of the *encomium* (vv. 8-13) continues the criticism of (some of) the Corinthians, framing it with a serious and purely sincere exaltation of love. Paul uses the Corinthians' most valued "spiritual gifts" in his unfavorable contrasts with love:

tongues, *gnōsis,* and probably also prophecy. Mention of the latter first lends some credibility to his statements since, as they well know and as he will make abundantly clear in chapter 14, he himself places great stock in prophecy. Dominating the comparison between love and the Corinthians' spiritual gifts is the contrast between the present and the eschatological future. Paul's previous teaching about "the present form of this world" that "is passing away" (7:31) and "the kingdom of God" (6:10) that will finally be realized at the *parousia* of Christ (15:20-28, 50-57) will have been sufficiently familiar to the Corinthians that he can simply allude to them here.

This contrast between the present conditions of life and the future fulfillment points to the basis of the fundamental misunderstanding between Paul and the Corinthian spirituals. What they value as the most important spiritual teaching and transcendent experience that rescues them from their mundane existence, Paul relativizes as limited and passing, not to be compared with what is to come. What the Corinthian spirituals experience as transcendence in the present, Paul denigrates as partial and elementary. This is seen in his shift of the focus to knowledge and the vision of the divine (vv. 9-12). The Corinthians thought their knowledge was full (6:12; 8:1, 4; 10:1-4), not partial (13:10); and they thought they were "mature" or "perfect," as opposed to being mere children (2:6-3:4)—the opposite of what Paul insinuates in verse 11.

Paul's subversion of the "mirror" image (v. 12) leads us to the essence of the issue of the Corinthian spiritualism he is attempting to counter. For Plato and the Platonic tradition, the mirror symbolized clarity (*Tim.* 72c; Plutarch, *Is. et Os.* 384a; Apuleius, *Apol.* 14). The kind of hellenistic-Jewish devotion to *Sophia* that seems to lie behind Apollos' teaching and the Corinthians' spiritual transcendence understood *Sophia* as "a pure emanation of the glory of the Almighty" and "a spotless mirror of the working of God" (Wis 7:25-26). As the mystical theologian Philo explained, knowledge of God by the rational mind alone is imperfect. Only when the rational mind is expelled by the divine Spirit in an ecstatic prophetic experience does one gain the full vision of God. In the ecstasy of their prophecy and glossolalia the Corinthian spirituals must have been experiencing what they considered a full knowledge or vision of God, made available through their ecstatic knowledge of *Sophia*, the very mirror of God's workings. Paul insisted they defer to the final rhapsody and face-to-face vision of God at the *parousia*. But his main point is that the love in the community that attends to others is the really enduring quality—or relationship—that would continue into the new age when mere spiritual experiences had passed away.

It is not quite clear how verse 13 ends both the paragraph (vv. 8-12) and the whole *encomium*, and why "faith" and "hope" suddenly appear at the end of this praise of "love." "And now" must have a temporal as well as concluding logical force. The present tense "abide" (which, together with "love never ends" in v. 8, brackets vv. 8-13) connotes something present that continues into the future—that is, something that remains, endures, persists on into the kingdom of God. Perhaps the best explanation of "faith, hope, and love" as a triad is their consistent appearance elsewhere at crucial points in Paul's summary exhortations (1 Thess 1:3; 5:8; Gal 5:5-6; Rom 5:1-5). Their presence elsewhere suggests that he commonly referred to them as overlapping and interrelated realities in the life of his assemblies. Since they overlap and interrelate, any schematization oversimplifies. Nevertheless one could think of (a) the *faith* that in the crucifixion and resurrection of Christ God has inaugurated the eschatological events leading to the new age, which enable the present and future life of the faithful; (b) the *hope* that enables the faithful to endure the sufferings and other problems of the continuing old age; and (c) the *love* that faithful have for one another, which holds the community together in anticipation of the completion of God's fulfillment. The greatest is love, because it endures in the solidarity of the community into the kingdom.

Argument for Preferring Prophecy to Tongues (14:1-25)

First Corinthians 14:1 serves as the epilogue of the praise of love, in which Paul, in good encomiast form, exhorts his hearers to imitate the virtue just praised. It also makes the transition into the next main step of the argument, referring back to the topic of "spiritual gifts" begun in 12:1 and picking up again on the exhortation in 12:31. Having redefined "spiritual things" in his own preferred terms of a wide diversity of manifestations of the Spirit given "for the common good" (chap. 12), and having indicated what he means by "building up" the community in his praise of love (chap. 13), Paul is now ready to address more directly the issue raised in the Corinthians' letter. Having just lauded a "more excellent way" in relation to the diversity of manifestations of the Spirit, he now proceeds to apply the latter as a criterion to the principal "spiritual gifts" at issue in the Corinthian community.

The argument in chapter 14 unfolds in clear steps. In 14:2-5 Paul states his main argument, ending with a repetition of his point in verse 5: Prophecy is to be preferred over tongues because, being intelligible, it can edify the community. He illustrates the point in 14:6-12, using himself as a hypothetical (and apologetic?) example, and repeats the main point at the end (v. 12). In 14:13-19 he concedes that tongues may be useful for the community if they are interpreted (v. 13), again uses himself as an example of why (vv. 14-15, 18-19), and yet again articulates the main point about the purpose of the gifts: "in order to instruct others" (v. 19). In 14:20-25 he shifts to an additional argument for prophecy instead of tongues, namely its effect on outsiders.

◊ ◊ ◊ ◊

In 14:1-25 Paul offered a sustained argument that prophecy is preferable to speaking in tongues because, being intelligible, it will edify the community. In the New Testament, the topic of "speaking in tongues" is confined to chapters 12–14 (Acts 2:4, 6, 8, 11 refer to different national languages). Our understanding is thus filtered through Paul's discussion alone. The phrase "speaking in tongues" may be Paul's, influenced from his time in Judea. The Dead Sea Scrolls (1QH 2:18; 4:16) reveal that the priestly-scribal community at Qumran was obsessed with the prophecy about speaking in strange tongues in Isa 28:11-13a, also cited here by Paul (v. 21). Other near-contemporary Jewish communities also knew of a paranormal experience of prayerlike or hymnlike speech uttered to

God in superhuman language, similar to the transcendent experience of what Paul describes as "speak[ing] in the tongues of . . . angels" (13:1). Such a phenomenon appears in the Testament of Job: "[Job's daughter, Hemera] received another heart, no longer to mind the things of earth, but uttered a hymn [to God] in the angelic language" (48:2-3a; cf. 49:2; 50:1a-2; 51:4; 52:7).

In the four main steps of his argument in 14:1-25 Paul characterizes speaking in tongues in four distinctive ways: it is personal speech or prayer to God (and not to other people, v. 2); it is like the indistinct sound of a flute or harp (lyre; v. 7); it is prayer in the spirit but without the mind (vv. 14-15); and it will appear to outsiders as madness (v. 23). It is therefore most suggestive that those very characteristics crop up in discussions of ecstatic prophecy by Philo, in whose writings so many other aspects of the Corinthian spirituals' language and viewpoint are paralleled. His discussions of ecstatic prophecy are invariably focused on a personal religious experience of the divine, not the revelation of a content to be communicated to others. The "prophet" becomes "filled with inspiration," or caught up in "ecstasy, divine possession and madness" *(mania)*. Philo draws some of his terms from a Platonic tradition that was ambivalent about whether the poet's or philosopher's inspiration was a form of possession that replaced the rational mind (*Phaed.* 243e-245c) or a transcendent ascension of the mind, a variation or confusion shared by many cultures. Dominant in Philo's descriptions of ecstatic prophecy, however, is the sense that "reason withdraws" or "the mind is evicted at the arrival of the divine Spirit" (*Heres* 259, 264-65; *Quaes. Gen.* 3.9; *Vita Mos.* 2.188-191). What is emitted, moreover, is vocal but not intelligible. Rather, the divine Spirit "plays upon the vocal organ [as upon a lyre or harp] and raises sounds from it" (*Spec. Leg.* 4.49). Thus (cf. the Corinthians addressed by Paul), only the wise person can be truly God-inspired and "plucked and played invisibly as the vocal instrument of God."

It appears that what Paul labels as "speaking in tongues" strongly resembled what Philo describes as ecstatic prophecy. Paul's strategy is apparently to deemphasize and regulate those aspects of the Corinthians' experience of prophecy that he found problematic (as "speaking in tongues") by advocating cultivation of prophecy as he understood and defined it.

14:2-5: Paul contrasts one who speaks in tongues and one who prophesies in terms of whom they are addressing and the effect (vv. 2-3). He is quite clear that the former "do not speak to other people" but only "to God." Judging from comparative material in Philo, the Corinthians' ecstatic speech was, in effect, communication within the divine world, a sharing in the worship of angel voices taken as an end in itself, the ultimate fruit of their devotion to *Sophia* (cf. Wire 1990, 145). Paul, on the other hand, insists on interpersonal communication, the criterion for which is the effective "hearing" of the hearers, appropriately rendered as "understands" in the NRSV. Paul's explanation is that the speaker in tongues is (literally) "speaking mysteries by a spirit." Whereas "mystery" in the singular has the technical meaning for Paul of "the/an apocalyptic plan of God (for the fulfillment of history)," as in 2:7-8 and 15:51-52 (and Rom 11:25-27), "mysteries" in the plural has the vaguer general sense of secret undiscerned things beyond understanding. Given Paul's other use of "spirit(s)" in the rest of this argument with reference to the spirit(s) of people (his own spirit or the prophets' spirits, 14:14-16, 32), "spirit" here may refer to "one's own spirit" rather than to the Spirit of God (NRSV). The one who prophesies speaks not to God, the source of such communication, but "to other people for their upbuilding," and so forth, the purpose of the various manifestations of the Spirit. Such edification of the whole community is the broader value and purpose that Paul urges upon the Corinthian spirituals in all three of his long arguments in opposition to their excitement about *sophia, gnōsis,* and *pneumatika* as personal possessions (3:10; 8:10; 12:23; 14:3, 4, 5, 12). "Encouragement and consolation" elaborate "upbuilding" (cf. Phil 2:1; 1 Thess 2:12).

The point set up by the contrast in verses 2-3 is explicit in verse 4. In arguing for prophecy over tongues for building up the assembly, Paul does not deny the value for the individual of personal empowerment that such tongues may provide. His concern is simply for the assembly as a whole. Thus in verse 5, as he repeats his main point he can express the genuine wish that all could enjoy tongues—but even more that they could prophesy, and he concedes that speaking in tongues could be useful for the community if only someone would interpret.

14:6-12: This step in the argument is framed as a hypothetical autobiographical illustration, closely linked with the next step, verses 13-19, which is more fully couched in terms of Paul's illustration from his own life and practice. That suggests that this part of the argument is apologetic, serving to explain why he did not emphasize tongues in his mission in Corinth as well as why (uninterpreted) tongues do not contribute to the building up of the assembly.

The obvious criterion for inclusion in the illustrative list of gifts or ways of speaking (v. 6) is intelligibility. The basis of Paul's point, of course, is that they were all recognized as Spirit-inspired, as well. But in addition, what Paul (or others) speak must "benefit" the group, and that is possible only if the utterance is intelligible.

14:7-12: Paul offers a series of analogies in 14:7-11. He picks up the musical instrument metaphor for the sounds emitted in ecstatic prophecy, standard in Philo's discussions, but gives it a distinctive twist: in order to mean anything to anyone else, to communicate anything, the flute or the lyre must give distinct melodies as opposed to indiscriminate sounds. The bugle must give the distinctive battle call or no one would get ready for battle. Verse 9 draws the analogy in terms of "intelligible" speech or of a distinct, recognizable message (*logos* has a wide range of meaning, from "word" to "message," but it always refers to something intelligible). "You will be speaking into the air" probably echoes the futile bugling. Verse 11 refers to what must have been a familiar experience in the cosmopolitan city of Corinth, the hearing of foreigners (literally "barbarians") speaking strange languages in the streets and other public places. At the beginning of verse 12 Paul applies the analogy, "So with yourselves . . . ," but simply assumes the conclusion to be drawn, that their communication must be intelligible to communicate anything worthwhile. He cannot resist mocking their being "zealots for the spirits" (AT), but then redirects the focus to what he insists must be the purpose of their striving: "building up the [assembly]." The term "spirits" (NRSV: "spiritual gifts"), probably refers to their human spirits that are the recipients of the divine Spirit's manifestations, parallel to what Paul writes about his own spirit and their spirits in 14:14-16. Paul is surely playing with the words. The sense is the same as in verse 1, being eager for "spiritual gifts." In accord with the analogies in verses 7-11, their "spirits" should be channeled into intelligible forms of communication such as prophecy (cf. v. 6).

14:13-19: Paul now applies the analogies of 14:6-12 to the meetings of the assembly. His use of his own practice as an illustration means that the apologetic aspect of his argument is far more prominent than it had been in verses 6-12. He is ostensibly encouraging interpretation of tongues for the building up of the community. In effect, he is explaining how tongues do not edify: Speaking in tongues is really prayer and thanksgiving directed to God (v. 2), not to the community. Verses 14-15 must be read together. With verse 14 Paul sets up a hypothetical situation ("for" in the NRSV is not part of the Greek text): "If I pray in a tongue, my spirit prays but my mind is unproductive"—(presumably for others) an unacceptable situation. To the rhetorical question "What should I do then?" (v. 15) he answers with the correction that he will pray and sing with the mind as well as with the spirit. If Philo's descriptions of ecstatic prophecy are any guide to the Corinthians' practices that Paul is addressing, then this is a pointed appeal to them to move their experiences in the Spirit into an intelligible interpretation by "the mind."

Verses 16-17 make clear that the intelligible productivity of the mind is not for personal edification, but for the benefit of others. The statement in verse 17 parallels as well as explains ("for") the statement in verse 16. Hence the "you" saying a blessing in verse 16 is the same as the "you" giving thanks in verse 17, and "anyone in the position of an outsider [idiōtēs]" (v. 16) is the same as "the other person" (v. 17). The context, moreover, is the internal life of the community, as stated implicitly throughout chapters 12–14 and explicitly in 14:1-19; 26-32. Hence "the one in the position of an *idiōtēs*" must refer not to "an outsider" (NRSV) but to someone who, in contrast to the one who prays, is not adept at "speaking in tongues." The claim in verse 18 is surprising considering the apologetic tone of verses 6, 14-15, 19. There can be no question about the continuing vitality of Paul's interaction with and inspiration by the Spirit, in apocalyptic visions or auditions and as the recipient of prophecies and "words of the Lord" (see especially 2 Cor 12:1-10; Gal 1:15-16). The rhetorical function of the hyperbolic declaration here, however, is to set up his main point in verse 19. He too (supposedly) values the personal edification of tongues. Nevertheless "in the assembly" (NRSV: "in church") again shifts the focus away from the individual cultivation of spiritual gifts to the movement and its assemblies. The dramatic contrast articulates his relative valuation.

14:20-25: With the blunt imperatives of verse 20 Paul moves to his second concern about tongues, their effect on outsiders or unbelievers. As in 13:11, he turns against the Corinthians some of their own favorite claims: that they were the mature, as distinct from being babes or children in spiritual matters (see on 2:6–3:4), and that their ecstatic prophecy was a sure indication they had transcended a mundane mode of life. The scriptural passage Paul cites in verse 21 is based on Isa 28:11-12. Citing prophetic texts as from "the law" was simply a habit from his own Jewish background (cf. Rom 3:10-19). He is setting up two applications of the recitation: the "people of strange tongues" are the Corinthians speaking in tongues, and the people God addresses (through those tongues) who do "not listen" are the outsiders or unbelievers who hear them. In verse 22 Paul appears to be reversing a claim by some of the Corinthians that tongues would somehow attract outsiders. Thus his application of the Isaiah prophecy makes two points straightforwardly: that tongues are a sign for unbelievers and that prophecy is a sign for believers. What he means does not become clear, however, until one reads his explanation in verses 23-25, which twists the meaning of his second point. He shows that tongues are a negative or counterproductive sign for outsiders or unbelievers who, upon hearing the Corinthians speaking in tongues, will simply reject them as "out of [their] mind," like the frenzied ecstatic devotees of the cults of Dionysus and Cybele (the Great Mother). In contrast to his discussion of prophecy as directed to the community itself in 14:2-19, however, he now claims that prophecy is a positive and productive sign for "believers" in the sense that when unbelievers hear it, they will be "reproved . . . and called to account," the secrets of their hearts will be disclosed, and they will bow down and worship God. With outsiders, as with members of the community (vv. 2-19), the intelligibility of prophecy makes the difference.

Procedures for Prophesying and Praying in Tongues (14:26-33 [-35])

Moving the focus back to the community itself in 14:26-33, Paul lays down instructions for procedure with prophecy and tongues at gatherings. He concludes the argument of chapters 12–14 with a threat against noncompliance in 14:36-38 and a summary in 14:39-40.

◊ ◊ ◊ ◊

14:26-33: As he shifts the focus to orderly procedure in the meetings (v. 26a), Paul also summarizes his concerns in the whole preceding argument. That when they come together "each one has a hymn, a lesson, a revelation, a tongue, or an interpretation" repeats his dominant point in chapter 12 about diversity of manifestations of the Spirit. That "all things [should] be done for building up" repeats the other main point in chapter 12, the thrust of the praise of love in chapter 13, and the exhortation about the use of tongues in 14:2-19.

While parallel, the instructions respectively for tongues-and-interpretation (vv. 27-28) and for prophecy-and-discernment (vv. 29-31) are also somewhat antithetical, with greater restrictions for tongues. They clearly aim to correct what Paul sees as disorderly practice. Verse 27 implies that many had been speaking in tongues simultaneously at meetings of the assembly (cf. v. 23). Contrary to the spontaneous, contagious flow of "tongues," Paul insists that "only two or at most three" should speak, "each in turn," and with someone interpreting. In fact, if there is no one who can interpret, they should be silent in the assembly and simply "speak to themselves and to God" in private. This is in accordance with what he has said about tongues in the preceding argument (vv. 2, 4, 17). The instructions about prophesying in verse 29 are less restrictive both in tone and substance. Only verse 30 brings any restraint. As long as they proceed one at a time, all can prophesy, "so that all may learn and all be encouraged" (v. 31).

Paul's stress on testing or evaluating prophecies (vv. 29, 32) provides a parallel for his insistence on interpretation of tongues. He had similarly listed "discernment of spirits" among the manifestations of the Spirit in 12:8-10 (but note its absence in 12:28-30 and Rom 12:6-8) because he was attempting to make such manifestations as diverse as possible in order to relativize tongues. However, the testing of prophecies or spirits was not peculiar to Paul's response to the Corinthian situation. In his earliest extant letter, Paul wrote to the Thessalonians, "Do not quench the Spirit. Do not despise prophesies, but test everything; hold fast to what is good; abstain from every form of evil" (1 Thess 5:19-21; NRSV footnote). He appears to be reminding them of something they already supposedly practice. The last two imperatives indicate what is to be done to the results of the testing. In 1 Thess 5:19-21, apparently, anyone in the whole assembly can be involved in the testing. In 1 Cor 14:29 Paul specifies the other prophets, who are potentially anyone. Paul seems to mean that prophecies are to be evaluated on the basis of their content, particularly as it bore on the group's behavior or action to be taken ("hold fast to what is good"). Prior to 1 Corinthians, testing the spirits may simply have been understood as part of prophesying. That two separate steps or gifts are involved may be the result of Paul's response to the Corinthian situation.

Given the known procedure in the Pauline assemblies of "discerning" or "testing" the spirits (12:10; 14:29, 32), the statement that "the spirits of prophets are subject to the prophets" must indicate that inspired divine utterance, working through the "spirits" of the prophets, is under the control of the whole community (represented by those who prophesy) for the sake of the whole community. Verses 32-33 conclude the paragraph introduced in verse 26, implying that tongues are acceptable only when interpreted. The term translated "disorder" in verse 33 means political disorder or party strife, thus almost the opposite of the "building up" that he is pressing upon his readers throughout chapters 12–14. "Peace" is an equally political term, with connotations for Paul of wholeness, but here it counters, even as it recalls (for residents of cities such as Corinth), the Roman imperial peace. "As in all the assemblies [NRSV: churches]" (which belongs with the rest of v. 33) continues the political imagery (the term for the Pauline communities [ekklēsia] being the same as for the civil assemblies of the cities in which they were located). Notably absent from this paragraph in 14:26-33 is any reference to guiding leadership or even a chairperson. The Pauline assembly at Corinth, and presumably those elsewhere, apparently met simply under the guidance of the Spirit. Perhaps that is all the more reason Paul was so concerned that the meetings be orderly.

14:34-35: The sequence of statements silencing women in the assembly are found in two different places in the ancient manuscripts: between 14:33 and 14:36 (NRSV) and after 14:40 (see NRSV footnote). This suggests that they may have been a marginal gloss that was subsequently interpolated into the text at two different places. Although some arguments for or against these statements as an interpolation include verse 33b or verse 36 (the NRSV includes both, along with vv. 34-35, within a parenthesis), there is no basis in the manuscripts for this longer version of an interpolation.

From what is known about the increasingly conservative attitude in the Christian churches toward women's roles in the generations after Paul (e.g., 1 Tim 2:9-15), it is easy to imagine why someone would make such an addition to 14:26-33, 36-40. These sentences silencing women intrude into the argument of chapter 14, which compares prophecy and tongues throughout. They also interrupt the conclusion to the argument in chapters 12–14, which otherwise parallels the conclusion to chapters 1–4, when it cites the situation "in all the assemblies" and pronounces an ominous threat (cf. 14:33, 36-38 and 4:17-21). Moreover, nothing in the intrusive statements has anything to do with the manifestations of the Spirit in the community. Again, the "all" in verses 23-24, 31, and "each one" in verse 26 assume that women pray and prophesy, and the silencing of women contrasts sharply with Paul's more egalitarian formulations about the relative authority and the mutual obligations of husbands and wives (7:1-16). Finally, despite several superficial verbal similarities, there are serious conceptual differences between the statements in verses 34-35 and their context, along with several non-Pauline expressions (e.g., "as the law also says"—without reciting a particular passage). If these statements silencing women and the paragraph in 11:3-16 are both original to 1 Corinthians, then Paul has to be addressing only married women, not all women, in 14:34-35, since in 11:5 he had already implicitly acknowledged that women were active in prayer and prophesying (Schüssler Fiorenza 1983, 230-33).

Threat and Summary (14:36-40)

Here Paul bluntly asserts his authority, together with a threat against noncompliance (cf. 3:15; 4:5, 21; 7:40), and then summarizes the whole argument of chapters 12–14. The two overstated rhetorical questions admonishing the Corinthian spirituals flow directly out of the sanctioning reference to "all the assemblies of the saints" in 14:33: Do they think they have a unique or special revelation that allows them to behave differently from the other assemblies? There is little textual or logical basis for connecting verse 36 with the (interpolated) statements of verses 34-35. Paul asserts his own authority with the same head-on formula he has used earlier (cf. 3:18; 8:2), picking up on one of the Corinthians' favorite self-designations: "Anyone who claims to be a prophet or spiritual . . ." (v. 37a AT; cf. 2:15; 3:1). Far from denying their claim to be prophets and spirituals, Paul is accepting it in order to insist on his own authority. "What I am writing to you is a command of the Lord" (v. 37b) refers to the whole argument in chapter 14, perhaps in chapters 12 and 13 as well. In verse 38, in a calculated oracular form, Paul pronounces judgment against anyone who does not recognize this particular assertion of his authority. Verses 39-40 summarize the argument of chapter 14. The appeal to "be eager to prophesy" is not meant to encourage more spiritual excitement in Corinth, but to press those keen on "tongues" to shift over to the intelligible prophecy that Paul has been advocating throughout this entire section of the letter.

◊ ◊ ◊ ◊

Paul's argument with the Corinthians in chapters 12–14 is a classic conflict between emphasis on individual spirituality and concern for development of community. It also involves two very different responses to social realities that are experienced as life denying and intolerable. As evident in the earlier sections of this letter, it was the Corinthians, not Paul, who cultivated spirituality. The experience of ecstatic prophecy would have been closely connected with the devotion to *Sophia* addressed in chapters 1–2, which had been influenced by hellenistic-Jewish religiosity whose language parallels that of the Corinthian spirituals in many ways: *Sophia* was known as "a spotless mirror of the working of God, and an image of his goodness," one who "passes into holy souls and makes them friends of God, and prophets" (Wis 7:26-27). The only connection that remains unclear is whether the Corinthians who had been caught up in ecstatic prophecy (chaps. 12–14) were the same ones who had experienced spiritual enlightenment in possession of *gnōsis* (chaps. 8–10). Judging from comparative materials, both ecstatic prophecy and spiritual enlightenment were manifestations of devotion to *Sophia,* although perhaps among different persons.

The ecstatic prophecy of the Corinthian spirituals—what Paul calls "(speaking in) tongues"—appears to have involved a transcendent paranormal experience of being caught up in the Spirit that included prayerlike or hymnlike utterances (to God/in the Divine). Paradoxically the experience of transcendence or loss of self in seizure by the Spirit provided the ultimate security for the believer. For the individual, such ecstatic experiences of union with the divine (Spirit) meant periodic and total (if temporary) escape from the troubles of an ordinary, perhaps oppressive and depressing, life.

Such ecstatic experiences and the accompanying behavior may be characterized as "childish" and "madness" by Paul, and as "regressive" by modern psychologists, but such "regression" can be creative. In mystical or spiritual form it can lead to an alternative self or life rooted in the childlike creative energies that have been overlaid or repressed by the social forms and contingencies of oppressive reality. The periodic seeming loss of self can be the means of establishing a new self above the social realities that emasculate, diminish, or deny it. Spiritual experiences like this could transform lives—and not only those of the social elite and economically well-off, such as the hellenistic Jews in Alexandria who joined the Therapeutics.

Studies of those involved in glossolalia in comparable modern circumstances are suggestive. Parallel to the disruption and displacement of people's lives in ancient Corinth, none of the people involved in a poor charismatic group in Mexico City had been born there. The experience of glossolalia transformed their individual lives in a way that was not simply internal or subjective. They would no longer participate in certain economic or social behavior normal in the larger society, such as dancing, drinking, smoking, or cinema, lest they lose their capacity for "tongues." "Afterward I felt strong, and all my problems were forgotten." "In the world one suffers much. But I am happy." Particularly important was the feeling of assurance and security in receiving manifestations of the Spirit, an assurance of eternal life (Goodman 1972, 25-27, 29, 40, 48, 87-89, 94).

Although it was focused on personal transcendence, the Corinthian ecstatic prophecy also involved intensive mutual support. The Corinthians' nascent spiritual identity would have been fragile and virtually unsustainable without regular reinforcement in repeated ecstatic experiences or a withdrawal from the problematic realities or both. The Therapeutics near Alexandria had withdrawn from the "turmoils and disturbances" of urban life to a contemplative monastic community. While the Corinthians enjoyed no such privilege, they did support one another in their common meetings for prayer and prophecy. In his paragraph laying down proper procedures for the gatherings of the whole assembly (14:25-33), Paul indicates that their meetings involved spontaneous outbursts of "tongues" in which several ecstatics prayed simultaneously.

Again, modern group practice of glossolalia is suggestive (see Goodman 1972, 30, 36, 80-81, 88-95). Although speaking "words that you don't understand yet they keep coming" is an individual phenomenon, such experiences usually happen in a small group, often in a worship context. After the first experience or two, subsequent episodes can be initiated with relative ease. Singing or clapping can set the mood. Then some members of the group or a leader pray for supplicants and even move into glossolalia as if providing an example to emulate. Many speak simultaneously in the midst of group prayer. The communities that cultivate such ecstatic speaking are usually small, and the ecstatic experiences provide a powerful cohesive force for the group. To drive another supplicant into trance is a constantly reenacted communal effort. Not surprisingly, of course, the same intense bond that holds the group together sets it off from others, including friends and close associates who may feel acute anxiety or inferiority about not having the gift. Possession of the gift, however, brings prestige in the community; it is proof of one's select status in the eyes of the group. Similarly for the Corinthian spirituals, as the inspired utterance of some drove others into ecstatic speech, they shared the common experience of transcendence in the Spirit. They experienced the dissolution of bodily boundaries that divided them from one another and the social barriers that deprived them of power over their own lives.

As with other aspects of the Corinthian spirituals' devotion to Sophia, the transcendence achieved through ecstatic prophecy broke with, but did not challenge or attempt to change, the dominant societal and cultural patterns. By participating in the inner divine life and attaining intense assurances of immortal life, the individual ecstatic transcended all the problems of an unsatisfying or oppressive social-economic life. Moreover, individual ecstatics benefited from the spontaneous support of others who enjoyed the gift. But the ecstatic prophecy of individuals apparently produced no vision of a life alternative to the one they had transcended, other than periodic inspiration by the Spirit. Modern glossolalists similarly do not usually make any noticeable break with the dominant cultural patterns, even though they depart from particular behavioral standards in their societies. Even the Therapeutics who lived in a monastic community near Alexandria were devoted primarily to individual cultivation of *Sophia* and the periodic rapture attained in divine inspiration (Philo, *Vita Cont.* 12); they had no vision of an alternative society.

By contrast to the transcendent individual spirituality of the Corinthian ecstatics, Paul focused on the life of a community. In his argument about spiritual gifts more than in his other arguments in 1 Corinthians we see the extent to which he emphasized the horizontal human social-political relations rather than the vertical relation of people with God. Judging from his repeated references to them (e.g., Rom 12:6; 15:19; 1 Cor 2:4-5; Gal 3:2-5; 1 Thess 1:5-6; 5:19-22), manifestations of the Spirit, including regular prophesying, must have been a prominent and integral feature of his mission in Corinth as elsewhere. As can be seen in his use of key political terms such as "the common good" and the common political analogy of the "body," the very purpose of the Spirit's workings were political: "To each is given the manifestation of the Spirit *for the common good*" (12:7, emphasis added). Paul thus insisted that spiritual gifts be used for the "building up" of the community. That meant for him that any prophetic manifestation of the Spirit had to be intelligible to the community.

Paul was so concerned that spiritual gifts benefit the community that he attempted to devalue, transform, and blunt the spontaneity of the Corinthians' ecstatic experiences in the Spirit. Clearly he felt that the Corinthian spirituals were overvaluing, even obsessed with, their ecstatic "tongues." It is possible, but not certain, that their excitement over possession of the gift was leaving other members of the assembly feeling spiritually inferior (see especially 14:16). Paul's creative device for taming their "zeal for the spirits" was the invention of a new spiritual manifestation tailor-made for the Corinthian situation: the "interpretation of tongues." He did not forbid, in fact he did not even discourage "speaking in tongues." He simply insisted that ecstatic utterance be transformed into some intelligible message for the community, on the model of a "revelation," "prophecy," "teaching," or statement of *gnōsis*. He did attempt to check the spontaneity of the spiritual ecstasies by prescribing limits on the number and insisting that speakers proceed one at a time, with interpretation. Paul insisted that the personal transcendence and the mutual support of small-group intensity generated by the contagious spontaneity of individual and shared ecstasy yield to the common good of the whole community. Indeed, for Paul mutual exhortation and edification were the general objectives of any communication in the assemblies. The greater gift, the better way, was to manifest mutual caring *(agapē)* in the community.

To note that Paul focuses on community as opposed to individual transcendence, however, does not adequately comprehend his argument on spiritual gifts. In this argument, as elsewhere in 1 Corinthians, Paul insisted that the Corinthian community embody an alternative society over against the imperial order that he believed was "passing away." For Paul it was precisely the "manifestations of the Spirit" that were making the communities of the new age a social-political reality. An international movement of "assemblies" was emerging precisely through the work of apostles, prophets, and teachers (such as himself!) and also through the "gifts of healing," "deeds of power," and various "forms of assistance [and] leadership" in particular local communities (12:9-10, 28). In the prophesying that would build up the assembly (14:4) Paul has in mind the kind of revelation, prophecy, or teaching on which the movement had been founded and nurtured—such as the *apokalypsis* (revelation) in which his own gospel and apostleship was commissioned (Gal 1:16). His conception of his mission and of the movement he was building was rooted in the Jewish apocalyptic tradition of revelations and prophecies through which people discerned how God was fulfilling his purposes in historical affairs despite, or rather against, the domination of empire. This very letter to the Corinthians was a means through which he was attempting to guide one of his assemblies in embodying his vision of a new society.

Particular aspects of Paul's argument in chapters 12–14 indicate some of the ways in which he envisioned his assemblies as an alternative society. Paul's use of the body analogy for the "Christ" movement was the very opposite of "conservative." This extended metaphor/analogy was used by the aristocracy in Rome and other city-states to manipulate the rebellious ordinary people into cooperation and coalescence in times of crisis. But Paul used it in argument against what he saw as a spiritual elite in order to relativize and democratize "manifestations of the Spirit." Paul construed the analogy to emphasize not unity but diversity (in the unity) for the common good. The Corinthian spirituals may not have been oblivious to unity, but theirs would have been a unity of sameness, all experiencing ecstasy of tongues, and a dissolution of embodied difference. Paul advocated embodied difference, an incorporation of diversely gifted and mutually contributing, interdependent, embodied persons. In direct opposition to the dominant aristocratic values and hierarchical order of imperial society, Paul used the body analogy to advocate egalitarian values. In 12:22-24, in particular, he insisted that the "weaker" and "less honorable" and "less respectable" members of the community should be given "greater honor" on the analogy of God's creation of the body. Most important of all was mutual "care for one another" and reciprocal solidarity in suffering as well as in rejoicing (12:25-26)—which was what Paul meant by "love" (chap. 13). Even the rhetorical style of Paul's argument shows how he envisioned his assemblies as an alternative to the dominant order. By suddenly shifting into the *encomium* on "love," he mocked aristocratic culture in its fawning focus on disembodied virtues or etherealized qualities abstracted from concrete social relations—precisely in order to call the Corinthian readers back into the kind of concrete social relations necessary to build up a community of solidarity over against an imperial order that, while "passing away," was still in power.

Despite his insistence on nonaristocratic, egalitarian relations being embodied in the Corinthian assembly as an alternative to the dominant social order, Paul cannot resist asserting his own authority, particularly at the end of arguments or steps in his arguments. After giving an unranked list of manifestations of the Spirit (12:9-10), he pointedly ranked apostles, prophets, and teachers as the most important in "the body of Christ" (12:28), leaving no doubt about who headed up the movement. More ominously, at the end of the whole argument (14:37-38; cf. 4:14-15, 21), he placed anyone who claimed to be a "prophet" or a "spiritual person" on notice that they had better defer to his authority.

It was apparent in chapter 7 that while Paul's rhetoric of equality was unusual in antiquity, he was also capable of using that rhetoric to persuade Corinthian women who had separated from their husbands to limit their newly attained freedom for the sake of their husbands' presumed lack of self-discipline. Yet it is difficult to imagine that the apostle who in chapter 7 took such a subtle approach to talking women out of their newly gained authority over their own bodies would in 14:34-35 be so blatantly authoritarian as to forbid women from speaking in the assembly's gatherings. The statements silencing women are also difficult to square with the important roles that particular women such as Prisca (Priscilla), Phoebe, and Junia played in Paul's own mission in Corinth and elsewhere (cf. Acts 18:2, 26; Rom 16:1-3, 7; 1 Cor 16:19).

If, however, 14:34-35 is taken as an integral part of the argument in chapters 12–14, there are implications for historical reconstruction of the situation in the Corinthian assembly and very serious implications for how Paul is understood. If these verses are really from Paul, then ecstatic prophesying by women was a relatively minor aspect of the practice of "tongues" among the Corinthian spirituals (it was the men involved who were not so easily silenced and required lengthy persuasion). If Paul did write 14:34-35, and was addressing only married women, then while he did not forbid single women who were "holy in body and spirit" (7:34) from prophesying in public gatherings, he nevertheless originated the distinction between unsanctified married women and specially sanctified single women that became important in later Christianity. If Paul himself was commanding all women to be "silent in the assemblies" (Wire 1990, 1994), then it was he who touched off the blatant subordination of women in the churches by subsequent "Paulinists" (e.g., Eph 5:22-24; Col 18; 1 Tim 2:9-15). Whoever may have been responsible for writing these statements silencing women, they came to be understood as Paul's own teaching, from the time Paul's letters were first collected in the ancient church right on up to the present. These statements, along with 11:3-16 and numerous other canonical "Pauline" passages, have formed the basis for the silencing of women in the churches, the assignment of women to secondary status in the life of the churches, and the general subordination of women in patriarchal society.

ARGUMENT(S) FOR THE RESURRECTION (15:1-58)

Paul begins a new argument in 15:1, although it is not clear precisely what the issue is until 15:12: Some of the Corinthians are saying "there is no resurrection of the dead." In his argument for the resurrection of the dead Paul attempts to pull the Corinthian spiritual people into his own eschatological orientation, to fix their eyes on the same goal toward which his whole mission is driven. His argument unfolds with a definite rhetorical strategy. In 15:1-11 he tries to establish a common ground with the Corinthians as a reference point for the rest of his argument. In 15:12-34 he argues the reality of the resurrection of the dead and then in 15:35-57 he explains "with what kind of body" the dead are raised.

Paul's argument here appears to adapt the hellenistic-Roman rhetorical form of *elaboration*. He places the "confirmation" of the rationale (15:1-11) prior to the statement of the "theme" and the "rationale" itself (v. 12), and then provides "elaboration" through several arguments, for example, "from the contrary" (15:13-19) and "from analogy" (15:35-41; Robbins 1996, 56-57). However, both the theme of resurrection of the dead and much of Paul's explanation are rooted in Jewish apocalyptic thought and have no parallel in hellenistic rhetoric. The controlling images and scenarios in 15:20-28 and 15:50-57, in particular, are distinctive to Paul's presentation of his apocalyptic vision of the imminent fulfillment of the eschatological events already set in motion by Christ's crucifixion and resurrection. While the logical reasoning in 15:13-19 is familiar from hellenistic philosophy and key language in 15:42-49—probably from the Corinthians—and is paralleled in hellenistic-Jewish literature, the controlling framework is Paul's apocalyptic orientation. The argument begins, moreover, with the citation of a pre-Pauline creed, which exhibits the compact language and parallel clauses that are typical of such materials.

Christ's Resurrection (15:1-11)

In this opening paragraph Paul attempts to establish ostensibly common ground with the Corinthians by reciting an already formulated creed that he had "handed on" to them. He begins on an entirely positive note, building up the importance of their standing firm in and being saved by the gospel, rhetorically giving them the benefit of the doubt before remarking on the serious implications of their denial that the dead will be raised (vv. 12-19). Coming immediately after his admonitions concerning the Corinthians' excitement over their own reception of revelations directly from the Spirit, his emphasis on himself as the conduit of the gospel by which they are saved, stacked up in six additional clauses (vv. 1b-2), is striking. Using what had become almost technical terms for the transmission of creeds and formulae basic to the movement (cf. those introducing the "words of institution" in 11:23), Paul reminds the Corinthians that he had presented to them the basic gospel that had preceded his own ministry and was shared by the movement generally (v. 3a).

The pre-Pauline "creed" cited in verses 3b-5 has a balanced four-line structure:

Christ died for our sins in accordance with the scriptures,
he was buried,
he was raised on the third day, in accordance with the scriptures
he appeared to Cephas, then to the twelve.

Paul adds emphasis to each assertion by prefacing each line with "(and) that." This four-line formula is more elaborate than other early formulae, and may have developed from a simpler antithesis of "died-rose" (e.g., Acts 17:3; 2 Cor 5:15b; 1 Thess 4:14; Rev 2:8). The expansion from "died" to "for our sins" may be influenced by early formulae of "Christ died for . . ." (e.g., Rom 5:8; 1 Cor 8:11; Gal 1:4) or from application to Christ's death of the "for you" in the "words of institution" (see on 11:24 above) or both. The second line of this creed serves to verify the reality of Christ's death, while the fourth line serves to verify the reality of his resurrection. Most of the language is non-Pauline ("for our sins," "in accordance with the scriptures," "buried," "raised," "the third day," and "the twelve"). "In accordance with the scriptures" (lines 1 and 3) probably refers to the Jewish Scriptures generally, and pertains to the whole clause, not simply to "died" or "for our sins" or to "was raised" or "on the third day."

Paul has included this creed in order to mention the witnesses who can attest Christ's resurrection (v. 5), which is the basis on which he will proceed to argue for the resurrection of the dead. The absence of women witnesses in this early creed suggests that others before Paul were conforming even fundamental formulae to more conventional patriarchal cultural forms. The unanimity of the Gospels (e.g., Mark 16:1-8; John 20:1-18) on the other hand, indicates that in the early Palestinian gospel traditions women were not only witnesses but the first witnesses to the resurrection appearances of Jesus. In verses 6-7 Paul expands the traditional list of witnesses, partly on the basis of traditions about Jesus' appearances. The key terms are Pauline ("more than," "still alive," "died"), and none of them is used elsewhere in fixed traditional formulae. By mentioning the "more than five hundred brethren" (NRSV: brothers and sisters), adding pointedly, "most of whom are still alive," Paul emphasizes the credibility of Christ's resurrection: Plenty of witnesses are still around! In adding "all" to "the apostles" (v. 7) he is surely distinguishing them as a larger, more inclusive group of witnesses to Jesus' resurrection than "the twelve" mentioned in the tradition (v. 5).

Paul includes himself in the list of witnesses in 15:8, presumably on the basis of the revelation he had of the exalted Lord commissioning him as an apostle (Gal 1:16). Beginning with the phrase "as to one untimely born," however, Paul—mindful of his critics in Corinth—broadens his agenda from resurrection witnesses to yet another self-deprecatory defense of his own apostolate. He acknowledges that he is not only the last but also "the least of the apostles" and "unfit" even to be called an apostle (v. 9; cf. his continuing self-defense in 2 Cor 2:16; 3:5-6). His previous persecution of God's assembly is his own obsession, which he understands as an amazing manifestation of God's grace in transforming an enemy into an apostle (see Gal 1:13-15; cf. Phil 3:6-8). That God's grace was not "in vain" is demonstrated, he says, by the fact that he "worked harder" than others in his mission (v. 10). In verse 11 Paul moves back to his main purpose in citing the common creed and expanding the list of resurrection witnesses. Since this basic gospel is common to all apostles, who were themselves witnesses of the resurrection, it is incumbent on the Corinthians to stand in it and to hold firmly to it.

The Reality of the Resurrection (15:12-34)

Paul argues the reality of the resurrection of the dead in three steps. In 15:13-19 he demonstrates the absurdity, even futility, of working from the premise of those who deny the resurrection of the dead. In 15:20-28 he argues the reality of the resurrection of "those . . . who have fallen asleep in Christ" on the basis of Christ's resurrection from the dead. And in 15:29-34 he argues for the resurrection of the dead from the practice by some Corinthians of being baptized for the deceased and from the goal of his own struggles.

◊ ◊ ◊ ◊

15:12-19: Paul's arguments for the resurrection of the dead and how to understand its reality will become clearer if we can glean some sense of what the Corinthians meant by saying "there is no resurrection of the dead." The interpretation of 1 Corinthians, as a whole, as Paul's response to an "(over)realized eschatology," so prominent in the last generation, was based on a misreading of 15:12 along with 4:8. This reconstruction projects back into the earliest community at Corinth the much later "false teaching" of Hymenaeus and Philetus that "the resurrection has already taken place" (2 Tim 2:17-18). But 4:8 provides no parallel to 2 Tim 2:18. The "already" in 4:8 is part of Paul's framing of the Corinthians' language of exalted spiritual status in terms of his own historical-eschatological perspective (see on 4:8-13). If the Corinthians were saying "the resurrection has already taken place," then it is difficult to understand why Paul, otherwise so well-informed about their favorite terms and general viewpoint, would have cited their position on this issue as "there is no resurrection of the dead." Most significantly, in 15:13-34 he presents an argument for the *reality* of the resurrection (against *its* denial), not an argument that the resurrection is still in the future (against a view like that in 2 Tim 2:18). The "(over)realized eschatology" interpretation of the Corinthians' view also segregates the denial of the resurrection from the other Corinthian positions Paul argues against earlier in the letter. It cannot be coordinated with the slogans in 6:12-13, the principle in 7:1, the statements of *gnōsis* in 8:1, 4, or even the Corinthians' terms that Paul borrows later on in his argument in 15:44-49.

The Corinthians' denial of the resurrection of the dead can, however, be correlated with the Corinthian principles and positions Paul argues against earlier in the letter. As reconstructed in this commentary, the views of the Corinthian spiritual people were similar to those expressed in the Wisdom of Solomon and by Philo. Paul's full citation of the Corinthian position should be taken seriously: "there is no resurrection *of the dead.*" It is surely significant that "the dead" occurs repeatedly in this two-stage argument (eleven times in 15:12-34; three more times in 15:35-52), whereas Paul's own term for the deceased is "one who has/those who have fallen asleep" (e.g., 7:39; 11:30; 15:6, 18, 20; 1 Thess 4:13, 14, 15). In certain hellenistic circles, including the hellenistic-Jewish philosophy represented by Philo, "the dead" *(ho nekros)* referred to the body as a "corpse," in distinction from the soul (mind or spirit), which was the true self and principle of its continuity. Centuries earlier, in a famous play on words, Plato had articulated a view that had become widespread in the culture: "The *sōma* is the *sēma* of the *psychē*," that is, "the body is the prison of the soul." Hellenistic-Jewish piety such as that expressed in the Wisdom of Solomon and Philo had long since assimilated such views of the soul (mind/reason) and the body from the general culture. Thus "Solomon," who has achieved true kingship, wealth, and immortality/incorruptibility in his devotion to *Sophia* (= Spirit), who passes into souls and makes them prophets, holds that the "perishable body weighs down the soul" (Wis 9:15; cf. 6:17-21; 7:8-14, 21-27).

Philo's description of the Therapeutics is particularly striking. Among them are elderly "virgins" who spurn pleasures of the body because of their devotion to *Sophia*. Seeking secure knowledge under the tutelage of *Sophia* and caught up in heaven-sent ecstatic prophecy, they have such an intense longing for "the immortal and blessed life" that they think of their "mortal life as having ended" (*Vita Cont.* 10-13, 18-20, 68). Similarly, the very Corinthians who had achieved high spiritual status (as powerful, wealthy, of noble birth, mature, and so forth) in their close relationship with *Sophia* (1:26; 2:6; 4:8, 10), who were avoiding sexual relations (7:1, 5), who possessed knowledge (8:1, 4), and who were caught up in ecstatic prophecy (chap. 14), had transcended matters of the body. They apparently did not view the body as evil ("the stomach [is meant] for food," 6:13), but simply as mortal, and as transcended ("it is well . . . not to touch," 7:1). The idea of a resurrection of the body that was "dead" (a corpse) was probably not repugnant to the Corinthians; it just made no sense to them.

Moreover, the problem behind 15:12, can be understood only superficially in terms of a Corinthian development of what Paul had taught. As discussed in the introduction, Paul's mission in Corinth involved an outsider addressing the Corinthians from a standpoint different in key ways from the hellenistic culture and understanding of reality into which the Corinthians had been socialized. If statements like those of the creed cited in verses 3*b*-5 were heard without the Palestinian Jewish apocalyptic (historical-eschatological) orientation in which the general resurrection of the dead was intelligible, the idea of the resurrection of Jesus would have been somewhat vague, susceptible of assimilation into another perspective or worldview.

In the first of three steps by which he argues for the reality of the resurrection of the dead in 15:13-19, Paul formulates the Corinthians' position as a foil in order to demonstrate its ostensibly disastrous implications. This step is a clever use of an "argument from the contrary," which draws a conclusion from certain premises. It seems doubtful, however, that the Corinthian spirituals would have understood, let alone shared, the Palestinian Jewish concept of the general resurrection on which the argument depends. Here and throughout the rest of chapter 15, moreover, Paul uses "the dead" to refer to deceased embodied persons, attempting to replace the Corinthians' understanding of "dead" as referring only to the body as separate from the soul or true self.

Paul states the basic argument in two brief steps in 15:13-14: If there is no general resurrection of the dead, then Christ cannot have been raised. If Christ has not been raised, then both the gospel he preached and the Corinthians' response in faith (see vv. 1-2, 3-8) are in vain. Verses 15-17 are best understood as expansions, in reverse order, of the double implication stated in verse 14b, with repetition of the same logical steps as in verses 13-14a. Not only had Paul and the other apostles been preaching "in vain"; if there is no such thing as resurrection of the dead, they had even been "misrepresenting God" as having raised Jesus (v. 15). Furthermore, the Corinthians themselves would still be in their sins and those who have fallen asleep in Christ have perished (15:17b-18). The point of this step in the argument is to demonstrate the disastrous consequences of the Corinthians' denial of the resurrection of the dead. From Paul's point of view, their premise is false; or more precisely, unacceptable. The concluding sentence drives home the point: We are utterly deluded, "of all people most to be pitied," if the hope we have staked in Christ is for this life only, and not for the new age, the resurrection life (v. 19).

15:20-28: Having demonstrated that the Corinthians' premise of no resurrection of the dead is false and unacceptable, Paul proceeds with the second step in his argument for the resurrection. His own premise is the basic gospel of the resurrection of Christ, witnessed and preached by all the apostles. The opening statement that "in fact Christ has been raised from the dead" (v. 20) directly counters the opposite premise in verses 14a and 17a. This is the last reference to Christ's resurrection, but the whole subsequent argument depends upon it. In the Jewish apocalyptic metaphor of final fulfillment, once the firstfruits are ripe, then the rest of the harvest is absolutely certain and soon to follow. Since Christ has been raised, the resurrection of the dead has begun and its completion will follow inevitably in a sequence of final events.

In 15:21-22 Paul restates the point in schematic, almost formulaic clauses (note the word order and lack of verbs in the Greek):

> For since through man death,
> also through man resurrection of the dead.

Already in 15:21-22 Paul is surely responding to a Corinthian distinction between a heavenly type of man and an earthly type of man, as he does more elaborately in 15:45-49. The idea of a "man . . . from the earth" (v. 47) derived from the account of the creation of "man(kind)" in Gen 2:7, and the idea of a "man . . . from heaven" (v. 47) probably derived from the other creation account in Gen 1:26-27 (see below on vv. 44-49). The Corinthians were probably using the generic Greek term for "man," *anthrōpos* (from the text of the biblical creation accounts), in reference to a higher or a lower type of people or both. Paul is thus picking up their (archetypal) term, casting it twice in an instrumental role, with reference first to death and then to resurrection of the dead. With verse 22 he quickly clarifies what he means in his own distinctive historical-eschatological statement, a sweeping overview of all history from Adam to Christ's *parousia*. If the Corinthians understood "man" as a type of humanity, Paul used the term for the historical figures who took the first, decisive action in two successive eras of history, although he does not elaborate. The "all will be made alive" probably has the overtone of all in the movement, given the overall eschatological context (see 15:50-57). The virtual personification of Death is rooted in Paul's apocalyptic worldview, in which superhuman forces are battling with God for control of society and history as well as individual lives (cf. Rom 5:12-21; Rev 6:8).

Verses 23-28 further explain the implications of the statements in 15:22. The long sentence in verses 23-24 (divided into two in the NRSV) restates basically the same two-step sequence as in verse 22, with "each in *his own* order: Christ the first fruits" (emphasis added), meaning the harvest has already begun, and then "those who belong to Christ," who are therefore sure to follow when the harvest is completed "at his [*parousia*]" (v. 23). Verses 23-28 should not be read in terms of an elaborate "apocalyptic order" involving a sequence of many different events (*contra* Conzelmann 1975, 270). The Greek term *tagma* translated as "order" in verse 23 indicates not a chronological sequence but a "division," as in a body of soldiers, or "order" in the sense of rank. Verse 24 begins with a weaker "then" (in Greek) than the "then" in the preceding clause ("then . . . those who belong to Christ," 23*b*). Thus verse 24 presents not so much another step in a sequence as an explanation of what will be happening when the resurrection is completed with "those who belong to Christ" at his *parousia*. The latter is "the end" in the sense of *the goal* (Greek *telos*), *not* "the end" in the sense of a termination or the "cosmic catastrophe." The two temporal clauses ("when . . . ," "after . . .") in verse 24 must be meant in apposition with "the goal," with the second clause subordinate to the first: Christ, who has been reigning since his resurrection and exaltation, will hand the kingdom over to God the Father "after he has destroyed every ruler and every authority and power," which is the purpose of his reign. The terms "every ruler" and "every . . . power" are political. Although they are not as particular here as the "rulers" who doomed themselves in crucifying Christ in 2:6-8, they are the imperial political institutions with superhuman power, not simply "demons" in a heavenly or spiritual realm (*contra* Conzelmann 1975, 272).

Verses 25-28 explain not only the implication of verse 24, but also what the resurrection of the dead means ultimately. The "must" in verse 25 translates the verb *dei*, which indicates what is necessary in God's apocalyptic plan. Paul also briefly cites two messianic psalms (Pss 8:6; 110:1), which are introduced by "for" in verses 25 and 27*a* respectively. A special problem in these sentences is whether the subject of "put all his enemies under his feet" (v. 25) and of "put all things in subjection under his feet" (v. 27*a*) is Christ or God. The key to reading the argument is verse 26, where Paul is still explaining his assertion in verse 21 that "the resurrection of the dead has also come through a human being." In verse 26 Paul finally proclaims that "death," which came through Adam (vv. 21-22), is "destroyed" as "the last enemy." Since Christ is clearly the reigning royal agent who destroys every ruler and power (v. 24), it is reasonable to understand Christ as the agent in verse 25. The citation of part of verse 1 of the "messianic" Psalm 110 (v. 25) provides a scriptural warrant as a bridge to the destruction of death: "For he [Christ] must reign until he [Christ] has put all his enemies under his feet." The citation of Ps 8:6 (v. 27a) immediately after the assertion that the last enemy, Death, is being destroyed, provides further scriptural explanation or proof. "For 'he [Christ] has put all things in subjection under his feet' " (NRSV footnote). That is what has already been set in motion with the resurrection of Christ, "the first fruits" of the resurrection of the dead. The resurrected Christ is now implementing God's "necessary" plan ("must," v. 25) of subjecting "all enemies/things."

But Paul's apocalyptic scenario is not quite completed, and he realizes that his recitations of messianic psalms may be confusing. He therefore explains that "when it [scripture] says, 'All things are put in subjection,' " this does not include God, who is ultimately "the one who put all things in subjection under him" (v. 27b). In verse 28 Paul finally explains how Christ's destruction of every power is related to his handing over of the kingdom to God (v. 24), the two subjections that will happen at "the end." He thus concludes his apocalyptic scenario with a distinctive image surely meant to designate agency and goal more than metaphysical existence: "so that God may be all in all." This conception of God as the sole, ultimate principle may also be directed against the Corinthian spirituals' focus on *Sophia,* whom they apparently viewed as both the efficient and formal cause of (creation and) salvation (see above on 8:6).

15:29-34: In the third step of his argument for the resurrection of the dead, Paul returns to a focus on the Corinthians' premise (see vv. 29b, 32b). In three seemingly unrelated steps signaled by sudden changes from third person to first to second, he proceeds first by posing rhetorical questions (vv. 29, 30-32) and then by admonishing the Corinthians with sharp imperatives (vv. 33-34).

Those "who receive baptism on behalf of the dead" (v. 29) appear to be the Corinthians who were baptized vicariously on behalf of deceased friends or relatives. It is clear from 1 Cor 1:13-17 that some members of the Corinthian assembly were keen on baptism of some sort. It also seems clear from the language in 10:1-4, and from Paul's sharp reaction to it in 10:5-13, that some Corinthians understood the Exodus narrative in explicitly spiritualizing terms, apparently even as a "baptism in the cloud and sea" (cf. 10:1-2). As noted above, hellenistic-Jews such as Philo understood the cloud and rock and the spiritual drink as *Sophia,* and the Exodus through the sea as the freeing of the soul from the body involving the agency of *Sophia* (the cloud). It is tempting to conclude, by analogy, that certain Corinthians viewed baptism as a rite that freed soul from body or from mortal corruptible realities in general, and that involved the agency of *Sophia.* Given the widespread standard cultural understanding of the relation of soul and body, it would have been only a logical extension to bring the benefits of a new teaching and ritual of *Sophia* to the souls of deceased friends or relatives by means of vicarious baptism. Paul appeals to just such an understanding of baptism in his argument. That is, he appeals to the common ground of expectation of some sort of life after death for which he sees evidence in their belief that they can generate a future or continuing life for the deceased through their ritual of vicarious baptism.

Moving again to his own hardships in (vv. 30-32; cf. 4:11-13; 9), he develops another argument from his own motivation to persist in his work in the face of danger and death. It is unclear just what connection he is making between his daily facing of death and his "boasting" (v. 31). The latter is apparently about the Corinthians, perhaps in the sense that their existence as part of his labors means that his struggles are not in vain (vv. 9-10). Far clearer is his reference, in a metaphor standard in hellenistic moral teaching, to having "fought with wild animals at Ephesus" in (v. 32). In 16:9 he refers to the "many adversaries" who had opposed him in Ephesus, the city in which he is writing this letter. His citation of Isa 22:13 (v. 32*b*) provides both a contrast to his own daily facing of death (in the confidence that there is a resurrection) and a transition to the ethical admonition in the next section.

The sharp imperative in verse 33 repeats similar warnings in 3:18 and 6:9, which were related to his objections to wisdom and wrongdoing, respectively. That he ends his argument for the reality of the resurrection of the dead with this abrupt and pointed moral admonition indicates that he sees a connection between the Corinthians' keen interest in *Sophia,* their ethical behavior, and their denial of the resurrection. In the well-known epigram "bad company ruins good morals" the plural term translated "company" (Gk. *homiliai),* would also have meant "speech(es)" or conversation. Paul is almost certainly casting aspersions on the "bad conversations" of *gnōsis* that accompany the Corinthians' "bad relationships" with *Sophia.* He views these as having a corrupting effect, leading them both to deny the resurrection of the dead and to problematic behavior. As at the end of the arguments in chapters 1–4 and 12–14, he closes with sharply ironic language in (v. 34): Sober up, as if from a drunken stupor. Further, he accuses those who claim to be full of *sophia* and *gnōsis* of having "no knowledge of God." Finally, he makes all this an admonition—and accusation—"to your shame"! (cf. 6:5).

The Manner of the Resurrection (15:35-58)

Paul's explanation of how the dead are raised also proceeds in three steps, with the second flowing directly into the third. In 15:35-41 he uses analogies from seeds and heavenly bodies as a basis for imagining the reality of the resurrection body. In 15:42-49, he borrows heavily from the Corinthians' own favorite terminology, some of which is already familiar from discussion of other issues, to present a picture of the resurrection body, now focusing more heavily on Adam and Christ as the historical and eschatological prototypes. In 15:50-57 this discussion flows into an almost ecstatic recitation of an apocalyptic "mystery" of the resurrection and the eschatological victory over death itself, an epilogue for the entire argument from 1:10 through 15:57.

◊ ◊ ◊ ◊

15:35-41: In posing the question in terms of "what kind of body," Paul speaks directly to the crux of the Corinthians' skepticism. By focusing on the body as the principle of continuity in the future transformation, he also casts the issue in his own terms and worldview. He could not conceive of people as disembodied, hence the continuity of human life required body. For him, apparently, resurrection life would be social-political, requiring embodied people.

With the hypothetical questions and his own response, Paul continues the sharp rhetorical attack with which he ended the previous section. The interlocutor's questions are almost mocking in their challenge (cf. the similar use of "how" [pōs], in 14:7, 9, 16). "Fool!" (v. 36) is a most severe put-down for those who had only recently become "wise."

The reference to the sowing of seed (v. 37) directs the questioner's attention to his or her own experience of nature, which was regarded as the source of wisdom in the (Jewish) wisdom tradition. The analogy of the sown seed that dies but then comes to new life was an appropriate choice given that the Corinthians seem not to have believed that a corpse—not part of the person's true self— could be resurrected. By means of this analogy Paul inserts the body as the principle of continuity *and* focuses on the future body to be taken by the new life that comes from the sown seed. The pointed adjective "naked" in the "bare seed" (NRSV) is surely an allusion to how the Corinthians viewed a soul that had achieved immortality, except that Paul uses the term for the seed/body that dies (see the continuation of the issue in 2 Cor 5:1-5). Paul's mention of different kinds of seeds ("perhaps of wheat or of some other grain," v. 37) sets up his point about different kinds of bodies in verse 38. Most important for drawing the analogy with resurrection is the introduction of God as the causative agent who gives the body to the sown seed. With the statement that each kind of seed has its own distinctive body, in verse 38, Paul sets up his move both to the different kinds of flesh (v. 39) and, in a further extension of the analogy, to different kinds of "bodies" and different kinds of "glories" related to those bodies (vv. 40-41). It is surely significant that the different kinds of bodies Paul mentions are precisely those of the creation in Gen 1. It may also be significant that he works in the radiant heavenly bodies, which in traditional Jewish apocalyptic literature were the key symbols for the martyrs raised to new life (e.g., Dan 12:1-3; 2 *Apoc. Bar.* 51:10). In this step of his argument, he is driving toward the distinction between the two different kinds of bodies and their glory, earthly and heavenly, which forms the center of the elaboration of different kinds.

15:42-49: Paul applies the analogies directly to the resurrection of the dead (vv. 42-44). In each of four parallel pairs of clauses he repeats the metaphor of the sown seed ("it [or "what"] is sown") and applies it to resurrection ("it is raised"), using antithetical terms. The antithesis of "perishability-imperishability/perishable-imperishable," distinctive in Paul's correspondence to precisely this context and the next paragraph (vv. 50, 52-54), must be from the Corinthians. The other three sets of antitheses are also borrowed from the Corinthians. The contrast between *psychikos-pneumatikos* (NRSV: "physical," "spiritual") is familiar from 2:13-15. "Weakness" versus "power" picks up on both Paul's comparison of himself with their transcendence (4:10) and on their high spiritual attainment in contrast with their social-economic origins (1:26-27). Finally, the contrast between "dishonor" (shame) and "glory" (honor) *(atimia-doxa)* refers clearly to their being "held in honor" versus Paul's "disrepute" *(endoxoi-atimoi,* 4:10), except that for Paul "glory" had connotations of the radiance of the resurrected ones, particularly in a Jewish apocalyptic context (Dan 12:1-3; 2 *Apoc. Bar.* 51:10).

Paul, however, is forcing the Corinthian language into new applications, a different pattern of meaning. For the Corinthians, *perishability* characterized the body while *imperishability* characterized the soul. He begins in verse 42b with what would have been for the Corinthian spirituals a conceptual jolt, that the "dead/corpse," which is *by nature* "perishable," could be raised in "imperishabiiity" (an idea he repeats three times in vv. 50-54). In verse 43, he applies and defers to the future the glory (honor) and power that (some of) the Corinthians claim to have realized spiritually in their exalted individual transcendence. The statement in verse 44a, also a virtual contradiction in terms to the Corinthians, explicitly applies their distinction between two types of people

(= souls/minds), *psychikos* (NRSV: "physical") and *pneumatikos* (NRSV: "spiritual"), to the historical body and the resurrection body, respectively. The *psychikos* type of soul, of course, was still only at an intermediate stage precisely because of its continuing association with the body. But the unprecedented idea of a "spiritual body," especially, must have been an utter oxymoron, as indicated by Paul's further explanation that "if there is a physical body, there is also a spiritual body" (v. 44).

Perhaps this oxymoron was precisely Paul's point—and why he dwells on the idea, twisting the Corinthians' terms and soteriological conceptualization into his own historical-eschatological orientation. Several key aspects of the issue engaged here are evident even from analysis of the text of verses 44-47, particularly once we realize that the *psychikos-pneumatikos* distinction was central to the Corinthian spirituals' newfound sense of transcendent identity. (1) The distinction of the two types of "man" is related to (rooted in) a typological reading of the creation of Adam in Gen 2:7, which Paul cites in verse 45. (2) The *psychikos* man is connected with Gen 2:7 (note "a living being *[psychē]*," v. 45), while the *pneumatikos* has no basis in that text. (3) Given the statement that "we have borne the image of the man" (v. 49), it would appear that Gen 1:26-27 must have played a role in the distinction. (4) Paul's pointed insistence on the priority of the *psychikos* before the *pneumatikos* (v. 46) indicates that for the Corinthians the *pneumatikos* must have held a priority of some sort over the *psychikos*.

The hellenistic-Jewish literature that has helped elucidate other aspects of the Corinthians' language of spirituality and praxis again proves helpful. Although Philo does not use the actual terms *pneumatikos* and *psychikos,* he cites repeatedly as an accepted idea a fundamental distinction between two types of "man" (soul or mind): the "heavenly" who, in Gen 1:26-27, was made in the image of God, as opposed to the "earthly man" who, in Gen 2:7, was made from earth and remained associated with earthy realities (e.g., *Op. Mundi.* 134; *Leg. All.* 1.31, 53, 88-95; 2.4). The only thing missing in Philo is the contrasting set of terms, *pneumatikos* and *psychikos,* which the Corinthians used in reference to much the same distinction of two types of "man" (soul/mind). It is clear, moreover, that the two "men" in Philo's discussions are paradigms or types of minds or souls. He exhorts intelligent souls to follow the model of the "man" made "after the (divine) image," while contrasting the lower type, "the earthly mind called Adam," to those who belong to the higher type, "the truly alive who have *Sophia* for their mother" (*Heres* 52-53). Not surprisingly, the distinction between "heavenly man" and "earthly man" as types of minds/souls is virtually interchangeable and synonymous with the distinction between the "perfect" *(teleioi)* and the "children" *(nēpioi)*, who represent, respectively, the advanced and the beginning stages in *sophia*. Particularly significant is the light Philo sheds on the priority issue. He writes of the "heavenly man" as having come into existence earlier or first, and of the "earthly man" as the "second man" (*Op. Mundi.* 134; *Leg. All.* 2.4-5). Yet the narrative or temporal sequence is almost incidental to a more fundamental sense of priority. Philo is asserting the ontological priority of the "heavenly man" to the "earthly man," a priority of origin and value.

From analysis of the text itself and a comparison with the Philonic analogy to the Corinthians religiosity and worldview, it is clear that Paul is drawing heavily from their language in 15:44-49. He does not mention Christ anywhere in this paragraph, which is unusual for Paul. Rather, he couches virtually everything in the Corinthians' term. Yet he does make subtle but key changes that indicate that his own historical-eschatological orientation still determines the pattern of thought. Thus he refers to "the first man, Adam" and "the last Adam" (v. 45) as individual historical figures, not as universal/spiritual archetypes. And coming from Paul, the statement that "the second man" is "from heaven" (v. 47) is an unmistakable reference to Christ's *parousia*. His emphasis clearly falls on the historical-eschatological sequence of the two men. He is not simply reversing the priority or value ("heavenly/spiritual" *vs.* "earthly/physical") of the two (types of) "men," as understood by the Corinthian spirituals. He is, rather, asserting a different kind of priority, according to the historical-eschatological pattern of thinking that he insists upon in chapter 15. Once that historical-eschatological sequence is established in verse 46, Paul then in verses 47-49, simply uses the Corinthians' terms for their transcendent spiritual status to characterize the resurrection reality, but now without the term "body." It is interesting that he is now speaking not just of those who will be resurrected but in inclusive terms of "we," even before he launches ecstatically into the "mystery" in the next paragraph.

15:50-58: Paul begins the final step in this argument with an indication that he is about to speak emphatically (v. 50a): "Flesh and blood cannot [are not able to] inherit the kingdom of God" (v. 50b). In the parallel statement (v. 50c) he again speaks the Corinthian pneumatics' language, ostensibly telling them exactly what they want to hear (the perishable [body/corpse] will not inherit the imperishable [quality of the transcendent soul]), but also setting up his final affirmation of the resurrection body (vv. 53-54).

Suddenly in verse 51 he launches into his own distinctive apocalyptic vision (vv. 51-52). As in 2:6-8, he identifies what he is about to relate as a "mystery," the Jewish apocalyptic term for God's plan of fulfillment hidden from the world but revealed to the assembly. His tone suggests intense excitement about the final transformation. "We" includes those who are still alive, as well as "the dead" who are to be resurrected. Since the final events are imminent, "we will not all die." Rather, in moving into the heightened reality of the new age, "the kingdom of God," "we will all be changed." The phrases "in a moment, in the twinkling of an eye" indicate how suddenly, instantaneously this will happen. "The last trumpet," used widely in Israelite and Judahite prophecy to signal decisive or final events, was commonly mentioned in Jewish apocalyptic literature as heralding the time of judgment or transformation into the new age. A comparison of verses 51-52 with 1 Thess 4:15-17 indicates that the "mystery" and "word of the Lord" revealed to and through Paul are particular to the specific situations in the Corinthian and Thessalonian assemblies, respectively. These were not set pieces, but new, ad hoc revelations, directed precisely to distinctive situations. In contrast with 1 Thess 4:15-17, Paul does not explicitly mention, let alone elaborate on, the *parousia* of the Lord in 15:51-52. Here he emphasizes the suddenness rather than the sequence, focusing on the general transformation rather than offering assurance that the dead in Christ will be raised first.

In verses 52*b*-53, Paul explains the "mystery" of sudden transformation, once more picking up the Corinthians' contrast between "perishable" and "imperishable," "mortal" and "immortal" (cf. v. 54*a*). In verses 53-54, after avoiding the term since verse 44, he again mentions the "body." Four times in successive phrases he refers to "this perishable/mortal *body*." The verb, "to put on"—literally, "to be clothed with"—is another standard apocalyptic image (cf. *1 Enoch* 62:15): By saying that the *body* becomes clothed with imperishability and immortality Paul is intentionally addressing and blocking the idea that the soul becomes disembodied when it takes on immortality. As is clear from his later attempt to speak to the same issue in 2 Cor 5:4, the sense here in verses 53-54 is that embodied people are not to be "unclothed" but further "clothed." In these sentences Paul is again speaking in what would be oxymorons to the Corinthians, collapsing what were standard distinctions not simply for them but for much of hellenistic culture in general, between the mortal/perishable and the immortal/imperishable. Here at the very end of his argument on the resurrection it is clear just how much Paul is insisting on his own historical-eschatological orientation.

The statement about the mortal body being at last clothed with immortality leads into an exultant acclamation of victory over Death and a direct taunting of the vanquished enemy (vv. 54-55). "The saying" Paul cites is a composite of Isa 25:8 (25:7 in NRSV) and Hos 13:14. The line from Isa 25:8 is used in keeping with its biblical context: On the final day of international deliverance, God "will swallow up death forever." Paul may have known the Isaianic prophecy in a form that included "victory," and may then himself have inserted "victory" into the Hos 13:14 prophecy (replacing "penalty"). He enhances the triumphant exultation over the personified "Death" by substituting "death" for "grave" in the second line and setting the defeated enemy in the vocative, "O Death."

The ecstatic exultation at the anticipated victory over Death in verse 55 flows naturally into the spontaneous "thanks be to God" of verse 57. Verse 56 interrupts with a brief statement about death, sin, and the law, topics of importance in the later letter to the Romans. In a letter otherwise completely and closely devoted to burning issues in the Corinthian assembly, this abrupt digression into sin and the law seems utterly out of place. There is no indication either in 1 Corinthians or in 2 Corinthians that these Pauline issues were a problem in Corinth. It is therefore probable that verse 56 is a gloss, added later (with Weiss 1910; *contra* Conzelmann 1975, 293; Fee 1987, 806). If it is original, then Paul would be interrupting a climactic passage in order to insert an aside about the cause of people dying. Over against the view that the body is *naturally* mortal and perishable he would be saying that death is brought about by the historical powers of sin and the law. The thanksgiving in verse 57 responds to God's victory over death, but it also embraces the argument as far back as 15:1-5, and echoes not only the affirmations in verses 20-28, but also those in 2:6-8 already called to mind by the "mystery" announced in verse 51.

"Therefore, my beloved" (v. 58) sets off the final exhortation, which concludes the whole set of arguments in the main body of the letter from 1:10 through 15:57. Significantly, Paul shifts from the stern admonitions and warnings that characterized his exhortations at the end of particular arguments (e.g., 4:14-21; 14:37-40; 15:33-34) to a positive, encouraging tone. It is surely also significant that, having omitted praise for their "(good) work of the Lord" (or "of faith") from the opening thanksgiving (where he was, instead, setting up the Corinthians for his criticism of their "speech" and "spiritual gifts"), he now focuses precisely on their "excelling in the work of the Lord" in the future. The word order, however, may contain a bit of a retrospective admonition about maintaining a focus on Christ: *if* it is "in the Lord," then "your labor is not in vain."

◊ ◊ ◊ ◊

Paul's goal for his community in Corinth, as for his mission in general, was the resurrection of the dead in the context of the *parousia* of Christ and the transformation of the faithful in transition to the kingdom of God. His gospel may have been Christocentric, yet he was oriented toward the fulfillment of history that he believed was underway in his own ministry. This goal, articulated in response to the Corinthian denial of the resurrection in chapter 15, was evident throughout the letter. It came to the surface in several connections, such as the political purpose of Christ's crucifixion according to God's mysterious plan (2:6-8), the goal of and sanction upon apostolic "building" (3:10-15), the sanction on the Corinthians' pretending to "judge" his apostleship (4:2-5), the political relations of the assemblies vis-à-vis the dominant political institutions (6:1-6), and the orientation of the community's celebration of the Lord's Supper (10:26). In chapter 15 Paul finally elaborated on some key aspects of the ultimate goal of his mission.

First Corinthians 15 is thus *not* a self-contained theological treatise (*contra* Conzelmann 1975, 249-50). Paul uses some of what must have been for him standard images, and he cites the crucifixion-resurrection creed at the outset. But chapter 15 is as much an ad hoc statement as any section in any of Paul's letters, directed to a specific issue, borrowing heavily the language of his addressees, and creating new combinations of images and ideas. Although he frequently used certain symbols of the future fulfillment, such as the new age, the kingdom of God, or the resurrection of the dead, Paul generally showed little interest in any fuller portrayal. He did so only when confronted with a problem regarding the resurrection in particular. Critical examination of passages in which this matter is addressed, 1 Cor 15, 2 Cor 5:1-5, and 1 Thess 4:13-18, suggests that he had not really given it much thought until it became a problem in Thessalonica and Corinth. In these texts he clearly tailored his discussion to the particular issues at stake in those communities. In fact, his resorting to new revelations (a "mystery" or "word of the Lord") suggests that he had no standard teaching to draw upon.

As noted in the exegetical analysis above, Paul developed his argument in 15:21-22, 29, 35-57 largely with terms borrowed from the Corinthians. The result was a sort of multicultural hybrid. His attempt to explain the resurrection of the dead/body to those who thought in a very different way and, for whatever reason, his use of their terms in doing so resulted in what must have been a puzzle to the Corinthians. It would be a misunderstanding of the ad hoc character of many of Paul's formulations in chapter 15 to press a metaphysical meaning on the terms he uses. Yet in the process of presenting the reality and manner of the resurrection to the Corinthians, he created new images, new combinations of terms, and new ideas. In constructing his arguments, Paul was hardly wedded to or partisan for some standard doctrine. He was ready to adapt others' terms and symbols, to combine them with his own key terms, to innovate and to create. Nevertheless, he insisted upon certain key terms and his own overall orientation toward the fulfillment of history in the kingdom of God. Here at the end of the argument on resurrection, the extent to which Paul insisted on his own historical-social-bodily orientation to reality attained greatest clarity over against an orientation that focused on disembodied and desocialized selves. Were we to "demythologize" the few terms and phrases in which Paul articulated his apocalyptic orientation, we would spiritualize his argument in the direction of the Corinthians he was addressing (*pace* Bultmann, as characterized by Conzelmann 1975, 249).

The view of the Corinthians addressed in chapter 15 is not appropriately described as "realized eschatology" (certainly not that "the resurrection has already taken place," since they denied the possibility of resurrection, 15:12). Indeed, there is no indication either in chapter 15 or elsewhere in the letter that the Corinthians had an "eschatology," in the sense of the end or fulfillment of history. Paul's message and ministry, however, might well be discussed in terms of eschatology, partly realized and partly imminent. He wrote in terms of an already realized salvation, whereby God has already inaugurated the eschatological events in the crucifixion and resurrection of Christ (2:6-10; 15:3-7, and so forth), and believers are already sanctified (1:2; 6:11) and enjoying the gifts of the Spirit, such as prophecy. The political, social, and ethical implications of the belief that the eschatological events are already underway and are imminently to be completed were dramatic: Believers were to deal with the world as if they had no dealings with it (7:29-31). Far from a tension between present and future, Paul displayed rather an anticipation of and eager longing for the completion of the eschatalogical events. That fulfillment, for Paul, however, was to include embodied persons and social life, at least for the believers, who belonged to his assemblies. The resurrection, and the wider realization of the kingdom of God of which it was a part, was, by Jewish apocalyptic definition and tradition, a collective historical (eschatological) event involving embodied people. Paul even envisioned it as a worldwide political event (15:20-28; cf. 2:6-8).

Judging from the language Paul borrowed from them and the way he used it in his own argument, the Corinthians who denied the resurrection of the dead appear to have understood themselves as (having become) a class of immortal, imperishable, heavenly, spiritual people (souls) who had transcended mortal, perishable, earthly realities, including the body. In their spiritual maturity, they had surpassed others, the *psychikoi* (earthly people), who were still somewhat attached to the perishable earthly-worldly realities. In fact, it is easy to imagine that they would have understood certain aspects of Paul's "realized eschatology," the disengagement from the world and relativization of sexual relations, as a gospel of liberation from troublesome bodily and other earthly realities. In their newly realized transcendent status, these *pneumatikoi* (spiritual people) would have been skeptical about and utterly disinterested in the resuscitation of their bodies, let alone in some new society of embodied people.

Paul's and the Corinthians' orientations toward reality were so different that it is difficult to discern just where the points of contact might have been. Perhaps Paul's achievement in chapter 15 was primarily to have forced some engagement between the two views. He did this in two steps of his overall argument, briefly in 15:20-28, and in more sustained fashion in 15:36-54. In the first two steps of his argument, he merely appealed to a tradition that the Corinthians had apparently not assimilated into their religiosity (15:1-11) and manipulated the dependence of Christ's resurrection on the reality (in his own worldview) of a general resurrection without explaining the latter in any way (15:12-19). In 15:20-28 Paul elaborated a bit on the final scenario of fulfillment as he viewed it, assimilating one set of Corinthian symbols, that of the two types of "men." He invited the readers to think of those two "men" as historical figures,

Adam and Christ. Of course, he also opened the way for later readers to transform and assimilate Adam and Christ into symbols of two types of humanity, fallen and transcendent.

In 15:35-54 Paul suggested, by way of the analogy of the sown seed, that there could be some sort of continuous personal identity, even through death and coming to new life, and he invited the readers to think of the body in that way. He then portrayed that new reality of the resurrected body in the Corinthians' own language of the spiritual transcendence of soul, inviting the Corinthians to think of the transformed body in the way they were thinking of the liberated, transcendent soul. That also opened up the possibility, of course, that later readers would come to think of the body as some transcendent spiritual reality. That also set up the possibility that readers no longer attentive to the rhetorical situation and ad hoc argumentative character of chapter 15 would come to understand this argument as a theological treatise explaining how resurrection is ontologically possible (Conzelmann 1975, 249, 281). Neither Paul nor the Corinthians were thinking in "cosmic" or "ontological" terms.

We might ask, finally, whether Paul needed to be all that worried about the Corinthian spirituals' denial of the resurrection of the dead. He was surely overreacting and overstating the supposedly adverse ethical implications of their "enlightened" skepticism. Except for a few members of the assembly who may have been offended at some persons' enlightened behavior in eating meat offered to idols, and a few men possibly distressed at their wives' new sexual asceticism, their behavior does not appear to have been socially problematic. Newly realized spiritual "power," "wealth," and "maturity" in their close relationship with *Sophia,* in fact, had brought a liberation from oppressive life situations and an enlivening new sense of self-worth for some of the Corinthians. On balance, the effect of the Corinthians' attainment of the transcendent "spiritual" level of existence was personal liberation for many, accompanied by a benign withdrawal from certain social relations.

Indeed, flexible as Paul was about the terms he used to explain issues, he also had an intense attachment to the particular worldview in which his gospel and his apostleship were inextricably embedded. To understand how that affected his insistence on the resurrection of the dead in his vivid apocalyptic portrayal of eschatological fulfillment, it is necessary to review the overall argument of the letter. Most significant in this connection, surely, is the key concern of his argument in the first long section of the letter: divisiveness must cease, the community must maintain its coherence, and the focus of excitement must shift away from *Sophia* back to the crucifixion of Christ, in which the rulers of this age were doomed. Closely related to Paul's eschatological orientation was his attachment to embodied personal and social-political life. He understood God's concern to be for people in social-political life. Forces such as death and imperial rulers had blocked realization of God's will. But God had finally set in motion events in which the ultimate concern for the fulfillment of human personal and social life, as intended, could finally be realized. Symbolizing the fulfillment in terms of political images such as "the kingdom of God" and "the *parousia* of the Lord," although it sounded vague, probably resonated with some hearers. Embellishing the fulfillment with statements about the body being transformed into immortality and imperishability, while perhaps sounding more substantive, in fact made them seem all the more fantastic. Moreover, to the hellenistic mind these statements would have moved the idea of social-political transcendence in the direction of ontological essences. In short, in the very paragraphs of chapter 15 in which Paul was insisting on the reality of the resurrection of the dead as that worldwide event through which the society of new age, the kingdom of God, would finally be realized, he may have penned the very formulations in which his later hellenistic-Roman readers would begin to spiritualize and defuse his anti-imperial political agenda.

THE COLLECTION, TRAVEL PLANS, AND APOLLOS (16:1-12)

After ending his argument for the resurrection of the dead with the crescendo of his apocalyptic "mystery" (15:51-52), Paul turns to matters that do not require extensive arguments: "The collection for the saints" (16:1-4), his own travel plans and the closely related visit to Corinth of his delegate, Timothy (16:5-9, 10-11), and the question of a visit to Corinth by Apollos (16:12). "Now concerning," in both verse 1 and verse 12, may indicate that the Corinthians had inquired about the collection and about an Apollos visit in their letter to Paul (cf. 7:1).

◊ ◊ ◊ ◊

16:1-4: Paul had presumably discussed a collection with the Corinthians before, either when still in Corinth or in his previous letter (see 5:9-11). The idea of taking up a collection for the poor among the saints in Jerusalem (Rom 15:26; cf. 2 Cor 8:13; 9:9, 12), which Paul has recently launched or revived, must come from the agreement reached between representatives of the Antioch assembly and the Jerusalem community. According to Paul's recollection in Gal 2:9-10, the "pillars" in Jerusalem—James, Cephas (Peter), and John—agreed that the Antioch leaders Paul and Barnabas could expand the movement among the nations (Gentiles), but that they should "remember the poor." The latter phrase suggests that in reciprocity and solidarity with the assembly in Jerusalem, the newly founded (Gentile) assemblies were to send economic assistance for the poor there. Some years later, in his letter to the Romans (15:27), Paul articulated the reciprocal rationale of the collection, which may also have been derived from prophecies (e.g., Isa 56:7) about the nations bringing tribute in gratitude to Jerusalem at the eschatological time of fulfillment. Since the other peoples of the world had come to share in the "spiritual blessings" of Israel, that is, the fulfillment of the promises to Abraham and his seed that through them all nations would be blessed, then the peoples should "be of service" to Israel in material goods.

Here in 1 Corinthians, Paul simply offers some practical advice about the collection. By mentioning that he has given the same directions to the assemblies in Galatia, he places the project in the wider framework of his mission. Paul's reference to "the first day of every week" indicates that there was already some special significance to it, probably as the day on which whole assemblies gathered for the Lord's Supper. In the synoptic Gospel tradition, the first day was remembered clearly as the day of Jesus' resurrection. The present instructions indicate that there was no organization of community finances in the Pauline assemblies. Each person is to "set aside and keep whatever he or she may gain" (v. 2*a* AT). The latter verb is quite general and might suggest, although it does not specifically refer to earning or income. The economy was not capitalist and many members of the community may have been slaves who did not have individual incomes. The procedure Paul specifies would guarantee that the resources would be accumulated over time, and would not have to be generated all at once when Paul finally came.

It is apparent that the collection entailed more than donation and delivery of money (v. 3). Beyond the gift, it was important that representatives of the peoples of the world accompany the collection to Jerusalem, probably as a demonstration to the Jerusalem leaders of the movement that Paul's labors among the nations had borne fruit. Paul's collection was a matter of the politics as well as of the economics of the movement and its apostles. These delegates were to be chosen by the assemblies themselves, and Paul would send them with letters of introduction and recommendation, a standard practice in business and political dealings in hellenistic-Roman times. The hesitancy that Paul expresses, "If it seems advisable [literally, "worthy"] that I should go [to Jerusalem] also" (v. 4), probably indicates just how uncertain he is at this stage about his own relationship to the leaders of the movement in Jerusalem. His anxiety about how his demonstration would be received only increased with his decision to bring the collection in person (Rom 15:30-32; 2 Cor 1:16).

[16:5-11]: Making arrangements for the collection brings up the question of Paul's travel plans (vv. 5-9). He plans to stay in Ephesus, where he is currently working effectively, though with opposition, until Pentecost (late spring). Then he will come to Corinth by way of Macedonia, where he will spend the summer and fall, finally arriving in late fall and perhaps spending the winter with the Corinthians. Instead, for some reason unknown to us, Paul may have gone to Corinth directly from Ephesus by sea, intending then to go on to Macedonia (cf. 2 Cor 1:15-2:4). That may have been the disastrous "visit of tears," involving an extreme crisis in his relationship with the assembly in Corinth, to which his further correspondence bears witness (2 Cor 2:14–7:1; 10–13; 1:1–2:13). Paul has already dispatched Timothy to Corinth as his delegate (to deal with the divisiveness there, 4:17), and he will likely arrive before Paul does (v. 10). Paul's commendation of Timothy (v. 11) is probably motivated by his anxiety that Corinthian hostility toward himself would be directed also at his delegate.

The Corinthians had inquired (perhaps in their letter) about Apollos returning to Corinth, but it is unclear whether they had merely inquired about when he might return or had asked Paul's approval for his return. It is difficult to know what lies behind Paul's comment that he had "urged him to visit . . . with the other brothers." The latter are probably Stephanas, Fortunatus, and Achaicus, leading members of the Corinthian assembly who were about to return from Paul in Ephesus, as implied in 16:15-18. It is likely that Apollos would be the last "servant" (3:5, 9) Paul would want to have reappear in Corinth. If this hypothesis is correct, it was to this eloquent Alexandrian that Paul attributed the Corinthians' devotion to *Sophia,* and hence the divisiveness in their assembly (see on 1:10-17; 3:1-15). The remainder of verse 12 is also puzzling. The Greek reads, literally: "And [emphatic] not at all was their [the] will that he come now." "Will" without a descriptive phrase could mean either God's will or Apollos' will. Either way of construing the statement could hide some spoken or tacit understanding between Paul and Apollos that the Alexandrian would not return to Corinth, at least for a time. Or, perhaps it was simply that Apollos, like Paul, was moving from place to place with his gospel, which would fit the comment, "He will come when he has the opportunity."

◊ ◊ ◊ ◊

Paul's comments about the collection enable us to see that the network of assemblies out of which Christianity eventually developed was not only a political-religious movement; it also had its own political-economic dimension. From early on, before Paul launched his independent mission to the nations, Christianity had its own means of practicing international economic solidarity and reciprocity, the "haves" sharing with the "have-nots" ("remember the poor," Gal 2:10). Not only did the local "assemblies" belong to a larger international movement or "assembly," but they shared economic resources across the nations and across considerable distances. That was something quite unusual in the ancient Mediterranean world or, for that matter, in any imperial situation. Diametrically opposite to the upward and centripetal movement of resources and wealth in the tributary political-economic relationship imposed by empire on subject peoples, Paul was organizing a lateral movement of resources from one subject people to another to be used in support of "the poor among the saints at Jerusalem" (Rom 15:26).

From Paul's own expression of anxiety about the delivery of the collection, however, it looks as though the delivery had become tied up with the internal politics of the movement. Having carried on his own energetic mission—departing from the policies of the original collective leadership in Jerusalem and Antioch—Paul now felt the need to obtain recognition of the legitimacy of his mission. This poses the issue of how the cooperative policies and mechanisms of an international social movement may be separated from the particular interests of its leaders. It also indicates that the movement had not found a way to "test the spirits" of the apostles who were energetically spearheading its remarkable spread and growth.

CONCLUSION OF THE LETTER (16:13-24)

In contrast with their openings, the conclusions of Greek letters around the time of Paul lacked standardized form, although some standard elements may be found. First Corinthians has, in sequence: a final exhortation (vv. 13-18), a final greeting (vv. 19-20), an autographic greeting (v. 21), a warning (which is unusual; v. 22), a benediction (v. 23), and a personal blessing of love (which is also unusual; v. 24).

◊ ◊ ◊ ◊

As he ordinarily does, Paul exhorts his readers to be "alert" because of the urgency of the eschatological situation in which they stand (cf. 1 Thess 5:6). "Be courageous" and "be strong" are common, general appeals. The other two exhortations seem specific to the issues of 1 Corinthians. "Stand firm in your faith" appears to sum up concerns such as those stated in chapters 10 and 15 (cf. 10:12; 15:1, 58), while "do everything in love" (AT) clearly repeats his earlier commendations of love (8:1, and chap. 13).

The NRSV translation obscures an awkward grammatical construction in verses 15-16, which may in turn betray some awkwardness in the three-way relationship between Paul, the household of Stephanas, and (some of) the other Corinthians. After beginning with a bold "Now I urge you [emphatic], brethren," he interrupts what he began to say with an intervening clause: "You know the household of Stephanas, that they are the firstfruits of Achaia and have appointed [set] themselves to the service of the saints." Only in verse 16 does he continue the exhortation: "to [in order that you] submit to such as these and to everyone who works and toils with them" (AT). Paul uses the term "submit" (NRSV: "put yourselves at the service of") only here in reference to relationships within an assembly. Fortunatus, Latin for "lucky" or "blessed," and Achaicus, Latin for "one from Achaia," were names commonly given to slaves (who may then have become freedmen). These two may be members of Stephanas's household, or they may have been simply traveling with him to visit Paul in Ephesus. That they are the ones visiting Paul and that he writes this brief recommendation for Stephanas and these warm words about all three in 16:15-18 suggests either that Stephanas or all three were the delegation from the Corinthian assembly that had brought the community's letter to Paul or that Paul was about to send this letter (1 Corinthians) back to the community with them, or both. The reference to Stephanas's household (which would include slaves and freed slaves as well as his spouse and children) also suggests that he is a man of moderate means, and therefore able to have been of material service as well as other service to (members of) the community, perhaps hosting gatherings of the assembly for the Lord's Supper in his house. That Paul here lays the mantle of his own authority on

Stephanas and his household suggests that they had been loyal to him through whatever conflicts had emerged in the Corinthian community. This would explain Paul's awkwardness as he exhorts the Corinthians to "submit" and "give recognition" to these devoted laborers in the "service of the saints."

16:19-24: Paul concludes 1 Corinthians by combining his standard greetings and grace with two unusual elements—a curse and a declaration of love. He includes greetings from the assemblies of the province of Asia (western Asia Minor)—the only such greeting in his letters—almost certainly as an additional way of inducing the Corinthians to discern the larger movement of which they are a part (cf. the other references to the movement in general or to the other assemblies in 1:2; 4:17; 11:16; 14:33; 16:1). Aquila and Prisca—usually mentioned with Prisca's name first (cf. Rom 16:3), suggesting that she was the more prominent leader in the movement—had been Paul's collaborators, supposedly in their common tentmaking trade as well as in the mission based in Corinth that resulted in the founding of various assemblies in Achaia and "the whole assembly" in Corinth. Originally from Pontus (northern Asia Minor), they were among the Jews who had been expelled from Rome by an edict of the emperor Claudius in the middle of his reign (41–54 CE), apparently after they had already joined the movement (Acts 18:1-3). After leaving Corinth they joined Paul in further collaboration in Ephesus and, as indicated here in verse 19, hosted a small assembly in their home there, just as they were to do a few years later in Rome (Rom 16:3-5). The book of Acts (18:24-28) attests a tradition that Prisca (in Acts, "Priscilla") and Aquila corrected Apollos about certain matters. Hence they may have had dealings with him in Corinth and elsewhere (e.g., Ephesus). If "all the brothers" (NRSV: all the brothers and sisters) in verse 20a are different from the members of the assemblies mentioned in verse 19, they are probably Paul's other coworkers based in Ephesus. In verse 20b Paul then calls the Corinthians to "greet one another with a holy kiss," an instruction found also at the end of other letters (e.g., 2 Cor 13:12; 1 Thess 5:26). The custom was apparently not confined to the Pauline churches (Rom 16:16; 1 Pet 5:14). However widespread such a custom may have been, it was apparently an Israelite/Jewish tradition within families and close friendships and a symbol of reconciliation (Gen 27:26; 33:4; 1 Sam 20:41).

Paul's addition of a special greeting in his own hand (v. 12; cf. Gal 6:11) shows that he dictated his letters, and our knowing this helps us appreciate the oral rhetorical forms in which they are "written" and then read to the gathered assembly. Perhaps the next element too, unique to his letter closings, was added in his own hand: "Let anyone be *anathema* who has no love for the Lord" (v. 22a). Although some of the terms may seem un-Pauline (e.g., *phileō* instead of *agapaō* for "love"), Paul does impose a curse like this elsewhere in a polemical context (Gal 1:8), and he has uttered equally sharp threats or judgments earlier in 1 Corinthians (cf. 3:17a; 5:4-5; 14:38). This harsh closing curse is simply one more indication of how seriously he takes the problems at issue in the divisiveness within the Corinthian assembly. The expression in verse 22b may be variously translated. *Maranatha* occurs only here in the New Testament, although its appearance at the end of the instructions for the Eucharist in *Did.* 10:6 is comparable. If the expression (simply a transliteration of Aramaic characters into Greek) is divided as *maran atha,* it would mean, "Our Lord has come! (See NRSV footnote.) Probably, however, it should be divided as *marana tha,* which means, "Our Lord, come!" Translated this way, it is likely a call for the *parousia* (coming) of the Lord in fulfillment and judgment, used in this case as a sanction on the curse Paul just pronounced. It fits well with the crescendo that he had reached with regard to the "mystery" of the Lord's coming at the end of chapter 15. Two final declarations (vv. 23, 24) then balance the preceding curse with highly positive elements. Calling for "the grace of the Lord Jesus" to be with the people is Paul's standard way of ending his letter, but what follows this is unique in 1 Corinthians. Even though he had just admonished some of the Corinthians, in rather sharp terms and on a number of issues, now at the very end Paul extends his own love to all in the community.

SELECT BIBLIOGRAPHY

WORKS ON 1 CORINTHIANS AND RELATED MATTERS
(BOTH CITED AND NOT CITED)

Barton, S. C. 1986. "Paul's Sense of Place: An Anthropological Approach to Community Formation in Corinth." *NTS* 32:225-46.

Bassler, Jouette M. 1992. "1 Corinthians." In *The Women's Bible Commentary*, edited by Carol A. Newsom and Sharon H. Ringe, 321-29. Louisville: Westminster/John Knox.

Beker, J. Christiaan. 1984. *Paul the Apostle: The Triumph of God in Life and Thought*. Philadelphia: Fortress.

Callan, Terrance. 1985. "Prophecy and Ecstasy in Greco-Roman Religion and in 1 Corinthians." *NovT* 27:125-40.

Cantarella, Eva. 1987. *Pandora's Daughter: The Role and Status of Women in Greek and Roman Antiquity*. Baltimore: Johns Hopkins University Press.

Carr, Wesley. 1981. *Angels and Principalities*. Cambridge: Cambridge University Press.

Castelli, Elizabeth A. 1991. *Imitating Paul: A Discourse of Power*. Louisville: Westminster/John Knox.

Chow, John K. 1992. *Patronage and Power*. Sheffield: JSOT.

Countryman, L. William. 1988. *Dirt, Greed, and Sex: Sexual Ethics in the New Testament and Their Implications for Today*. Philadelphia: Fortress.

D'Angelo, Mary Rose. 1992. "'Abba and 'Father': Imperial Theology and the Jesus Traditions." *JBL* 111:611-30.

Davis, James A. 1984. *Wisdom and Spirit: An Investigation of 1 Corinthians 1:18–3:20 Against the Background of Jewish Sapiential Traditions in the Greco-Roman Period*. Lanham, MD: University Press of America.

de Boer, Martinus. 1988. *The Defeat of Death*. Sheffield: Almond.

DeMaris, Richard E. 1995. "Corinthian Religion and Baptism for the Dead (1 Corinthians 15:29): Insights from Archaeology and Anthropology." *JBL* 114:661-82.

Elliott, Neil. 1994. *Liberating Paul: The Justice of God and the Politics of the Apostle.* Maryknoll, NY: Orbis.

Forbes, Christopher. 1986. "Early Christian Inspired Speech and Hellenistic Popular Religion." *NovT* 28:257-70.

Furnish, Victor Paul. 1984. *II Corinthians.* AB 32A. Garden City, NY: Doubleday.

_____. 1993. "Theology in 1 Corinthians." In *Pauline Theology Vol II: 1 & 2 Corinthians,* edited by David M. Hay, 59-89. Minneapolis: Fortress.

Garnsey, Peter. 1970. *Social Status and Legal Privilege in the Roman Empire.* Oxford: Clarendon.

Garnsey, Peter, and Richard Saller. 1987. *The Roman Empire: Economy, Society, and Culture.* Berkeley: University of California Press.

Gooch, Peter D. 1993. *Dangerous Food: 1 Corinthians 8–10 in Its Context.* Waterloo, Ontario: Wilfrid Laurier University Press.

Goodman, Felicitas D. 1972. *Speaking in Tongues: A Cross-Cultural Study of Glossolalia.* Chicago: University of Chicago Press.

Harrill, J. Albert. 1995. *The Manumission of Slaves in Early Christianity.* Tübingen: Mohr-Siebeck.

Harris, Gerald. 1991. "The Beginnings of Church Discipline: 1 Corinthians 5." *NTS* 37:1-21.

Hay, David M., ed. 1993. *Pauline Theology, Vol II: 1 & 2 Corinthians.* Minneapolis: Fortress.

Hays, Richard B. 1989. *Echoes of Scripture in the Letters of Paul.* New Haven, CT: Yale University Press.

Hock, Ronald F. 1980. *The Social Context of Paul's Ministry: Tentmaking and Apostleship.* Philadelphia: Fortress.

Holladay, Carl R. 1990. "1 Corinthians 13: Paul as Apostolic Paradigm." In *Greeks, Romans, and Christians: Essays in Honor of Abraham Malherbe,* edited by David L. Balch, Everett Ferguson, and Wayne Meeks, 80-98. Minneapolis: Fortress.

Horsley, Richard A. 1976. "*Pneumatikos vs. Psychikos*: Distinctions of Spiritual Status Among the Corinthians." *HTR* 69:269-88.

_____. 1977. "Wisdom of Word and Words of Wisdom in Corinth." *CBQ* 39:223-39.

_____. 1978a. "How Can Some of You Say 'There Is No Resurrection of the Dead'? Spiritual Elitism in Corinth." *NovT* 20:203-31.

_____. 1978b. "Consciousness and Freedom Among the Corinthians: 1 Corinthians 8–10." *CBQ* 40:574-89.

_____. 1979. "Spiritual Marriage with Sophia." *VC* 33:30-54.

_____. 1980. "Gnosis in Corinth: 1 Corinthians 8:1-6." *NTS* 27:32-51.

_____, ed. 1997. *Paul and Empire: Religion and Power in Roman Imperial Society.* Valley Forge, PA: Trinity Press International.

Hurd, John C., Jr. 1965. *The Origins of 1 Corinthians.* New York: Seabury.

Jones, Amos, Jr. 1984. *Paul's Message of Freedom: What Does It Mean to the Black Church?* Valley Forge, PA: Judson.

Judge, E. A. 1980. "The Social Identity of the First Christians: A Question of Method in Religious History." *JRH* 11:102-17.

_____. 1984. "Cultural Conformity and Innovation in Paul: Some Clues from Contemporary Documents." *Tyndale Bulletin* 35:3-24.

Kirchhoff, Renate. 1994. *Die Sünde gegen den eigenen Leib: Studien zu porne und porneia in 1 Kor 6,12-20 und dem sozio-kulturellen Kontext der paulinischen Adressaten.* Göttingen: Vandenhoeck & Ruprecht.

Kloppenborg, John S. 1978. "An Analysis of the Pre-Pauline Formula in 1 Cor 15:3*b*-5 in Light of Some Recent Literature." *CBQ* 40:351-67.

Kraemer, Ross S. 1989. "Monastic Jewish Women in Greco-Roman Egypt: Philo on the Therapeutrides." *Signs* 14:342-70.

MacDonald, Margaret Y. 1990. "Women Holy in Body and Spirit: The Social Setting of 1 Corinthians 7." *NTS* 36:161-81.

Marshall, Peter. 1987. *Enmity in Corinth: Social Convention in Paul's Relations with the Corinthians.* Tübingen: Mohr-Siebeck.

Martin, Dale B. 1995. *The Corinthian Body.* New Haven, CT: Yale University Press.

Martin, R. P. 1984. *The Spirit and the Congregation: Studies in 1 Corinthians 12–15.* Grand Rapids, MI: Eerdmans.

Meeks, Wayne A. 1983. *The First Urban Christians: The Social World of the Apostle Paul.* New Haven, CT: Yale University Press.

Mitchell, Alan C., S.J. 1993. "Rich and Poor in the Courts of Corinth: Litigiousness and Status in 1 Corinthians 6:1-11." *NTS* 39:562-86.

Mitchell, Margaret M. 1992. *Paul and the Rhetoric of Reconciliation: An Exegetical Investigation of the Language and Composition of 1 Corinthians.* Louisville: Westminster/John Knox.

Munro, Winsome. 1988. "Women, Text and the Canon: The Strange Case of 1 Corinthians 14:33-35." *BTB* 18:26-31.

_____. 1990. "Interpolation in the Epistles: Weighing Probability." *NTS* 36:431-43.

Murphy-O'Connor, Jerome, O.P. 1978. "Corinthian Slogans in 1 Cor 6:12-20." *CBQ* 40:391-96.

_____. 1981a. "Tradition and Redaction in 1 Cor 15:3-7." *CBQ* 43:582-89.

_____. 1981b. " 'Baptized for the Dead' (1 Cor XV.29): A Corinthian Slogan?" *RB* 88:532-43.

_____. 1983. *St. Paul's Corinth: Texts and Archaeology.* GNS 6. Wilmington, DE: Michael Glazier.

_____. 1988. "1 Corinthians 11:2-16 Once Again." *CBQ* 50:265-74.

Pearson, Birger. 1973. *The Pneumatikos-Psychikos Terminology in 1 Corinthians.* SBLDS 12. Missoula, MT: Scholars Press.

Pickett, Raymond. 1997. *The Cross in Corinth: The Social Significance of the Death of Jesus.* JSNTSup 143. Sheffield: JSOT.

Pogoloff, Stephen M. 1992. *Logos and Sophia: The Rhetorical Situation of 1 Corinthians.* SBLDS 134. Atlanta: Scholars Press.

Robbins, Vernon K. 1996. *The Tapestry of Early Christian Discourse: Rhetoric, Society, and Ideology.* London & New York: Routledge.

Rohrbaugh, Richard. 1984. "Methodological Considerations in the Debate over the Social Class Status of Early Christians." *JAAR* 52:521-46.

Schmithals, Walter. 1971. *Gnosticism in Corinth: An Investigation of the Letters to the Corinthians.* Translated by John E. Steely. Nashville: Abingdon.

Schüssler Fiorenza, Elisabeth. 1983. *In Memory of Her: A Feminist Theological Reconstruction of Christian Origins.* New York: Crossroad.

_____. 1987. "Rhetorical Situation and Historical Reconstruction in 1 Corinthians." *NTS* 33:386-403.

Sellin, Gerhard. 1986. *Der Streit um die Auferstehung der Toten: Eine religionsgeschichtliche und exegetische Untersuchung von 1 Korinther 15.* Göttingen: Vandenhoeck & Ruprecht.

Sider, R. J. 1975. "The Pauline Conception of the Resurrection Body in I Corinthians XV.35-54," *NTS* 21:428-39.

Sigountos, James G. 1994. "The Genre of 1 Corinthians 13." *NTS* 40:246-60.

South, James T. 1993. "A Critique of the 'Curse/Death' Interpretation of 1 Corinthians 5:1-8." *NTS* 39:539-61.

Stowers, Stanley K. 1984. "Social Status, Public Speaking and Private Teaching: The Circumstances of Paul's Preaching Activity." *NovT* 26:59-82.

_____. 1990. "Paul on the Use and Abuse of Reason." In *Greeks, Romans, and Christians: Essays in Honor of Abraham J. Malherbe,* edited by David Balch, Everett Ferguson, and Wayne Meeks, 253-86. Minneapolis: Augsburg Fortress.

_____. 1995. "Greeks Who Sacrifice and Those Who Do Not: Toward an Anthropology of Greek Religion." In *The Social World of the First Christians: Essays in Honor of Wayne A. Meeks,* edited by L. Michael White and O. Larry Yarbrough, 293-333. Minneapolis: Fortress.

Theissen, Gerd. 1982. *The Social Setting of Pauline Christianity: Essays on Corinth*, edited by John H. Schuetz. Philadelphia: Fortress.

Thistleton, Anthony C. 1977-78. "Realized Eschatology in Corinth." *NTS* 24:510-26.

Thompson, Cynthia L. 1988. "Hairstyles, Head-Coverings, and St. Paul: Portraits from Roman Corinth." *BA* 51:99-225.

Tomson, Peter J. 1990. *Paul and the Jewish Law*. Minneapolis: Fortress.

Trompf, G. W. 1980. "On Attitudes Toward Women in Paul and Paulinist Literature: 1 Cor 11:3-16 and Its Context." *CBQ* 42:196-215.

Tuckett, Christopher M. 1983. "1 Corinthians and Q." *JBL* 102:607-19.

Walker, William O., Jr. 1989. "The Vocabulary of 1 Corinthians 11:3-16: Pauline or Non-Pauline?" *JSNT* 35:75-88.

Wedderburn, A. J. M. 1981. "The Problem of the Denial of the Resurrection in I Corinthians XV," *NovT* 23:229-41.

_____. 1987. *Baptism and Resurrection: Studies in Pauline Theology Against Its Greco-Roman Background*. Tübingen: Mohr-Siebeck.

Welborn, L. L. 1987. "On the Discord in Corinth: 1 Corinthians 1–4 and Ancient Politics." *JBL* 106:83-113.

Willis, Wendell L. 1985. *Idol Meat in Corinth: The Pauline Argument in 1 Corinthians 8 and 10*. SBLDS. Chico, CA: Scholars Press.

Winter, Bruce W. 1991. "Civil Litigation in Secular Corinth and the Church." *NTS* 37:559-72.

Wire, Antoinette C. 1990. *The Corinthian Women Prophets: A Reconstruction Through Paul's Rhetoric*. Minneapolis: Augsburg Fortress.

Wiseman, James. 1979. "Corinth and Rome I: 228 B.C.–A.D. 267." In *Aufstieg und Niedergang der römischen Welt* II.7.1, edited by Hildegard Temporini, 438-548. Berlin: DeGruyter.

Witherington, Ben, III. 1993. "Not So Idle Thoughts About *Eidolothuton*." *Tyndale Bulletin* 44:237-54.

Yarbro Collins, Adela. 1980. "The Function of 'Excommunication' in Paul." *HTR* 73:251-63.

COMMENTARIES (BOTH CITED AND NOT CITED)

Barrett, C. K. 1968. *Commentary on the First Epistle to the Corinthians*. HNTC. New York: Harper & Row. — Commentary on author's translation of the Greek text. Still views Corinthian community as divided into parties, with Paul arguing against Gnostics on the one hand and against Jewish Christians on the other.

Conzelmann, Hans. 1975. *1 Corinthians: A Commentary on the First Epistle to the Corinthians*. Hermeneia. Philadelphia: Fortress. — Translation of a respected 1969 German commentary. A compendium of comparative references to particular terms, verses, and issues, with heavy doses of German theological discussion.

Fee, Gordon. 1987. *The First Epistle to the Corinthians*. New International Commentary. Grand Rapids, MI: Eerdmans. — Intended for evangelical readers. The most extensive and detailed of recent commentaries, in conversation with other positions and a wide variety of previous interpretation.

Harrisville, Roy A. 1987. *I Corinthians*. Augsburg Commentary on the New Testament. Minneapolis: Augsburg. — Readable commentary written for laypeople, working primarily from previous German Lutheran tradition of interpretation.

Holladay, Carl. 1979. *The First Letter of Paul to the Corinthians* LWC. Austin, TX: Sweet. — Readable commentary written for laypeople, with well-grounded interpretations.

Murphy-O'Connor, Jerome, O.P. 1979. *1 Corinthians*. New Testament Message 10. Wilmington, DE: Michael Glazier. — Brief, readable, solid commentary with frequently original angles on passages and issues.

Orr, William F., and James A. Walther. 1976. *1 Corinthians*. AB 32. Garden City, NY: Doubleday. — Accessible to general reader, with detailed notes on terms and phrases in the Greek text and interpretative comments on the arguments. Not as strong as other volumes in this series.

Schrage, Wolfgang. 1991–. *Der erste Brief an die Korinther*. EKKNT 7. Zürich: Benziger Verlag. Neukirchen-Vluyn: Neukirchener Verlag. — Detailed multivolume scholarly commentary in German.

Schüssler Fiorenza, Elisabeth. 1988. "1 Corinthians." In *Harper's Bible Commentary*, 1168-89. New York: HarperCollins. — Brief but packed commentary that opens up clearly the many interrelated issues in the Corinthian community and in 1 Corinthians.

Talbert, Charles H. 1987. *Reading Corinthians: A Literary and Theological Commentary on 1 and 2 Corinthians*. New York: Crossroad. — Accessible interpretation of large units of Paul's arguments, with frequently innovative angles. Assumes that in 1 Corinthians Paul is responding to an "overrealized eschatology."

Weiss, Johannes. 1910. *Der erste Korintherbrief*. MeyerK. Göttingen: Vandenhoeck & Ruprecht. — Older German commentary. Divides the letter into fragments that represent evolution of Paul's theology.

Wire, Antoinette. 1994. "1 Corinthians." In *Searching the Scriptures, Vol. Two: A Feminist Commentary*, edited by Elisabeth Schüssler Fiorenza,

156-95. New York: Crossroad. — Brief commentary focused on the prominence of women in the Corinthian community, based on Wire's book listed above.

Witherington, Ben, III. 1995. *Conflict and Community in Corinth: A Socio-Rhetorical Commentary on 1 and 2 Corinthians*. Grand Rapids, MI: Eerdmans. — Accessible discussion of Paul's arguments step-by-step, with attention to social conditions and customs.

INDEX

Abraham, promises to, 36
Achaia, 29, 30, 32, 225
Achaicus, 33, 46, 103, 225
Acts, book of, 29, 30, 46
Adam, 204-5, 212, 219
age, this, 49, 58
   the rulers of, 58, 76
Alciphron, 31
alternative society, the assembly as, 82, 94,
   100, 113, 145-47, 163-65, 194
ancestors (Israel), 134
angels, 155, 176
apocalyptic
   literature (Jewish), 40, 58-59, 88, 150,
     194, 213
   scenario, 206
   worldview, 70, 84, 88, 150, 197, 204,
     211-12, 217-18
Apollos, 34, 36, 37, 43, 44-45, 63-65, 76,
   77, 126-27, 148-49, 223
apostle, 39, 63-64, 124-25, 147, 173
   Corinthians attachment to, 33
   Paul's self-defense of being an, 124-25,
     146, 148
apostolate, 199-200
   rights to, 124-27
Apuleius, 31
Aquila, 30, 226
aristocracy
   Greek, 31, 51
   spiritual, 32
Aristotle, 158
asceticism, sexual, 96, 98, 106-11, 202, 219
assembly, 29-30, 32, 39, 40, 74, 76, 88-89,
   145-46, 173, 188, 194, 221-27
   Corinthian, 29, 64, 75, 79-80, 82-85,
     89, 159-60, 182
     spiritual people in the, 57, 60, 61,
       77, 93-94, 107-8, 126, 134-38,
       144-45, 169, 178-79, 190-93,
       210-12, 218-19
   in houses, 30, 32, 55, 159-60
   whole, 32, 46, 159-60, 163-65, 183

associations (collegia), 26, 149
authority
   individual ethical (exousia), 90, 97,
     122, 124-27, 129-32, 143, 150
   over another's or one's own body/head,
     97, 108, 110, 153, 155
   Paul's apostolic, 44, 67, 72-73, 77, 79-
     81, 189, 195

baptism, 45
   on behalf of the dead, 206-7
   into Moses, 136, 151
Barnabas, 125
betrothed, 104-5
boasting, 42, 51, 64-65, 79, 128, 176
body, 89, 91-94, 107, 110, 140, 162-63,
   166-67, 171-73, 202, 209, 214, 219
   analogy of, with city-state, 167, 171-
     73, 194-95
   of Christ, 140, 173

calling, prophetic, 128-29
Cenchreae (town near Corinth), 24, 30
Cephas (Peter), 45, 125, 221
Chloe's people, 33, 44
Christ, 45, 66-67, 119-20, 136-38, 144,
   149, 150-51, 204-6, 219
   body of, 92
   crucifixion of, 47-54, 62-63, 123, 216
   martyrdom of, 37
   parousia of (coming of), 36, 41, 65, 68,
     161-64, 212-13, 215, 220, 227
   See also Jesus
church. See assembly
circumcised-uncircumcised, 100-101, 114
cloud, as symbol of deliverance, 135
collection, 221-23
commission, Paul's, 129, 149
common good, 167, 169-71, 193-94
community
   building up of, 36, 117, 180, 182, 186,
     193-94
   discipline, 78-83, 88-89

CPSIA information can be obtained at www.ICGtesting.com
Printed in the USA
LVOW06s1855300913

354763LV00006B/1059/A